PORTRAIT OF EDINBURGH

Also by Ian Nimmo

Robert Burns: *his Life and Tradition in Words and Sound*
Crossing the Tay

THE *PORTRAIT* SERIES

Portrait of the Broads
J. Wentworth Day

Portrait of the Burns Country
Hugh Douglas

Portrait of Cambridge
C. R. Benstead

Portrait of the Chilterns
Annan Dickson

Portrait of Cornwall
Claude Berry

Portrait of the Cotswolds
Edith Brill

Portrait of Dartmoor
Vian Smith

Portrait of Devon
D. St Leger-Gordon

Portrait of Dorset
Ralph Wightman

Portrait of County Durham
Peter A. White

Portrait of Gloucestershire
T. A. Ryder

Portrait of the Highlands
W. Douglas Simpson

Portrait of the Isle of Man
E. H. Stenning

Portrait of the Isle of Wight
Lawrence Wilson

Portrait of the Isles of Scilly
Clive Mumford

Portrait of the Lakes
Norman Nicholson

Portrait of Lancashire
Jessica Lofthouse

Portrait of London River
Basil E. Cracknell

Portrait of the New Forest
Brian Vesey-Fitzgerald

Portrait of Northumberland
Nancy Ridley

Portrait of Peakland
Crichton Porteous

Portrait of the Quantocks
Vincent Waite

Portrait of the Scott Country
Marion Lochhead

Portrait of the Severn
J. H. B. Peel

Portrait of the Shires
Bernard Newman

Portrait of Skye and the Outer Hebrides
W. Douglas Simpson

Portrait of Snowdonia
Cledwyn Hughes

Portrait of the Thames
J. H. B. Peel

Portrait of the River Trent
Peter Lord

Portrait of the Wye Valley
H. L. V. Fletcher

Portrait of Yorkshire
Harry J. Scott

Portrait of EDINBURGH

IAN NIMMO

ILLUSTRATED
AND WITH A MAP

ROBERT HALE · LONDON

First published in Great Britain 1969

SBN 7091 0588 6

Robert Hale & Company
63 Old Brompton Road
London S.W.7

PRINTED IN GREAT BRITAIN
BY EBENEZER BAYLIS AND SON, LTD.
THE TRINITY PRESS, WORCESTER AND LONDON

CONTENTS

	Preface	13
I	People	15
II	Saturday Night . . .	48
III	Old Town	54
IV	. . . Sunday Morning	94
V	New Town	100
VI	Seats of Learning	133
VII	Seats of Wisdom	148
VIII	Ceremony	156
IX	Culture	170
X	Tomorrow	187
	Index	203

ILLUSTRATIONS

1 Looking down the Royal Mile to the Tron Kirk with St Giles' on the right *facing page* 40

2 Panorama from Calton Hill. On the skyline from left to right: St Giles', the spire of Tolbooth St John's, the broken line of the Castle, and the Scott Monument. The monument in the foreground is to Dugald Stewart, the philosopher *between pages* 40 *and* 41

3 The Atomic Age, but visitors still go to the Castle to look at Mons Meg in wonder *facing page* 41

4 St Giles' 64

5 The City Chambers on the Royal Mile, once the Royal Exchange 65

6 The Canongate Tolbooth still plays its part in history as a museum 80

7 One of the ornate gateways to the Palace of Holyrood, with Arthur's Seat in the background 81

8 Randolph Place below the dome of St George's Church 104

9 Edinburgh from the Castle ramparts looking over the Forth to Fife *between pages* 104 *and* 105

10 Coates Crescent, typical of New Town architecture *facing page* 105

11 Whitehorse Close, one of the finest examples of restoration work in Britain 112

12 Chessel's Court, another Royal Mile restoration triumph 112

13 Greyfriars Bobby on his stance on George IV Bridge 113

14 The Duke of Wellington outside Register House 128

15 Children playing in St James Court 129

16 Almost a symbol of Edinburgh, a line-out of schoolboy rugby jerseys below the Salisbury Crags 144

17 The whale bones at the entrance of Jaw Bone Walk across the Meadows 145

18 Part of the impressive quadrangle of Edinburgh University 160

19 High on Arthur's Seat 161

20 A sign reminding of Roman times at Cramond 184

21 & 22 One of the most dramatic sights in Scotland, the Forth's famous twin bridges . . . the graceful new road bridge and, below, the structural wonder of last century carrying the railway across the Firth *between pages* 184 *and* 185

23 Portobello sands at sunset *acing page* 185

Map of Edinburgh *pages* 10–11

PICTURE CREDITS

A. D. S. Macpherson: 1, 2, 3, 4, 5, 6, 7, 8, 9, 10, 12, 14, 15, 16, 17, 18, 19, 20, 22; W. A. Sharp: 21; The Scotsman Publications Limited: 11, 13, 23.

ACKNOWLEDGEMENT

THE poem 'Peevers in Parliament Square' by the late Dr John Oliver in chapter I is reprinted by permission of his sister Miss J. M. Oliver.

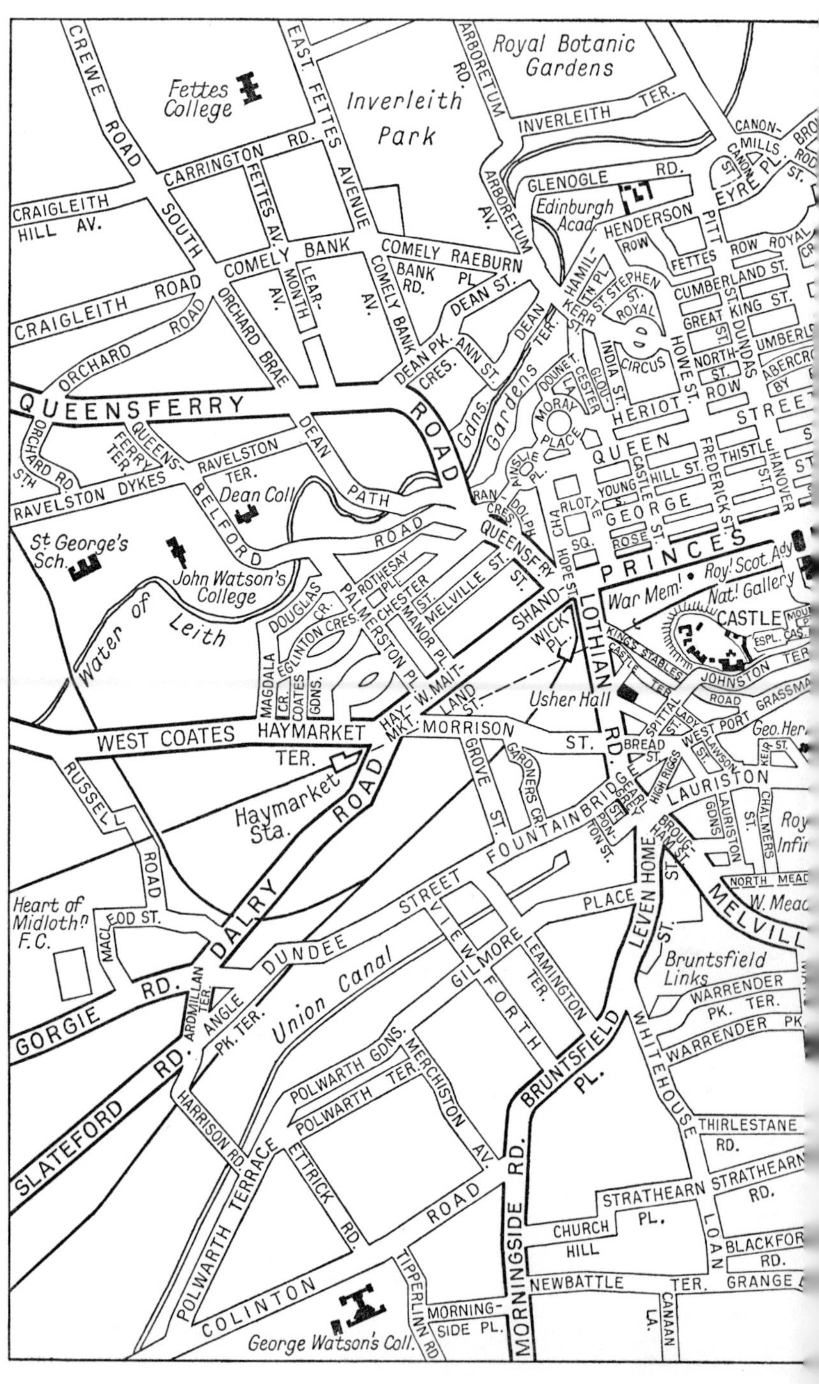

Fettes College
Royal Botanic Gardens
Inverleith Park
CREWE ROAD
EAST FETTES AVENUE
ARBORETUM RD.
INVERLEITH TER.
CARRINGTON RD.
FETTES AV.
GLENOGLE RD.
Edinburgh Acad.
CRAIGLEITH HILL AV.
SOUTH
COMELY BANK
COMELY BANK RD.
RAEBURN PL.
HENDERSON ROW
PITT ST.
EYRE PL.
CANONMILLS
CRAIGLEITH ROAD
ORCHARD ROAD
LEARMONTH AV.
COMELY BANK AV.
DEAN ST.
FETTES ROW
CUMBERLAND ST.
GREAT KING ST.
ST. STEPHEN ST.
ROYAL CIRCUS
ORCHARD BRAE
DEAN PK. CRES.
ANN ST.
DEAN TER.
INDIA ST.
GLOUCESTER
HOWE ST.
DUNDAS ST.
NORTHUMBERLAND ST.
QUEENSFERRY ROAD
DEAN PATH
MORAY PLACE
HERIOT ROW
ABERCROMBY PL.
QUEEN STREET
ORCHARD RD.
QUEENSFERRY TER.
RAVELSTON TER.
Dean Coll.
Gardens
AINSLIE PL.
CASTLE ST.
HILL ST.
FREDERICK ST.
THISTLE ST.
HANOVER ST.
RAVELSTON DYKES
BELFORD ROAD
YOUNG ST.
CHARLOTTE SQ.
GEORGE ST.
ROSE ST.
PRINCES ST.
St. George's Sch.
John Watson's College
ROTHESAY PL.
CHESTER ST.
MELVILLE ST.
QUEENSFERRY ST.
HOPE ST.
Roy! Scot. Ady
War Mem!
Nat! Gallery
Water of Leith
DOUGLAS CR.
EGLINTON CRES.
PALMERSTON PL.
MANOR PL.
SHANDWICK PL.
LOTHIAN RD.
CASTLE
ESPL.
KING'S STABLES
JOHNSTON TER.
MAGDALA CR.
COATES GDNS.
W. MAITLAND ST.
Usher Hall
CASTLE TER.
GRASSMARKET
WEST COATES
HAYMARKET TER.
HAYMKT.
MORRISON ST.
BREAD ST.
WEST PORT
Geo. Her.
RUSSEL ROAD
Haymarket Sta.
ROAD
GROVE ST.
GARDNERS CR.
LAURISTON
CHALMERS
Roy. Infir.
FOUNTAINBRIDGE
PONTON ST.
HOME ST.
Heart of Midloth! F.C.
McLEOD ST.
DALRY
DUNDEE STREET
VIEWFORTH
PLACE
LEVEN ST.
NORTH MEADOW
MELVILLE
GORGIE RD.
ARDMILLAN TER.
ANGLE PK. TER.
Union Canal
GILMORE
LEAMINGTON TER.
Bruntsfield Links
WARRENDER PK. TER.
SLATEFORD RD.
HARRISON RD.
POLWARTH GDNS.
POLWARTH TER.
MERCHISTON AV.
BRUNTSFIELD PL.
WHITEHOUSE LOAN
THIRLESTANE RD.
POLWARTH TERRACE
ETTRICK RD.
ROAD
STRATHEARN PL.
STRATHEARN RD.
CHURCH HILL
BLACKFORD RD.
COLINTON
TIPPERLINN RD.
MORNINGSIDE RD.
NEWBATTLE TER.
GRANGE
MORNINGSIDE PL.
CANAAN LA.
George Watson's Coll.

EDINBURGH
SCALE
0
1/4
1/2
3/4
1 MI.
PILRIG ST.
WALK
LEITH
EAST CLAREMONT ST.
McDONALD RD.
BELLEVUE
ANNANDALE ST.
HOPETOUN ST.
HOPETOUN CRES.
EAST LONDON ST.
BROUGHTON ST.
UNION ST.
ALBERT ST.
ST. CLAIR ST.
HAWKHILL AV.
LOCHEND RD.
LOCHEND AV.
SLEIGH DR.
Hibs. F.C.
ALBION ROAD
BRUNSWICK ROAD
ELGIN ST.
MONTGOMERY ST.
HILLSIDE CR.
EASTER ROAD
LONDON ROAD
ROYAL TERRACE
Lochend Pk.
LOCHEND RD. STH.
MARIONVILLE ROAD
ALBANY ST.
FORTH ST.
PICARDY PL.
YORK PL.
ELDER ST.
Cath.
National Mont
Nelson Mont
REGENT TER.
REGENT ROAD
MONTROSE TER.
ABBEYHILL
SPRING GDNS.
ROYAL PK. TER.
MEADOW PK. TER.
WATERLOO PL.
G.P.O.
NORTH BR.
WAVERLEY ST.
CALTON RD.
St. Andrew's Ho.
Waverley Sta.
CANONGATE
Palace of Holyroodhouse
St. Margaret's Loch
John Knox Ho.
HIGH ST.
HOLYROOD ROAD
St. Giles Cath.
COWGATE
SOUTH BR.
CHAMBERS ST.
Univ. of Edinburgh
Ro. Scot. Mus.
NICOLSON ST.
PLEASANCE
HOLYROOD PARK
SALISBURY CRAIGS
Dunsapie Loch
ARTHUR'S SEAT 823'
TEVIOT PL.
BRISTO ST.
POTTER ROW
GEORGE SQ.
MIDDLE MEADOW WALK
BUCCLEUCH PL.
BUCCLEUCH ST.
CLERK ST.
ST. LEONARD'S ST.
MEADOW LA.
East Meadow Park
DRIVE
PARK RD.
Duddingston Loch
S. CLERK ST.
BERNARD TER.
EAST PRESTON ST.
DALKEITH ROAD
Royal Edinburgh Hosp.
ARGYLE PL.
HATTON PL.
CHALMERS CRES.
SALISBURY RD.
NEWINGTON ST.
CAUSEWAYSIDE
MINTO ST.
GRANGE ROAD
FINDHORN PL.
RATCLIFFE TER.
EAST MAYFIELD
PRIESTFIELD ROAD
PLACE
LOAN
GRANGE

To

WENDY and ALASDAIR

so that they may never forget the city of their birth

PREFACE

My first tangible memory of Edinburgh is as a very small boy walking hand-in-hand with my father up winding Johnston Terrace. In his half-teasing way he told me about Scotland's capital. "This is a great and wonderful city," he said, "a city of surprise. Why, I wouldn't blink an eye if we saw the ghost of Prince Charlie sauntering down the Royal Mile or if a herd of wild elephants came marching round this corner." At that precise moment a herd of elephants did march round the corner. They were real ones, in single file, holding on to each other's tails with their trunks. A blare of music preceded them, then followed six white horses pulling a stagecoach of cowboys and cowgirls, the band and a caravan retinue behind. The truth, of course, was that the circus had come to town, but the suddenness of its appearance so close to my father's words and the incredulity on his face confirmed the miracle. Since then I have come to expect anything from Edinburgh, and the old city has seldom disappointed.

To write a book about Edinburgh is at once a privilege and a challenge. Edinburgh truly is a fine city, full of beauty and character, its history almost the story of Scotland itself. There is material for entire books down almost every close off the High Street. What I have tried to do in this one is present a panoramic portrait of Edinburgh, broad and expansive, yet here and there taking a close look at particular aspects, which I think may be of special interest or because, selfishly, they follow my own predilections. At times I have written in criticism. Elsewhere I have explained that the outsider may criticize Edinburgh only in fear of swift retribution, an insider only if he is of long standing and if an admirer. There I stake my claim, and I hope the sincerity in the criticism will be obvious to readers, for I am one of the city's most ardent admirers.

During the research and writing of this book I have had much help and many kindnesses from Edinburgh citizens of all ranks. I am particularly indebted to the following: Mr J. Stanley Cavaye, Chairman of the Edinburgh Voluntary Guides, for his advice, help and friendship; Mr J. B. Frizell, the former Director of Education; Mr Tom Hurst, Secretary and Treasurer of The Royal Infirmary; Mr Max McAuslane, Editor of the *Evening News,* for his permission to reproduce in part two of my articles from his paper; Mr Philip A. Stalker for his assistance on church affairs; Mr William Watson, Features Editor of *The Scotsman*; Mr Albert D. Mackie; Mr J. Brian Crossland; Mr Craig Ogilvie; Mr Murray Grant, *The Scotsman's* librarian, and the staffs of the National Library of Scotland and the Edinburgh Central Public Library; my father for his encouragement and wisdom; and my gratitude to Edinburgh writers past and present, who have recorded and reflected the affairs of the city over the years with devoted dedication.

Edinburgh I.A.N.

I

PEOPLE

THEY say that Edinburgh folk are cauldrife, that the teethy east wind and sea haars long since froze the marrow in their bones until the cold has even sunk into their senses. Aloof, snobbish, distant, especially to strangers. In Edinburgh all are strangers. A city of pease brose and grand pianos. Shake an Edinburgh man by the hand and you hazard finger frostbite. In Glasgow they ask if you have had your tea, in Edinburgh they say—you'll have had your tea. Austere, humourless, dour, mean—that is what they call Edinburgh folk.

How much is true and how much a confidence trick, a myth begun years ago by Edinburgh's great and boisterous rival, dear old, dirty old, friendly old Glasgow? The joke being that in its own way Glasgow is one of the most snobbish cities in Britain, ridden with class and social consciousness on a descending ladder of inverted snobbery that glorifies those long-drawn warbling vowels and glottal stops, fish suppers, Rangers, Celtic, bunnets and Sauchiehall Street.

The outstanding difference between Edinburgh and Glasgow folk is that basically Capital citizens are an aristocratic breed. It is true. Not just the difference between a vast, cosmopolitan, industrial city of over a million people and another of half its size. The differences are much more subtle. After all, Edinburgh's hardmen are just as tough, but fewer; Glasgow's society set are no less gracious than in the Capital; the throng on Argyle and Princes Streets are apparent siblings; there is little to choose between the industrial interests, although perhaps money is a force of greater motivation in the west, their yardstick of success.

But in Edinburgh something of the Capital's age and the

richness of its history has brushed off on its citizens. This is also true. The story of Edinburgh is very much the story of Scotland. It is a sad story in many ways, but colourful and proud.

The Edinburgh character has been forged from it, a process of age, centuries in the making, developing through wars, privations, revolutions in Church and State, re-routing the path of history. It has evolved through the fire-and-brimstone days of Knox, and his religious stormtroopers; the extroverts of the Robert Burns era and before it; the golden years of cultural renaissance; the uncertain dark days of invasion, unstable government, intrigue and murder in high places.

The echoes of history still sound for Edinburgh citizens, whether native or newcomer, whether French, Italian, Belgian, Pole, Norwegian, Nigerian, Greek, Indian or Pakistani—and there are communities of all of those in Edinburgh, and more—for time is atmospheric in the old city, and the experiences wrought by time have been imbued by the public to such an extent that there is no other city in the world whose citizens have such a sense of history and involvement in the story of their own town.

Of course, there are a number of more tangible facts we know about Edinburgh people. The last tally taken showed that there were more than 468,000 of them, 9 per cent of the total population of Scotland. At least two thirds are born and bred in the city, the birth rate is higher than the death rate, and there are more women than men compared to the rest of the country.

Over the years Edinburgh has had a steady population increase, even greater than in Scotland as a whole, although recently it has fallen slightly behind. Back in 1801 there were 90,768 people counted in the census, and then the numbers really began to move. By mid-century the figure had more than doubled to 208,000, and at the dawn of the twentieth century, it had reached 413,000. Since then the rate of increase has subsided, especially over the last twenty years.

In the second half of the last century Edinburgh had its best years of recruitment to the expanding city. As transport and accessibility improved, so the numbers began to swell, drawing the transfusion of new blood from all over Scotland, from Highland and Island stock, hard-working lowland folk from the surrounding districts, Borderers, and even an element from overseas. Yet over the next quarter century, which included the First World War, there was a considerable loss, not merely a result of battle toll, but a definite migration out of Edinburgh and the country. The movement has continued and Edinburgh still loses her sons, a few more every year, to all the corners of the world.

Among those 468,000 citizens, we know that drunkenness is on the increase, that about 160 will be divorced each year (where both parties are resident), approximately 30,000 crimes and offences will be committed, and that vandals will cost the tax-payer some £40,000. Which makes Edinburgh no worse than any other large city today, and better than most.

We also know that people care in Edinburgh. They care about all sorts of things: education; car parks; George Square; ring roads; rugby; football; Princes Street decorations; tradition; dignity; the neighbours across the street, even if they don't know their names; and particularly they care about old people. Old people are a problem. In the Capital they have an inherent silent pride forbidding many from seeking help. They regard themselves demeaned failures by accepting a handout, especially National Assistance, which they consider is for those flighty young ones incapable of managing their own affairs. Behind the disguise of crisp starched curtains, chalked steps and burnished door knobs many an old couple slowly starve or freeze to death while practising the impossible housekeeping geometry of stretching an inadequate old age pension that can never meet the demands made upon it, no matter how far it is elastically extended.

But Edinburgh takes the welfare of her senior citizens seriously. There is a kind of glowing dedication about those involved. Apart from the excellently run official organizations like Edinburgh and Leith Old Peoples' Welfare Council, Dalry House, Margaret Tudor House, Lamb's House, Leith Benevolent Association and the Red Cross, there is an army of private volunteers, often attached to churches, who are fired with the same kind of zeal as shown by city preservation societies. Where ancient Edinburgh is concerned—and that includes people as well as buildings—Edinburgh is indeed a city of passion.

Even the city down-and-outs are well catered for. This odd tribe of urban nomads, comprising junkies, meth drinkers, alcoholics, ne'er-do-weels, misfits, beatniks, as well as genuine homeless workers, men and women, in search of a roof and temporarily hard up, who turn the Grassmarket area into a kind of eastern bazaar scene, can find a bed for 3s. a night, with clean sheets if they are lucky, and a meal to go with it.

There is much of pride, poverty and irony about Edinburgh people. More of them go to fee-paying schools than in any other city in Britain, if not the world, and for years thousands lived in some of the worst slums in Europe; a confirmed bingo-addicted city with a turnover of thousands of pounds, and a locally unsupported international festival of music and arts that loses a fortune; a city of great churches and churchmen, but religiously apathetic citizens; a teaching hospital famous throughout the world as a pioneer in saving lives and easing suffering, and a death toll among middle-aged men from coronary thrombosis and lung cancer that has reached alarming proportions.

Yet Edinburgh folk, if statistics prove anything, are a hardy clan. The natural increase in population, the excess of births over deaths, gives an indication of their gristle. Families tend to be smaller in the Capital, and the infant mortality rate is becoming increasingly lower. Until nowadays it has been a tightly-knit community, cliquish, patrician, withdrawn, for it must be admitted that not all of those Glasgow snipers are unjustified in their criticism. Even now there is hardly a leg-breaking stampede to put out welcome mats to new residents, especially if they are unfortunate enough to have an accent associated with one of the less sophisticated English industrial areas. Perhaps that is why only 12 per cent of the population comes from furth of Scotland. Yet visitors can never complain about Edinburgh hospitality.

They are afforded the full bountiful treatment, no matter if they speak babbling Hindi or lilting Scouse. Their money is good, of course, although anything so distastefully vulgar is an affront to Edinburgh's delicate taste. The real reason that so much warmth is shown to tourists is because they *are* tourists, an ephemeral, Borealis race, here today and gone by the end of September, when the coffee mornings and afternoon tea sessions can continue uninterrupted, and Edinburgh can be its normal douce self again, through the drab, tourist-free, china-chinking winter.

Since the war, however, Edinburgh people have become much less insular, more outward-looking. Attitudes have altered, the mood of the city has changed. But tradition dies slowly in a great city like the Capital, a way of life does not disappear overnight. There remains a residue of the Old Brigade, particularly among the city's elderly ladies. They are magnificent. Edinburgh is a city of types, and these haughty-eyed matrons, graciously splendid and so befitting an ancient capital, are to Edinburgh what royalty is to Britain. Elegant, dignified, proud, bewildered at the eye-blink speed of the changing world about them, they study *The Scotsman* leaders daily, take afternoon tea at four, and think big, expansive thoughts.

Some take their places on various city organizations of a useful, helpful, counselling nature, providing a bowl of rice for India's starving multitude, a word of advice to erring young girls in trouble, upholding the traditions of Scotland at home and abroad. They are timeless, excruciatingly respectable, devoted to their causes, not of their generation, deserving admiration and very much a part of the city scene.

A younger generation of the Mark Two variety are ready to take their place for the future. You can see them over their coffee in Jenners, the Edinburgh Bookshop, Darlings. Here, Glasgow would say, eyeing the tweeds, the furs, the model hats, the general air of felicitous, restrained opulence, is the Land of Snob. They would be wrong. It is just the Edinburgh coffee set hard at it. Perhaps there are overtones of snobbery, more easily detected among the lower echelons frequenting other establishments, but in Edinburgh coffee and afternoon tea are traditional. The patrons meet in the same way that parliamentarians use the Lobby. It is an exercise in social science, a further education class, a hallowed Edinburgh institution.

There is much talk in Edinburgh outside coffee houses and the town council chambers. It is one of the characteristics of Edinburgh people that they are outspoken. They will say what they believe, with little regard for the consequences, even if it makes them look, as we say in Scotland, half daft. There are more half daft characters in Edinburgh than in any other city in Britain. There is a danger here to sentimentalize over Edinburgh and its people. The lives of Capital citizens follow much the same pattern as in other large cities. Life is real and life is earnest and there is a fair portion of everything that makes it good, bad, hopeful, bearable or indifferent. Through its people there are reflections of love, hate, pride, misery, religion, crime, honesty, poverty, wealth. That is life, and it is also Edinburgh. But people make cities and create their character, and Edinburgh is a city of distinctive character which, carried to its conclusion, means that the citizenry of the Capital are also distinctive. Perhaps because Edinburgh is a capital they have been attracted to it like homing moths to bright lights, or perhaps, because it is such a city of character itself, it is character-forming.

It is certainly not to say that Edinburgh folk appear in any way different from those in other towns, yet there is undoubtedly a propensity to produce characters to a remarkable extent. The real Edinburgh character is a complex combination betwixt a worthy, a nonconformist and an eccentric, and the city has mass-produced them over the centuries.

Just think of those incredible old judges who sat on the Scottish bench in the eighteenth century. Bedecked in rustling gowns and powdered wigs, quaffing port and munching biscuits, faces suitably solemn and with an air of dignity befitting their positions in society, erudite, witty, full of earthy commonsense, and thoroughly, unashamedly eccentric.

There was Lord Gardenstone, for instance, who once kept a pet pig which followed the noble lord around like a loving dog. People said it even shared his bed until it grew so large and heavy that the collapse of the four-poster was imminent, when it was forced to spend the night on the floor, nestled in his lordship's best cloak.

Lord Hermand was preoccupied with the glories of days long gone. The publication of Scott's *Guy Mannering,* reflecting these balmy times, moved him so deeply that he carried the book constantly with him, poring over its pages whenever he had a chance.

His conversation was monopolized by *Guy Mannering,* which eventually bored his friends to frenzy point. As bores go, they would say, Hermand is artesian. At one point he even produced *Guy Mannering* in court to illustrate his argument over some remote legal point, and insisted, in spite of anguished pleas for mercy from his fellows, in reading out the whole of the High Jinks chapter. It was noticed how he was shunned for a time after this. Hermand could also take his dram better than most, and could be counted upon to retain his feet on a hard night until the last body hit the floor. For him drinking was almost a virtue. Once when a friend had been killed in a drunken altercation, Hermand leaped to his feet crying, "Good God, if he will do this when he's drunk, what will he not do when he's sober."

The stories revolving around the woolly Lord Monboddo are legion. Perhaps one of his strangest notions was his unshakeable belief in human tails. It is said that he was known to hide near houses where new babies were awaited so that he could be readily on the scene to see the poor infant before the midwife amputated its tail. Lord Arniston was not beyond measuring the time a judge spoke with a sandglass, as if he were boiling an egg, and if the speaker waxed verbose, the instrument would be ominously thrust under his nose and shaken threateningly.

Lord Kames, an orator of quite outstanding ability, could cast a snake-like spell over the court, bending wills this way and that to meet his requirements, gently caressing them the while with his golden tongue. Unfortunately, he had a nasty habit of affectionately calling his closest friends by the most obscene names. Then the magic would be splintered. After holding his audience spellbound with his flights of rhetoric, he would crash-land them with a merry: "Weel, that's that, ye auld b—, ah'll be seein' ye!"

Lord Braxfield had also a sharp tongue. A man of brilliant

intellect, yet so uncouth that his wit, for which he was famous, contained so much calculated coarseness that few examples of it are with us today. He gave the poor Jacobites a sair time, ruthlessly venting his fury on them as a political measure. It was once pointed out to him that all great men had been reformers, even Christ himself. Braxfield glowered his reply. "Muckle he made o' that," he said. "He was hangit."

Much of our knowledge of this period emanates from another of the great judges and Edinburgh characters, Lord Cockburn, who set down the passing scene in his fascinating *Memorials of His Own Time*.

This was Edinburgh's golden age, the renaissance when Scottish thought and culture came out of the shadows. Cockburn lived during the transition period, a reformer himself but able to look back with sympathy into the preceding dark days, and understand them. The reforming zeal of the new age, as in all revolutions, was ready to sweep the slate clean, despising tradition, seeking different values. Lord Cockburn was the steadying influence, the man who brought objectivity to bear on the changing Edinburgh, and, reformist though he was, he would speak out against change for the sake of change, quietly indicating what was of worth from the old days as he stepped cannily in the new. It was to Cockburn's credit that Princes Street and the Mound remain in magnificence, and it is in his name today that Lord Cameron, a prominent member of the Cockburn Association and another famous law lord, tries to keep sanity in preserving Edinburgh's amenities from possible follies of a misguided public.

There is a very amusing poem, written by the late John W. Oliver in 1954, which suggests that there is no shortage of characters among the present crop of distinguished Edinburgh men of law.

We know this for a fact, although whether they are so bohemian as to be peevers-players[1] is another matter. Mr. Oliver wrote the verses after seeing a beautifully executed peever-court in the centre of Parliament Square.

[1] Hop-scotch players.

They're playin' at Peevers in Parliament Square,
In Parliament Square, in Parliament Square;
And judges and pleaders and writers are there,
A' ettlin' to play at the Peevers.

They run oot like stour when they're by wi' their trokes,
To the beds, chalkit oot like a muckle square box
Atween Chairlie's horse and the grave o' John Knox—
A gran' place to play at the Peevers!

The Lord President's sel', when the pleaders are mute
And he's fain hae a change frae forensic dispute,
Has challenged the Lord Justice Clerk to come oot
To see wha'll be best at the Peevers.

And the Writers and Advocates, gethert aroun,
They a' held their braiths and nane daurt mak' a soun,
As ilk ane cam forrit and kiltit his goun,
Syne yerkit awa at the Peevers.

They stood on ae leg wi' nae shoogle or swither,
And the Peevers they skiffed frae ae square to anither,
And the hale Bench and Bar were sune roarin' thegither
To see them sae gleg at the Peevers.

But the Lord Justice Clerk, he was soople and strang,
And it seemed he juist couldna dae onything wrang;
But the President could—and it wasna that lang
Till he awned himsel bate at the Peevers.

And the Lord Justice Clerk said, "In maitters o' Law,
My Lord, there are nane that come near ye ava;
In fact, ye're the flooer o' the Parliament Ha',
But ye're no worth a dawm at the Peevers."

But that nicht, when the mirk happit Parliament Ha',
And Pleaders and Writers had a' gane awa,
The mune lookit doon, and a ferlie she saw
At the place where they'd played at the Peevers.

For she saw a dark shape that gaed slinkin' aboot
Aroun' Parliàment Square wi' a pail and a cloot;
And syne it bent doon, and it clean wipit oot
The beds where they'd played at the Peevers.

So the bonnie white beds noo are a' wede awa;
They're clean dichtit oot ayont hope o' reca',
And they're sighin' and sabbin' in Parliament Ha';
For they canna get playin' at the Peevers.

Then there were those extraordinary characters of a later era and lower social aspirations, the multifarious army of street traders, entertainers, waifs, crackpots, Bible-thumpers, discontents, no-gooders, and do-gooders, who were one of the city sights in themselves only fifty or sixty years ago. Many are still remembered, some with affection, most now with pity. But what a gathering! What an astonishing mixture of humanity, the whole drama of life concentrated virtually on one street, a compelling fascination to stroll down the Royal Mile's memory lane. . . .

Like Coconut Tam at his stance opposite the old Temperance Hotel, a kenspeckle, humpy wee man, outsize lugs supporting a frayed bowler, jacket sleeves turned back to the elbow to make them fit. Over his right arm he sports a malacca stick, and under his scraggy beard the shirt collar is of the fly-away variety. As the citizens of Edinburgh pass about their business his battle cry sounds above the rattle of hansom cabs juddering down the Royal Mile: "Coco-nit! Coco-nit! Come an' buy, ha'penny a bit!" Yes, Coconut Tam himself, standing half-bent on the pavement with his wares spread out before him—and all around the sounds, sights and smells of the Edinburgh at the turn of the century. Coconut Tam, or Tam Simpson to give him his real name, had his home in Potterrow behind the Empire Theatre. He was just one of a host of characters like Pie Davie, Moodie Heels, Caw'nle Dowps, Register Rachael, Burn the Bible, Mutton Hole Wullie, Walking Dick, Farthing Bob of the Watergate, Betsy Mustard of the Canongate and, only a dozen or so years ago, Gramophone Grannie, who entertained the queues outside the Playhouse

Cinema. Gramophone Grannie, or Mary Russell, of Portsmouth Square, ca'd the handle of her record machine with the firm belief that the people who went to the pictures were the meanest race on earth. Yet she could boast with pride that she never took a penny off the parish in her life.

There were the street singers and musicians, and in the old days many were really accomplished performers. Davie Arkley and Jamie Mair, who used to tuck his big spade beard inside his coat to keep his neck warm, were almost a theatre show in themselves as they made their rounds among the closes of the Old Town. Albert Parkin, with his wee mongrel dog at his heels, was another favourite and a fine artist on the violin. He could argue with considerable knowledge about the various merits of fiddle-makers from all over the world. His beat was High Street and the Mound. One winter's night a passer-by asked him if he felt the chill. Albert shook his head with a smile and slowly unfastened the six raincoats that he was wearing to show the five warm jerseys below. The go-as-you-please competitions at the Old Star Picture House were always an attraction to him, and when he competed he never failed to walk home with the first prize of 10s. Swing Charlie, the blind musician, was a welcome turn, and Poemy Dick could pick up any tune on his melodeon after hearing it only once.

Perhaps some of Edinburgh's old characters deserved more pity than publicity, although in their own right they were splashes of colour in the city. Beef was one of them. He was given no other name—just Beef. With a tall lum hat on his head, a long swallow-tail coat to his back which almost swept the street, he could make a pound of steak disappear from a butcher's shop before you realized it was missing.

But on the occasions when someone saw the blur of his hand, the poor man would be chased down Easter Road with a pack of urchins, women and an angry butcher on his heels shouting: "Beef! Beef! Beef!" until the whole street was chanting the name.

Feechie, the Duddingston letter carrier, knew what it was to have a crowd of small boys screaming behind him as he hefted his big bag of mail up to the G.P.O., and old Moudy Cheese, who wandered the city streets around the 1880s, became so exasperated at his tormentors roaring his nickname that he decided to leave the country. Off he sailed to New York, but as he stepped off the gangway to set foot in America and start a new life, up went the cry again: "Here comes Moudy Cheese!" News of his arrival time had already been advanced to former Edinburghians in the skyscraper city.

One of the most famous of all Edinburgh characters was Theodore Napier, who strolled around the Capital's streets in full Highland dress, complete with sword. His white hair fell on his shoulders in cavalier curls, and his eagle's feather was fixed to his balmoral by a silver buckle. A great supporter of the Jacobite cause, he refused to drink any toast except to "The King oe'r the water".

Once at an Edinburgh banquet he was heavily criticized for his lack of good manners in failing to rise for the loyal toast. Leaping to his feet with a snarl, he ferociously challenged his critics to a duel—with dirk or battleaxe. One look at this wild man was enough. The answer was silence. Australian-born, he had some property and business interests there, and eventually acknowledging that the Stuart cause was indeed lost, he returned home, to the relief of many.

Although some of Edinburgh's characters were in the advanced stages of eccentricity, the citizens were always ready to take them to their heart. Dr Cochrane, the Lawnmarket chemist, was one. He performed a multitude of duties like attending births, pulling teeth, and keeping the poorer folk happy with bottles of Gregory's Mixture. His black skull cap was familiar in the poor districts, children knew him for his sweeties, widows and the destitute for the fly sixpences he slipped them without waiting for thanks.

Even Funeral Wullie was a weel-liked chiel in his tall hat, baggy black clothes, and gloomy face. Looking like a hoodie crow he would wait outside the infirmary gates for the funeral processions to pass, and he was never happier than when he found a place in the leading cab. Funerals were his great preoccupation, yet he refused to attend when a child was involved. The death of the very young depressed him unbearably.

Another man in black was the Bible-punching street preacher, Daddy Flockhart, who had a regular stance at St Giles, where he called hellfire down on the heads of a good-natured citizenry. Wee Daddy's turn of phrase brought a smile even to dour kirk faces, only to have them quickly wiped off again with the threat of the man with the horns. "If ah had ma wey," he would shout, "Ah'd fill Mons Meg fu' o Bibles and fire salvation doon the High Street. Aye, when ah go tae Heaven ye'll be tryin' tae hing on tae may coat tails, but ah'll put on a short jaiket that day and fool ye!"

Tarry Jean was another character who would have preferred sympathy to jeers as she wheeled her tarry barrels up to her house in Aird's Close in the Grassmarket. She collected them from all over the city, before breaking them up and selling them for kindling, to scratch a meagre living.

Scranner Mary was considered one step down the social ladder, but her profits were worth the indignity. Mary was up at 4 a.m. to scrape around the city garbage cans and rescue the oddments that were for the dump. There was never a pot of gold, but the junk merchants were generous with their pennies, and nowadays, although the scranners are hunted by the police, the scrap and rag business has become a profitable trade.

Hogmanay at the Tron was always a big attraction for the characters of the Old Town. Many turned out to toast in the New Year with the hope that the next would be a little more rewarding. Ginger Jack was sure to be there with his lungbursting machine, and Old Carrots never did better business with his height and weight contraption. Blind Bess, with her head wrapped in a tartan shawl and white stick by her side, sold sweet Seville oranges with a serene smile on her tranquil face, until someone tried to give her short money or a dud coin, then Bess would let them have the full blast of her tongue with language and invective that would do credit to the dockers of Leith.

These were some of the colourful citizens familiar to all and part of the kaleidoscope of the Edinburgh scene. But, of course, the whole Edinburgh story is sprinkled with characters who for one reason or another stood out from their fellows, some by their eccentricity, intellect, circumstance, others by force of personality. Like famous Jenny Geddes, the first stool-thrower, or so history says, at the great St Giles' riot of 1637, when Charles I tried to introduce his new Liturgical service for the Church of Scotland. The independent Edinburgh spirit never has been easily swayed, and Jenny, with her cry of "Out fausse thief," and her well-aimed stool at Dean Hanna's lug, typified the city's and church's determined thrawnness to think and act with freedom.

Bowed Joseph was another. General Joseph, as he was called by the mob of the Old Town, ruled as dictator in spite of all that the city fathers and the law could do, until his death when he fell off a stage coach on his way home from Leith races after an over-convivial evening. A Cowgate cobbler, stunted, deformed, yet with extraordinary strength in his arms, Bowed Joseph could call the baying pack of rabble to heel with one piercing whistle. At least 10,000 of his followers, it is said, could be gathered within the hour, ready to do his bidding. The city officers were powerless and even sycophantic in their dealings with him. General Joseph was in charge, and his justice, though fair, was swift and final.

One of the great characters of the city was fishwife Meggie Ramsay, from Newhaven. Meggie was an acknowledged beauty in her day, but the bite of her tongue was even more famous than her looks. Once one of Edinburgh's gay young men about town decided to hold a fish supper in the village, and during the evening took the chance to deliver a stinging attack on the fishy smell of Newhaven. It was too much for Meggie. Up she jumped, shaking her fist. There was not a man there would dare stop her. "Deil scrape the parlin face o' ye," she cried. "The last I saw ye, ye were in the Auld To'buith for debt. Forbye, ye're owin' me saxpence for the brood o' oysters ye got the water caddie tae wile oot o' me. I'll be obliged tae ye for it this verra meenit. Smell! Ye'll dowm a guid honest stink where there's nane. In fact, the To'buith is whiles like tae gar me faint."

One of Meggie's stances was at the head of Lady Stair's Close off the High Street, a corner where some of the city's nobility lived. One of her calls was to Principal Baird's house, who at that time lived in Allan Ramsay's old home in Ramsay Garden. It was one of the Principal's special pleasures to hear Meggie's sweet cry of "caller ou-ou . . ." come echoing back from the grey Castle rock.

Today only a few characters remain to attract a smile and wink in city streets: a poor soul who sports three hats all worn at once, trekking the centre of town with rucksack on back; a negro, dungaree-clad on working days, steps out at the week-end in immaculate sartorial splendour, complete with shooting-stick; a lady of enormous proportions who parades Princes Street like a princess. On the same street, shoulder-rubbing with the proletariat, other characters on a higher social rung: writers, poets, business men, academics, clerics, medics, socialites, distinctive from their fellows, colourful without demonstration, mostly unassuming, yet definitely different, with minds and principles of their own, and the courage to stick by them. But in this age of sameness and monotonous facsimiles of each other Edinburgh's characters have taken a pounding.

Slowly they are disappearing, as that all-engulfing, Brobdingnagian bureaucratic machine, hard jammed on a course of individual suppression, sucks them in, works them over, cajoling, indoctrinating, soothing, hinting, then regurgitates them, not in triplicate, but in millions of puppet people, looking, acting, thinking alike. Not just in Edinburgh, or even in this country, but halfway across the world. That is a problem. Thank goodness there is a rebel or two left in Edinburgh still and some seemingly abnormals who though behind their backs receive knowing smiles and fingers tapping heads, are probably the sanest of all.

And what about the wee folk, the Edinburgh children? Give or take a complexion and a language or two, young people are the same the world over, reality-insulated, wide-eyed in awe at their own great adventure in their earth-rooted galaxy of make-believe land. High above their heads in Edinburgh the age-old castle broods, the tenement canyons of the Old Town look down on the Royal Mile and the historic wynds and closes where many of the famous names in Scotland walked and talked. Edinburgh's child is oblivious to the splendour. He sees it because it is there, a fact, but for him without significance. In childhood we accept the world for what it is. Whether it is a cheerless flat in Easter Road or a mansion in Fairmilehead, to youngsters it is merely a place to stay, a flat and a mansion, home, facts without conclusions.

The castle and the High Street are the same for the boy in a Barnton villa as for the little girl with her broken doll playing along the pavements of Niddrie, Craigmillar or Leith Walk. Life is real and hard or happy, just as they find it, and the turrets of the castle or the big iron cannons are only parts of that life, something to play around or perhaps to dream over. There is the same innocence, the same sensitive wonderment on both their faces. They have their own world with their own secret key to its door. To us it is always shut. For the very young life is such an exciting exploration, so full of strange discoveries, that historic pride is of little moment, even if someone took the trouble to explain to them what it meant.

But if the beauty of Edinburgh and its story meet with the unimpressed, matter-of-fact stare of a five-year-old who has shared the life and death struggles of television spacemen and fast-shooting cowboys, it has also made its impact. For it is fact, and children never miss facts; it is there to be seen, the castle, the symbol, always there, high on the hill so that every citizen must lift his head to view it. As children grow older there is comprehension in those facts and gradual pride, not always self-admitted, and a sense of ownership.

Which may account in no little way for that air of superiority among Edinburgh folk, for it is not every city that has an ancient castle and architectural splendour at the bottom of the back garden.

Those spacemen and cowboys have changed the pattern of Edinburgh childhood. Television spirits them off the streets at five o'clock, and gives them new games to play and new heroes to emulate, when at one time they were left to find their amusement through their own inventiveness. As the decaying tenements crumble and families move into the suburban housing schemes, the children leave behind many of their traditional games and the haunts that have been familiar for generations. There are no queues nowadays outside the Scabby Alice and the

Alabam, or, to give them their more polite names, the Palace and The Alhambra. The Money Bag, better known as the George, up in Morningside, is seldom full. Even the cinemas themselves are vanishing. Bingo and television have taken over from many of the former stamping-grounds and pastimes, but with all a child's genius for adaptation and assimilation into new surroundings, new games or new versions of the old, and a whole new series of nicknames are soon specially produced.

The secret signs and hieroglyphics chalked on close walls ("Ah widnae draw oan ma ain wa', mister, Ah'd only dae it oan somebody else's"); the peever-beds of the lassies scrawled on the pavements; the strange, impassioned cries from a group of boys huddled at the kerbside: "Keps! Nae Keps! Nae high nickle! Bombers!", then, in lower tones as their game of bools swings this way and that, "Ah'll gie ye twa glessies for a jaurie or fower steelies"; the weird chants accompanying the girls at their skipping, or as they play their stotting ball games; it is all a fascinating study, a peep into the world that is barred to us.

The lassies have done well to retain in their play what was best of the old days, in spite of house-proud mothers in their new semi-detacheds who do not particularly relish peever-beds scribbled outside their front doors. How many of the old rhymes come back over the years:

Nievie, nievie knick knack,
Which haun' will ye tak'
Tak' the richt, tak' the wrang
Ah'll beguile ye if I can.

or:

Sugarallie water
Black as the lum,
Gether up peens
An' ye'll get some.

or for use in one of their counting games:

Eetle ottle black bottle
Eetle ottle out,
Shining on the mantelpiece
Like a silver threepenny piece.

The girls are quick to use any topical situation that lends itself to rhyme. It is almost possible to trace the major events over the years in these street operettas. They reflect love, war, soldiers, home-comings, school, murder, films, television and the odd happenings that occur from time to time in the neighbourhood. Going back to the First World War, the lassies in their long ankle-length dresses and black hand-knitted stockings were singing,

Bluebells, dum-dum shells
Eevie ivy over,
Charlie Chaplin went to France
To teach the ladies how to dance.
First your heel and then your toe
Then ye go
Big birlie-o.

And as time marched on the two big stars of the cinema screen of the late 1930s were projected thus:

One, two, three a-leerie
I spy Wallace Beery
Sitting on his bumbeleerie
Kissing Shirley Temple.

Many of the old favourites are still played. Dodgie, Allevo, Be-bo-babbity, donkey, rounders, french cricket, kick the can, chessies in season, heiders, three-an'-in, ballie, doublers, hoppies, skiffies, bools in all their forms, which include guttery, holie and ringie, although plonkers and dollickers are hardly ever heard of now, like chuckie-stanes, a game that seems to have altered out of all recognition.

If ye stan' oan a line ye'll br'ak yer spine
If ye stan' oan a crack ye'll br'ak yer back.

Green peas, mutton pies,
Tell me where my Jenny lies,
I'll be there afore she dies
Tae cuddle her in my bosom.

Hearts ever, Hibs never.

Imagine the thoughts of some foreign visitor on hearing a group of innocent lassies chant:

Eentie teentie fingerty fell
Ell dell demon ell
Urky purky tarry rope
An tan toosie Jock.

These are the games, the thoughts, the streets, the castle, the closes, the sweetie and toy shops, the new housing schemes, the whole world of the children of Edinburgh, and, with only a few minor changes, the world of bairns anywhere. We should smile upon them as they pass, for, even as we watch, the door to that enchanted land is closing upon them, but mercifully never enough to keep out another generation of new wee ones to take their place.

The vanishing backstreets and closes still remain a rich slice of Edinburgh life. They provide a finishing school in the arts of self-preservation for the children who live in them, a preliminary training ground for the varying fortunes of adulthood. Do not confuse the closes of Edinburgh and Glasgow. In spite of an army of responsible Glasgow citizens living in closes—a symbol of respect if your flat is in a half-tiled wally one—among outsiders they still wrongly reflect Gorbals and gangland, a whiff of danger round each dark corner. Edinburgh closes are associated with the wynds and passages of the Royal Mile, where the city's aristocracy once lived. But there are other closes, too. Many, many of them, mostly in grey and ageing tenements, where generations of honest Edinburgh citizens spend their lives and which they call home. In Edinburgh a close as often as not is called a stair to distinguish it from those of the Old Town, and life on an Edinburgh stair has its own individuality and colour.

Never underestimate the stair-folk. Much of worth and pride is there, only unexpected for those unfamiliar with the tenement traditions, just as there is much of everything in life, good and bad, perhaps enhanced and exaggerated because of the tightly knit community. Most of all there is realism, and the acceptance of it, and one of the great virtues of Edinburgh people, tolerance. There are none of the problems of religion or race that bedevil Glasgow.

Apart from the odd shouting match and punch-up on a Saturday night, Proddies and Papes, Piscies and Wee Frees, Pakistanis, Norwegians, Irishmen, Englishmen, Poles and Chinamen live happily enough with their long-established Edinburgh neighbours in amicable armistice. Much is to be learned from the close inmates of Abbeyhill, Leith, Fountainbridge, Gorgie, Canonmills, Slateford, Broughton, Leith Walk and many another part of Edinburgh's tenement lands. Today there are many Capital citizens living prosperously in comfortable staid suburbia who had their beginnings on one of the city's stairheads. They say that it takes every kind to make the world. In microcosm they are all found up an Edinburgh working-class close.

Take for example Mrs Gilhooley. She lived in the fourth-floor flat of a drab tenement building that had done service for a hundred years. She was a big woman in every way. Tall, undulating, and wobbly in her stoutness, with arms that some girls would have been pleased to use for legs, and legs like over-filled sausages. As she scliffed about in a pair of worn baffies, stockingless, permanently peeny-clad, there exuded from her an impression of military imperiousness. Here was a woman who was always right, you could tell at a glance. Her roar, to emphasize the point, was like the thunder of mighty waters. Mrs Gilhooley had thirteen children and a wee shilpit husband, who held down a job in Leith docks. The Gilhooley stamp was across the faces of them all, eleven boys and two girls. Dark and straight of hair, dark eyes, wide mouths. Except for one, the eighth. His hair was bright ginger, eyes grey, mouth rosebud.

Life in the little flat was a thing of incredulity. The family slept cross-ways in three beds, two drawers, and a blanket on the floor. Noise was the most astonishing first impression. Deafening, of course, but by shouting at varying pitches of crescendo and with some adroit lip-reading they were able to converse with a degree of comprehension. Almost every article and stick of furniture in the flat was capable of producing noise response, and every child was skilled in obtaining it to a maximum. Even the baby in the go-chair had the ability to discover sound effect in a plate of mashed turnip. The radio blared; the toddler Gilhooley and the crawler Gilhooley screamed, chortled, snuffled or hiccuped as the mood took them between knocking things over or together; the elder Gilhooleys whooped, thudded, squealed and chanted; the canary warbled; the cat meowed, occasionally howled if cajoled with a sharp instrument; Mr Gilhooley girned; and above all was the volcanic rumble of Mrs Gilhooley. At feeding times, especially lunch, when a cousin and sister Gilhooley arrived to make use of the free canteen service, bedlam was church-like in comparison.

When school was out at four o'clock, thirteen jammy pieces were consumed to stave off starvation until tea at 5.30 when father Gilhooley arrived home. The children changed into their play clothes and the din began in earnest. Clothes were always a problem. They were handed down one to the other until the smallest walker was wearing short trousers hitched up to his chest that reached half way between knee and ankle. From the earliest, babies were the dolls of the house, live playthings that gave the Gilhooley children the premature responsibilities of parenthood, and they accepted it willingly. They fought constantly with everyone and everything, especially each other, unless one took a licking from an outsider, when the clan instinct reasserted itself and the pack came baying in defence. They were as tough and self-reliant as young hawks.

Tuesday and Thursday were bingo days for Mrs Gilhooley, and on Friday and Saturday evenings the Gilhooley himself donned his tawdry finery and with a suede-shoe shuffle sauntered pubwards to debate with his cronies on the week's happenings: the connivings of politics, the myopia of football referees, management-labour relations, the female sex in general and in particular the misfortune of espousing a mountainous member with pugilistic tendencies. Sometimes it was necessary to continue the deliberations in the house of a friend with the aid of a "cairry-oot", and on such occasions the belated Gilhooley, deeply conscious of the transgression, would make his way up the narrow stairs to his home preceded by the aroma of a conciliatory fish supper.

Saturday morning was bath time for the older members of the family. They trooped along to the local swimming pool, two towels between them, one for the girls, the other for the six boys. The great unwashed of Edinburgh had gathered for their weekly cleansing. Money was scarce and times could be hard. There was the occasional visit to the pawnbroker, and once Mrs Gilhooley found herself forced to enter between the imposing graffiti-covered portals of the Ministry of Social Security. But in the poorer districts people still practise help thy neighbour and when the pinch came, injury or illness, there was always a helping hand, someone with an extra bowl of soup, another to do the washing or muck out the house. Where hardship is commonplace there are no inhibitions of pride to prevent asking for help or giving it. Compassion and understanding remain one of the great qualities of the poor.

Not that the Gilhooleys considered themselves underprivileged in any way. If some unwitting sociologist had even suggested it, Mrs Gilhooley was quite capable of answering with a left hook. And who was to argue with her? Who could deny that the children did not appreciate life and find pleasure and happiness in it? Who could say that it held no meaning or future for them? Certainly there were periods of extreme poverty, scrimping and half-rations, but that is life, it happens in every walk of it, and the Gilhooleys were better equipped than most to deal with such contingencies. Their priest called them the salt of the earth. It would have been a courageous man to tell Mrs Gilhooley otherwise.

Then there was wee Mrs Rubena McKinnon, always on the hop, jog-trotting around her house, polishing, dusting, tidying, fidgeting continually, swiping at imagined dust specks. Mrs McKinnon was a member of the Brethren. She went to one of the city Meetings, attended twice on Sunday, and on Wednesday and Saturday evenings. She said grace before meals, held a Bible-reading and prayer session every night, giving thanks for preserving her during the day, and another session in the morning when she woke to find she was still there. She frowned on television, radio, cinema, jeans, short skirts, tight trousers, dancing, smoking, drinking, Catholics, bigoted splinters of the Brethren, and other works of the Devil. She knew that the end of the world was nigh when God's wrath would be terrible, and that only she and a small handful of like believers were to be saved. She had dedicated her life to that day. She was solemn, reserved, kind and friendly enough when spoken to, a lover of children, suspicious of strange men, skinny, frumpish, industrious, generous and middle-aged.

But Mrs McKinnon, or Bible Beanie as she was called behind her back, did not anticipate her salvation by sitting at home ticking off the days.

After her husband died, she was hard put to keep on her decrepit home. It was sited in a dreary, unsavoury tenement with a gloomy close entrance, by day a playground for children and dogs, a platform for gossips and aged tenants to deliver their sermons, at night almost sinister, a place for loiterers, lovers, and, because there was a pub only a few yards away, occasionally a urinal. Mrs McKinnon did not specially want to live there, but she was used to it, and it was within her budget at a scrape.

To help out she did a weekly washing for two elderly brothers who lived nearby, and there was a lady with a young family glad of her help in cleaning and polishing around her house. All this Mrs McKinnon did for a few extra shillings. But to ease the financial burden still further, she took a full-time job, helping out in a draper's shop owned by a decent, God-fearing, ailing woman, an elderly member of the Brethren. She set about her duties with a will, and, because her employer was quite frail, she was soon running the place. The two got on extremely well together, but as the poor woman grew weaker and weaker, Mrs McKinnon was forced to look after her at home, dispensing comfort in prayer, reading the text calendar and long passages from the Bible. When the old lady eventually passed on, Mrs McKinnon found she had been left the entire business. For the first time in her life she faced the future without a financial care in the world.

Now you might have thought that at last Mrs McKinnon could enjoy a little comfort herself, even luxury in her life. Not so. You might have thought that she would have bought herself a small bungalow somewhere, or even a nice flat where people with like bank balances could live in respectability. To be honest, she did give it consideration. But then she got to thinking. What would the two old gentlemen do with no one to take in their washing? She did not think or perhaps did not want to think, that they would simply find someone else. What would that kind, harassed lady and her children say? They had had such a trouble to obtain a suitable person, someone who took care and bothered. What would the neighbours think? They really were quite nice, and she got on well with them all. If she flitted to a better-class area they might even have called her snob.

So Mrs McKinnon did not move. She stayed in her slummy old close and became richer and richer. She brushed and washed the disgusting stairs every Friday evening, became a char for the kind lady and her children on her Wednesday half-holiday, took in the washing for the aged brothers on a Saturday, ironed it on Monday and delivered it *en route* to her Wednesday afternoon stint. In the meantime she carried on at the shop. The Meeting was attended with the same devotion. She increased her donation to cover five overseas missions, and during her summer holiday (a new extravagance) she visited a Meeting in Aberdeen, as well as travelling to a Bible conference in Glasgow.

Of course, the ownership of the shop was never mentioned openly, and the neighbours were unaware of her true position. But they guessed and added the words mean and stingy to the other names they called her. Only behind her back. To her face they were just the same. And Mrs McKinnon was happy.

Mrs Gilhooley and Mrs McKinnon lived within fifty yards of each other. Taken out of context they appear almost bizarre. But in their own environment of Edinburgh's tenement and working-class areas they are not particularly noteworthy or even exceptional. They are merely part of the vast army of Edinburgh citizenry, ordinary people with all the faults, virtues, qualities and idiosyncrasies of ordinary people, and if you look very closely into the faces of the passing crowd, you will see the reflections, quite clearly, of both of them.

Of course, the Capital is not short of citizens who really do stand out from the masses. People who have forced their way into public recognition by their own qualities as individuals and because of their exclusive difference. Their names appear in the newspapers for what they have done or said. Sometimes for what they have not done or not said. They are celebrities, personalities, characters. They come from every walk of life. Some hate it, others adore the distinction. Edinburgh is full of them.

The extraordinary Sir Compton Mackenzie is one of them, an author who actually looks like one, a conversationalist of such engaging brilliance that he ranks among the world's top twenty of grandiloquence. Compton Mackenzie is the arch rebel, the recalcitrant hero. To promulgate an opinion on a course he should not follow is to see his will harden on that very course. Against all counselling, and with anguished cries from his friends dirling his ears, he lent his face and his name to Grant's Standfast, and became one of the all-time great whisky salesmen, his achievements still to be marvelled at in awe. There is the same stubborn individuality of thought in his writing. His work defies classification. The flighting romantic, the dissecting historian, the rib-tickling humorist, the philosopher, realist, satirist, each succeeding success acclaimed by the very critics who advised him to channel his genius along one categorized, adventureless path. He had to wait two years before a publisher would accept his first book, yet he made up his mind not to write another until the first had been printed and was open before him. The fighter of officialdom, supporter of the lost cause, the burning advocate of Scotland's political independence. Perhaps the most astonishing feature about this remarkable man is his memory.

He winters in shivering Edinburgh (extraordinary in itself considering that he chooses to spend the rest of the year in mild France), browsing among the 12,000 books in his Drummond Place home, entertaining his friends with the graciousness of the Chevalier, the impish eye of an Allan Breck, robed for the most part in night attire that in flamboyance is pure film set and there, among good company, with a glass at his side, a cigar for his fist, he has time and inclination to think and reflect, to cast his mind back to the early days of his youth, his childhood, even into babyhood. As his autobiographies are published with amazing rapidity, so his memory-power and grasp of detail become more obvious. "The first thing of which I have any clear memory is when I was seven months old," he will tell you. "My nurse lifted me out of my pram to watch some black and white rabbits playing in a field." He can clearly remember the nurse's name and the colour of her dress.

There are indeed many vivid memories to recall with pleasure: people of fame, fortune and nonentity; travels around the world; adventures as a Royal Marine captain, a counter-espionage chief in the Aegean; writing days; talking days; Hebridean days; exciting, stimulating days; and now, well into his eighties, relaxing, enjoyable, thoughtful Edinburgh days. But never retirement, for there is always the chance, almost inevitably, that even now he will go on to surprise and delight us yet again, and who knows in what form his genius will manifest itself next time.

Back in 1962, Sir Compton dedicated his book on *Moral Courage* to yet another of Edinburgh's great characters. It reads thus: "To Wendy Wood whose friendship I have enjoyed for thirty-five years, and who, throughout those years has never failed to show the moral courage of a Scottish patriot."

Wendy Wood. Her very name is a battlecry, a skirl on war-pipes given flesh, the conscience of Scotland firmly rooted in Howard Place. Who in Scotland does not know her, who has not been exasperated at her capers, captivated by her charm, admired and loved her. Wendy Wood, the patriot, the artist, the author, the crofter, the orator, the dreamer, the jag in the Scottish thistle. There is no limit to the woman. Up there on her rostrum at the Mound, the green cloak and Ross skirt flaunting pennants, Wendy is irresistible. The friend of the bobby who nabs her at a frolic, the confidante of his inspector; she has deliberately had herself arrested to campaign against the appalling conditions in the very prison in which she spent her sixty days—Glasgow's old Duke Street jail, now thankfully demolished, with her help; she has appeared in court for failure to pay a dog licence, a protest against the government which pockets this money for itself,

Looking down the Royal Mile to the Tron Kirk with St Giles' on the right
(overleaf) Panorama from Calton Hill (*for details see page* 7)

GLADSTONE'S
LAND
SALTIRE
SOCIETY

although south of the Border it is for the use of local authorities; she has presented with her compliments a rigormortised procession of long-deceased rats to a startled city officer, banging them down on his desk with a thump, until nearby property was rid of the pest; she has picketed the Border; humbly presented her case to the august body of the General Assembly of the Church of Scotland for the return of the Thrie Estates, Scotland's ancient parliament; she has annoyed everyone in the country worth annoying, and won their respect.

Indeed, Wendy Wood has a delicious yarn or two to tell spanning more than seventy years: of ink eggs thrown with unerring aim; of buckets of whitewash put to unconventional use; of pirate radio; protest marches; sinister capers at darkest midnight; noble causes lost and won. She can also tell—with all the sensitivity of the artist—lump-in-throat stories of devotion to Scotland from lords and ladies, her friends; from tinkers, tourists, workaday business and shirt-sleeve men, also her friends; of pride and dedication to her own great passion—her homeland.

The Lord Provost's chair, one of the oldest and most honoured civic positions in the world, has attracted a fair proportion of characters since the great George Drummond of the eighteenth century: the boisterous, elegant Sir Will Y. Darling, with his tile hat and silver-topped cane; the gentle Sir John Falconer, pioneer of the Festival; the humorist, Sir Andrew Murray; the Dick Whittington, Sir James Miller, who also became London's Lord Mayor; and, more recently, that controversial crabapple, Sir Duncan Weatherstone, of the twinkling eyes and affable quip that so often became a newspaper headline. There was a fellow. Tall, bald as a ball in billiards, a game he played daily, sweet and sour, hot and cold, overspilling with cheer or spleen as the day demanded, and intensely passionate in his love for Edinburgh. At least one newspaper office kept a cuttings book of his sayings, including such choice items as the occasion when he asked the Beatles for a £100,000 donation to the Festival, which he had once described as "money for old rope". Loquaciously forthright when he thought that Edinburgh would benefit, or would not, he had the country continually talking about himself and his city

The Atomic Age, but visitors still go to the Castle to look at Mons Meg in wonder

during his term of office, and this is the hallmark of a professional ambassador, the true tradition of an Edinburgh character with a mind and will of his own.

Albert Mackie is built in with cobbles and haar, the hawk-eyed, outspoken, lyrical MacNib, who has graced Edinburgh's newspapers for years with those timely, sweet-humoured philosophies in verse, often extravagantly irreverent, sometimes the dispenser of knifing criticism, yet sugar-coated, and always amusing, even for those institutions he outraged or the people whose egos he punctured. Here is Mr Edinburgh himself; witty, couthy, earthy, balding, asthmatic, likeable, a great teller of tales, a noser into odd corners of the city, a shoulder-brusher of toppers and bunnets; for Edinburgh people are his great preoccupation, particularly those once called the working class, or the unfortunates categorized into a social strata several rungs lower.

Dr Harry Whitley, parish minister as he likes to be called, a proud title for someone who is such a force in the kirk, has for his parishioners the High Streeters of the wynds and closes; his pulpit is Scotland's great Mother Kirk, the High Kirk of St Giles', although title and rank have little meaning for him. Like all good ministers he is as much a friend and confidant of the tenement folk—whether they are members of his flock or not—as he is of the large number of dignitaries who come to listen to him expound each Sunday in his well-known short sermon that is a twelve-minute burst of enlightenment and passion straight from Harry Whitley's heart. He is quite a character, this former brewery hand and social worker in Edinburgh's slumland. He knows the underside of the city, the crime and violence, and he can hit hard enough himself on occasion, even fiercely when the situation demands it. Not with the knuckles, of course, but with a truth and repugnance of sham, dishonesty, intolerance and evil that will not be denied. He is never one to pull his punches; his truths hit home from time to time and people get hurt, and when that happens they have a habit of hitting back, which often turns him into a figure of controversy. Contention and outspoken Dr Whitley are never long separate, but his downright attitude over things he does not like is to be admired, even if you do not agree with him. In his day he has been branded a militant communist and a Scottish Nationalist, as well as an activist member of the other three big political parties, and these are a few of the kinder things he has been called. In fact, Dr Whitley is giant-hearted, compassionate, a lover of mankind, a sincere pricker of pomposity in all its forms. He will tell you his aim is to make St Giles' the voice of Scotland. It is an ambition realized many years ago.

Only a few hundred yards down the Royal Mile broods the historic, centuries-worn Canongate Church, kirk of Holyrood House, the parish church of the palace, still playing its important part in a new age of history, creating history again with the Rev Dr Selby Wright in its pulpit. Tall, solemn of face, yet with a ready humour, sensitive to other people's troubles, he has the gift of conveying emotion in words. At one time Selby Wright had the largest congregation in the world, ten million at least, during the dark war days when his familiar, friendly voice as radio padre brought comfort and courage. A man deeply interested in human problems, especially those of the young and aged, a sympathy and understanding of humanity, so that he can communicate at all levels, whether among the old folk he meets as chairman of Edinburgh and Leith Old People's Welfare Council, a soldiers' drumhead service at the castle, the multifarious crowd who gather as the grey dawn breaks to hear him preach a May Day service atop Arthur's Seat, or among royalty as he visits Holyrood Palace as chaplain to the Queen.

Over at St Cuthbert's another of the same mould, the minister of gaiety, once an amateur football goalkeeper of international standard, The Very Rev Dr Leonard Small, who in his year as Moderator of the General Assembly, looking like an escapee from the seventeenth century, did so much to have the image of the Moderator accepted as a man of the moment in a religiously apathetic age. There was a task! But, like some revered Olivier with Scotland as his stage, he presented an engrossing series of quick change performances. Voila!—Dr Small, the submariner; Dr Small, scientist; Dr Small, lifeboatman; Dr Small, football coach; Dr Small, the pilot; Dr Small, firefighter, a never-to-be-forgotten sight as he stood in his Moderator's antique raiment, the walking-out dress of a seventeenth-century gentleman, with its frilly lace embellishments, black silk knee-breeks revealing leg-clutching stockings, silver buckled shoon—a fireman's hat clapped on his head, hose in hand, and a large grin to his face. And, of course, Dr Small, the hard-working, deep-thinking, parish minister, one of the outstanding preachers Scotland has produced in the twentieth century, a man who enjoys every minute of life.

A postcard, written in childish characters and addressed to "Uncle Willie, Edinburgh" will be delivered without question to Chief Constable William Merrilees, O.B.E., of the Lothians and Peebles Constabulary. The postal authorities know their man and his works. Incredible. A man branded as a terror by the criminal element, is the beloved 'uncle' of thousands of handicapped and under-privileged children over the whole of South-east Scotland. Willie Merrilees, in his own lifetime an institution and a legend. His knowledge of Edinburgh is exhaustive. He studied the city from the underside, sweeping clean many murky places as he studied, and built a reputation extending far beyond our shores. Born into hard times in humble beginnings, the streets and docks of Leith gave him his education. Compassion for the fallen, gentleness for the weak, courage to risk his own life many times to save lives. A happy Christian home was his background, giving him sturdy independence; but social burdens bearing on helpless shoulders, the distribution so obviously uneven, roused a hatred of injustice wherever it showed. Not least a sense of humour to inspire the laugh to halt a tear. Willie Merrilees passed through the school of life, and graduated at the university of experience.

His story is well enough known. He saved so many people from drowning that he almost lost count; the master of disguise, he once passed as a baby in a pram; ruthless as a crime fighter, outspoken as a critic, cherubic-faced Willie, under minimum height and with a fingerless hand, rose to the top of an exacting job, and when retirement age came was persuaded to stay on as Chief Constable of his present force, and continue his work for the common good. Throughout his career Willie Merrilees worked tirelessly to help the poor, with a special interest in handicapped children and old folk. He has attracted a host of willing helpers to his cause, ready on call. From time to time he must prove his worth as a policeman, with ruthless efficiency, but when work is over he again becomes that familiar cheery William Merrilees, halo aglow, leading his private band of hope on a great and wonderful crusade.

The gentle, timid-looking Lord Clyde, Lord Justice General and Lord President of the Court of Session, resolution in his fragility, and understanding in his heart; an Edinburgh Academy boy, a former dux no less, like his father before him, and his son after. Witty, intellectual, lucid in thought and word, a great delver into subjects antiquarian. Or his colleague of the Bench, big, affable Lord John Cameron, conversationalist of delight, a lover of the arts and things beautiful, yachtsman and amateur artist of sensitivity, imprisoning for life the kaleidoscope waters around Ullapool on glorious seascape canvases. William MacTaggart, President of the Royal Scottish Academy, quiet, undemonstrative for an artist, yet with commanding authority springing from respect of ability, his work the seeming antithesis of the man, until you know him, rich in striking colour, alive, intense.

Sir Thomas Innes of Learney, Lord Lyon King-of-Arms, is a splash of vivid colour himself on the Scottish scene, gaunt, bushy of eyebrow, moustache and unruly white hair, a walking caricature figure, with the little appealing eccentricities of the thinker. When the Lyon roars, people tak' tent. But Sir Tam's roar is falsetto, more squeak than roar, as he sits at his desk in Register House, the only court of heraldry in the world in daily session, and lifts the telephone to proclaim in a voice like the tinkle of a penny trumpet, but with majestic dignity and bizarre effect, "Lyon here!" Not that Sir Tam's thunder does not carry authority. Indiscreet are those who would cross him in matters armorial or genealogical. Living in his timeless world of ancient insignia, coats of arms, pursuivants, fesses, chevrons, escutcheons, heralds, unicorns, sinisters, dexters and the entwined roots of aged family trees, Sir Thomas is omnipotent. Indeed, it would be foolish to argue with him, for he may still have the right to chop off your head. Scholarly, outspoken and passionately Scottish, Sir Thomas has done his country signal service in giving meaning and worth to Scottish titles and, just as important, affirming with vehemence and on every occasion his belief in Scotland.

Tommy Walker, in spite of his controversial and distasteful waygoing from the Heart of Midlothian football club, a team he had served with such dedication both as player and manager, remains one of the great legendary figures of soccer. The gracious, modest gentleman of the football field, a Church of Scotland divinity student until the interruption of the war when he was commissioned, then later an inspiring lay preacher and inside-forward of rare ability, who reached the soccer heights, in Scotland and England, and because Hearts is the most fickle team in the first division, also the blackest depths. In a city of such past soccer thoroughbreds as the poetry-in-action Gordon Smith; Laurie Reilly, the gay opportunist; the eel-like Bobby Johnstone; Willie Bauld, master of the header; Alfie Conn of the thundering shot; Jimmy Wardaugh, scorer of goals extraordinary and many, many others, the memories of the long-suffering Edinburgh football faithful still turn wistfully to the golden days of Tommy.

Tiny Pilkington Jackson, the sculptor, 5 feet 4 inches in his thickest-soled shoes, the creator—with the help of an extending ladder—of the largest and most dramatic piece of statuary produced in recent years, the bronze Bruce once more astride his caparisoned steed on the field of Bannockburn. Charles d'Orville Pilkington Jackson, Cornish born, mind as sharp as his chisel, as chivalrous as the age of his masterpiece, an Edinburgh man since the Boer War, an honour that he should have stayed in the city, a disgrace that it took Scotland so long to raise the money to pay for the work.

Alastair Dunnett, another incomer, like Lochinvar came, out of the West—to edit Scotland's great national quality newspaper, *The Scotsman,* and there always was something cavalier about the man; a visionary and adventurer; pioneer of sea canoeing, forcing the Minch in a force six gale when the fishing boats were running for shelter; a journalaut[1] of the newspaper world,

[1] A neologism analogous of astronaut.

probing and discovering new spheres to give *The Scotsman* a scintillating list of firsts in its field. A thinker, too, a realistic dreamer, a nationalist in the best sense, a public speaker of impromptu brilliance, a man who found wisdom by plunging his arms in life up to the oxters, which is the kind of word he would use.

Moray McLaren, one of the last of the old Bohemians, a student of Edinburgh and its past, an authority on Scott and Stevenson, raconteur, snuff-taker, fisherman, author, playwright, conversationalist of dedicated urbanity, married to Lennox Milne, who has graced the Scottish stage for years. Tom Fleming, theatre reformer and actor of outstanding ability, an idealist and courageous sticker to his principles. A host of critics, artists, poets and writers. Norman McCaig, Tom Scott, Robert Garioch, W. G. Gillies, Sydney Goodsir Smith, and his father, Sir Sydney Smith, one of the greatest authorities of forensic medicine in the world, or fellow medico, Professor Norman Dott, brain surgeon of international repute.

Their names come fast, from every social strata, without attention to merit or importance. They are the people of Edinburgh in all their fascination, their complexities, their idiosyncrasies. Some are in the public gaze, some nonentities. All have one common denominator—individuality. Today it is a quality of great and precious rarity. As those sinister, uncompromising gods of conformity, conventionality and similarity in thought and expression gather their increasing armies of faceless cypher people, Edinburgh remains a beleaguered outpost against their insidious march. This city is famed for its characters, eccentrics and half-dafts. Study them carefully for they are a dwindling race. But as long as they remain part of the Capital scene, there is surely hope for the world.

II

SATURDAY NIGHT . . .

THEY are airting out Gorgie way, plastic macs at the trail, for the sky is clerical-grey and rain-smir smudges car windows. They fill Gorgie and Dalry roads and the public houses along them, jostling, shouting, galloping, goading, laughing, serenading all the way back to Haymarket; a surging river of people, singly, in groups, in maroon regiments, spated tributaries and eddies gushing to join the main flood, babbling down Henderson and Ardmillan Terraces, trickling from every close and opening. They come by bus and car and taxi. There is hooting, fist-waving, and cursing from space-hungry drivers with time strictly rationed, for speed is a snail and the police have sealed off the sideroads. Some try to force the entry-blocking No Parking signs, infiltrating from the rear or five cars in enfilade attack on one cramped car-length of room, but the Law has patience and humour and deadly intent, and there is much redirection of the miscreants via Dalkeith.

At precisely 2.30 p.m. the barman in the Tyncastle Arms calls "Time!" At first the bellow is as a plaintive cheep, and goes unheeded. More engrossing matters are on hand, for the talk is of football, of golden goals past and present, of balmy cup-winning days and barren excruciating years in the soccer icefields, of cultured flying wingers with intellectual left feet, of thick-thighed half-backs who could splinter a post with a flick of the head from forty yards, of agonizing sleepless nights when, on bended knee, faces haggard and mask-like, they invoke across the gulfs of darkness eleven well-intentioned demon bodies incarnate to enter the souls of the Hearts' first team, a kind of devil's holiday in hell, and by some black satanic magic win European

Cups by the barrowload and all honours glorious. Then a frenzy of elbow bending as beer mugs bang the bar in machine-gun staccato. Ah, the faithful think to themselves, wistfully, as they move to the enclosure and terracing gates, if only the Hearts' players' reactions were as fast.

At 3 p.m. on the dot, with the rain beginning to stot from the pavements and drookit queues shuffling and fidgeting at the turnstiles, the referee wheeps his pea. Silence falls on the Tyncastle Arms. It is left bereft. All that remains are empty, ringed glasses and a distinction—the pub with one of the most enjoyable drinking-up times in the city.

In Princes Street the wet shopping pavement is a jousting ground. Sedate and elegant ladies cut, thrust and parry with umbrella lances, the primitive survival instinct of a back-to-the-wall commando in the deft prods, stabs and slashes to vulnerable eye, ear and nape of the neck. On guard! But there is no warning or chivalry, only silent cold-eyed venom. Inside the big stores range the baying packs of bargain hunters. To lift an article for closer examination is to have it torn and ripped from the hand as the mob pounces, honed elbows and stiletto heels flashing, masters of infighting. Bruised and battle-fatigued males brood in the backwaters, set faces telling their own stories.

The other side of Princes Street is a casualty collecting station, where the old folk rest their bunions and the exhausted find new strength from the sodden tranquillity of the gardens. The rain is lessening, the evening promises, and the fury of the shopping has almost abated. Yet the Saturday denizens of Princes Street show little good humour. Unlike other days of the week, smiles and relaxed chuckles are in short supply. Princes Street on Saturday afternoon is a tense street of snarls and ill manners. A stroll in search of good humour along its length discovers only one genuine hearty laugh. It is outside Waverley Station when an elderly gentleman slips while trying to board a Number 26 bus. After doing a backwards tango, he measures his length in the gutter. The faces of some bystanders crinkle with mirth, and one lady goes into whooping convulsions. But that hardly counts. . . .

By 5 p.m. Tynecastle has disgorged. The shopping commuters from Fife, clutching their half-crowns, stream back across Forth to Dunfermline, Cowdenbeath, Kirkcaldy, the Edinburgh suburbia of the future. City restaurants are at their busiest, shop assistants begin to eye the clock. The pink *News* proclaims the sports results, the bus station overflows. George Street begins to empty and look its douce self again, for crowds and cars never did suit its particular kind of dignity. Singing and music drift upwards from the Ross Bandstand, punctuated fortissimo now and then by the two-tone klaxon of the diesel trains in the rock fissure below. On the Princes Street pavement aloft the crowds gather to watch and listen for free. Dr Thomas Guthrie, the divine of last century, turns his stone-statue back on the frivolity, and stares away up Castle Street. The cinema queues lengthen outside the Odeon, Playhouse and Cameo. Bingo addicts, mostly middle-aged women, still with their shopping bags and parcels, at last with curlers removed, clickety-click their way a little farther down the road to mothers' ruin. Up at the Simpson Maternity Pavilion, sharp on the stroke of 7.30, a queue of quite another nature, a long, bashful, self-conscious line of coy and blushing new fathers.

It has stopped raining. Fingers of mist trail across the Pentlands, clutching still at Allermuir and Caerketton, while giant castle clouds tower and tumble above. The sun, white and watery, slowly gains strength and colour, dappled shadow is cast again below Princes Street garden trees, and the pigeons magically reappear to strut and pout like vain town councillors. The canyon walls of the Old Town suddenly appear brighter, the silhouette sharper, wet roads and rooftops sparkle and shimmer, the gardens are greener, the throng on the streets more vivid. For those with senses to appreciate, it is wondrous. Not merely the lowlying outcoming sun, nor the contrast after a gurly day, nor because cloud is now quickly vanishing from the blue-green evening sky. It is that strange, glowing, luminous Edinburgh light that clarifies, magnifies, and reflects the city scene, a thing unique, seen but not understood or scientifically explained, a freak of atmosphere that shows the city off in its finest livery, and it remains until

Edinburgh is in shadow, except where the sun still holds the castle and Arthur's Seat in a golden royal spotlight, and until that too dims to the coming night.

Now is the time of the great Edinburgh metamorphosis. The face of the city changes, the pace and mood changes. It takes a million lights to make a city and now, one by one, they flick on, in chains along the main thoroughfares, in glittering clusters, multi-coloured along the shop fronts, hanging single stars high on the castle.

The harried, purposeful citizenry of the afternoon now stroll and saunter aimlessly, relaxed laughter never distant. The working clothes have been slung in a corner, and Edinburgh is pleasure bent. The bright lights beckon; dancing and beat as the young ones get in the scene, swinging ancient Edinburgh, chemin and cobbles, history and hippies, centuries and saxophones, blues and blackjack in Georgian splendour, spit and sawdust down among the backstreet pubs of Leith.

Saturday night out is fish and chips at the Deep Sea then over to Fairlie's for the jiggin'. It is bhuna at Jamils, goulash at George's, oysters at the Café Royal, fresh trout at the George, chateaubriand at the Caledonian, Edinburgh Fog at L'Aperitif, chow mein, smorrbroed, cannelloni, pilaff or a native, honest MacGregor's Special at the Epicure, with a dram for the haggis and a piper to go with it.

Saturday night is green baize, a pack of cards and an Italian croupier; it is smoke, beer and a giggle at the Black Bull; a lover's walk on Calton Hill; a piano recital in Heriot Row; a debate on nihilism or a cuddle in the corner at the students' union; a song at Milne's; a contemplative daunder along Portobello prom or with the ghosts of the old New Town; a smashed telephone kiosk somewhere in the city.

By 10.10 the pubs are locking up, ejecting their habitués into whirling space. There are grunts, sniggers, shouts, dropped carry-outs, swear words, vomitings, commiserations, felicitations, thick-tongued camaraderie. Now here is a man with a suit to his back but no shirt to his front, a knotted white silk scarf hiding his hairless modesty; a silent, crumpled figure slumped at the rear of a bus trundling through the night until final destiny with the garage; a trio of vocalists; a loquacious, jolly lurcher gesturing at two solemn policemen; a blank-eyed, stringless puppet youth being deposited in a taxi, but the driver does not want him. At midnight they are still feeling their way home, joined by the Cinderella young people from the dances and teen clubs whose parents insist on bed by 12.

Those million lights are vanishing fast, pearls falling from a string, utter darkness their foil. For the castle guard it is the eclipse of the city, piece by tiny piece, indiscriminately—click, click, click—as slumber calls. They mark the gulf of Arthur's Seat, a raven's wing void, a dozen pinpoints to the south that is Colinton, a glitter that could be Craiglockhart, a glimmer that is Grange. To the north the car lights flash along the Fife coast beyond the sable nothingness of Forth, overflowing its blackness towards the city, the lights of Granton, Newhaven, Pilton floating upon it. And suddenly, lo, where they have just looked—Colinton has gone, Craiglockhart almost engulfed. But there is revelry still on Princes Street and on the Royal Mile, bathed in the centuries-recalling tungsten iodine lights, producing an effect far better than all the corporation's restoration work, that stirs the imagination so that the gay voices of the young folk could be Dawney Douglas and Willie Dunbar with their Crochallan Fencibles retiring after a hard evening.

Now appear the people of the night; unfamiliar, retiring, little-known figures, hidden behind the curtain of the day. The down-and-outs whose beds are a pile of bus tickets or newspapers on a park bench, who rise to walk the streets at three in the morning, slapping the chill from numbed legs and arms, finding luxury in the heat-retaining brick walls of a certain bakehouse. The dog-men who tread a restless path through the dark hours, sad-eyed curs loyally lolloping at their heels, man and dog waifs alike, understanding between them. The man who finds sleep on a corporation night bus, jiggelty-jogging his way around the city, from midnight until the last run at 5 a.m., pitied by the conductors who grudgingly accept his fare, shaking him into reality only when they must; the anguished, the pained, the lonely, desolate people, for whom sleep is but a clutched hour or two, the day a nightmare, the night a release shortlived.

The police know them and sympathize and let them be. The police who are part of the furniture of the night themselves, who feel its peace, its beauty, its threat, who observe it in all its detail: Sunday papers on sale at 2.30 a.m. outside the G.P.O.; the last of the meandering celebrants; lovers and loafers in shadowy doorways; the long-distance lorry men rumbling south as they catch up on overtime; the bustle at the entrance to the Royal Infirmary, doctors and nurses fending off death after a car crash, as a blue-flashing ambulance arrives at the Queen Mary, a new life well launched on its way.

The sounds of deepest night are all around. Even in rubber soles the police can hear their own footsteps, and that in a city is indeed a strange thing. They hear the distant, muted rattles from Waverley Station, trains stopping, starting, shunting; milk cans clattering; doors banging; the cry of a baby in a high tenement, the sleepy, soothing answer from a parent; a snore from an open window; the skirl of an owl; the dry creak from a swinging shop sign; the scrape of Saturday night refuse blown along the gutter; and a myriad small unintelligible sounds that could mean a mouse scuttling under a door, a drip of water plopping in rhythm, a moth fluttering at a window. Then all noise stops. The police halt in their rounds, almost by compulsion, and watch in fascination the extraordinary spectacle of a great city asleep. It is a time for wonder and thought and private reflection. Dawn is an hour away, a new day approaches, and with the first grey light the spell will be broken; but Sunday promises fair.

III

OLD TOWN

THE symbols of old Edinburgh stand for all to read. Castle for a warrior, abbey for a churchman, palace for a king, the high Land tenements between to hold the people. Bound within the rigid grip of a defensive wall, young Edinburgh had to reach upwards for growing space, so reached and grew. Democratic enough, rich and poor alike sharing the same roof, jostling each other daily in the closes leading to their homes, the high Land tenements, the forerunners of the modern skyscrapers. Problems enough; water was scarce and sanitation non-existent. Nightfall solved many, and too often the warning cry, "Gardy-loo!" sent the wary sprinting for cover, leaving the unwary under a pile of garbage and slops tossed from an upstairs window. Edinburgh was no worse than other towns of the period; output was the same, only her buildings were higher.

The young town began one bow shot from the castle entrance and clung to the rocky ridge sloping down towards Holyrood. An encircling wall guarded the growth, entrance and exit being at two defended gateways, the Netherbow Port at the foot of High Street, and the Upper Bow near the castle. The Castle, Castlehill, Lawnmarket, High Street, Canongate, Holyrood Palace—the Royal Mile. No street in the world can produce such variety, such varied emotion. Edinburgh, the city of three queens, the town within a town, marches with her past as few cities in the world can do, and history is not so dead in the Scottish capital.

Here is the stage with the centuries as a backcloth. Here stepped the kings and queens, nobles and commoners, priests and ministers, councillors, and plain, ordinary people, each stepping into the scene as the times dictated, to play out his or her part in the most stirring drama ever presented.

Drama indeed it was. Love, hate, greed, fear, courage. Ambition brought the clashes that brought the bloodshed. The lesson was never learned. Great men fell as greater men rose, to drive a new idea in a different way, to the same inevitable end. One pace into the wynds and closes and those vanished years are felt at once. It is then easy to imagine that the sigh of the wind up the grey old stairways whispers the secrets of a thousand years and echoes the cries of long-dead swordsmen.

This is the story of Edinburgh's Old Town. What a tale! As James Barrie once said, "Who could hope to tell all its story, or the story of even a single wynd in it." It is true. But we can stroll its length through the centuries, from ancient castle all the way down to Holyrood and Arthur's Seat, and see and think and wonder. This chapter is such a walk through time.

Stand on the summit of the Castle Rock and look around. Here is where it all began ere history had been born to record the beginning. Look back through time for a brief space, and see the landscape as it appeared to those vague men and women who came here for the first time to build a home. Turn from man's works, and little is changed. Below, Forth rolls restlessly forward as she has rolled for thousands of years. Berwick Law still stands in the east to point a way to the chill North Sea. The kingdom of Fife holds the north; and as far as the eye can see rear the eternal hills, whose names alone conjure up a thousand tales for Scottish ears—Grampians, Ochils, Pentlands, Lammermuirs, Moorfoots; while the lion shape of Arthur's Seat towers over old Dunedin, as it always did.

Dunedin, the fortress, Edinburgh's oldest name. It was made of wood in those pre-history days, wooden stakes and poles, not hard to find, for the vast forest of Drumsheugh was all around. Vanished marshes, burns and lochs like Corstorphine, Craigcrook and Holyrood were familiar to the tribes who sought the safety of the high ground on Arthur's Seat and Calton Hill and the Castle Rock. The Romans came and saw and left again; Columba's missionaries, St Ninian and St Cuthbert, brought their message. Rock of ages indeed. Pict, Roman, Celt, Angle, Scot, each in his turn marched from the mists of time, made his imprint here, then marched on into the void and history. Only the Scot remained, a part of them all and more, and this great rock became an anvil, on which the mountains and the rivers, the centuries and their storms, the plough and the sword, combined to hammer out the character that made the Scot and moulded his nation.

Perhaps only Scots truly understand Scots, though they run openly for all to read. Branded the dourest and most unemotional of the four nations, they created the most beautiful and emotional memorial of any nation, and dedicated it to their war dead. They set it, as it just had to be set, in the most prominent position of their rock.

The National War Memorial, not church, not shrine, not exactly memorial—it creates and breathes its own elusive atmosphere. Pride predominates—not sorrow, pride—and something else. It is here where the living rock is underfoot, and the bronze figures of Scotland's sons and daughters, equipped for war, march without movement across the bare stone walls. More than men were cast to the furnace, and this is not forgotten. Here are the stubborn but patient mules humping their loads to the deadly trenches; the pigeons which flew through battle storm with vital message; the lowly mouse, the innocent canary that warned the sapper of invisible dangers as he burrowed his dangerous way underground—all are here—remembered.

Blenheim to Salamanca, Sebastopol to Modder River, Ypres to the Rhine. Across the world—across the years. Same story, same end. So came the great slaughter, and again the drums rolled, the pipes wailed. Scotland stirred, gathered the names of her sons, privates to general, who fell in a common cause, and locked them in time on equal terms with the older and more illustrious names of Wallace and Bruce. Here each year come the Scottish people, high rank and low, to mark the end of the killing, while the pipes sob the sorrow of Scotland and weep over what was lost, what might have been, and what might be again.

The old and the new are never long separate. A few paces to

the rear stands Margaret's Chapel. Margaret, the English princess who fled north when William the Conquerer invaded her land in 1066, was wrecked on the Fife coast, taken to Dunfermline, then the Scottish capital, where she wed Malcolm Canmore, King of Scotland. In due time she crossed the Forth, created her chapel, linking Church with State for the first time, uniting many warlike factions. Margaret died in 1093, shortly after hearing that husband and son had been killed in battle near Alnwick. The castle was under heavy attack, and her remaining sons, taking advantage of a misty day, lowered her body down the sheer face of the rock, took horse and headed for Dunfermline. There, Margaret still sleeps peacefully in her first Scottish home.

It is a tribute to Scotland's first great queen that the fighting men who have garrisoned the castle for over 900 years linked to defend her chapel against all comers, including that arch destroyer, Time. Even The Bruce, who devastated castle and fortifications to deny their use to the enemy, after daring Lord Randolph's attack up the rock face, spared Margaret's Chapel. Today, fresh flowers still glow between the grey walls, set there by Edinburgh ladies whose names are Margaret. History in Edinburgh may slumber but never really dies.

> There's a divinity that shapes our ends,
> Rough-hew them how we will.

The thought comes from the chiselled stone built into the wall of the building facing the memorial. The initials and date are as clear as the day they were freshly cut, the interlocked letters, *M-H,* the year—1566. A year of hope for Mary Stuart, Queen of Scots, and Henry, Lord Darnley, her husband. Hope! It was all that was left for the ill-starred Stuarts to clutch. Poor Mary. Beauty was hers, tragedy was her portion. The dice was loaded against her from the beginning. At eighteen laughter-loving Mary had become a legend as well as a queen, something beyond the cramped understanding of the religious factions scrabbling for the control of men's souls, and the power that goes with it. Happiness ever came bitterly. Here, in a tiny room, Mary's son was born to make history, and set a problem unsolved to this day.

Here, on 19th June 1566, she held out her two-hour-old baby to the sullen-faced Darnley, saying, "This is your son, my Lord . . . so much your son that I fear it may be worse for him hereafter. . . ." Then, to Sir William Standen, "This is the prince who, I hope, will first unite the two kingdoms of England and Scotland."

Even as she spoke, the storm was gathering bleakly round Mary's head, aided considerably by that grim-faced reformer, John Knox. Just one year later it broke, when an explosion at Kirk o' Field, a house on the outskirts of the town, killed Darnley and roused the factions. Four months later, in June 1567, her own lords made Mary a prisoner, forced her to resign her throne to her infant son, James VI, and set her on the long road that was to end on the scaffold at Fotheringay.

Elizabeth of England was friendly, and quite sincere in the letters she addressed to "My Dear Cousin". But Elizabeth, in her own way, was fighting the pressures surrounding every throne, and who can turn events? Mary Stuart passed into history, and in March 1603, Sir Robert Carey rode 400 miles from London in sixty-two hours, strode into Holyrood Palace and announced that Elizabeth was dead. James of Scotland was England's King.

Mary's inspired hope of thirty-seven years before had come true. Or had it? There are still some who believe that England's first James was not a Stuart. They insist that Mary's baby son died while she was touring the Borders, and that the Countess of Mar, who had charge of the young prince, substituted her own child, her second son.

Much has been written on this matter and much 'evidence' produced. Not least is a portrait of James, showing few of the facial characteristics of the Stuarts, but bearing a startling resemblance to John, Earl of Mar, who, say the theorists, was the King's elder brother. The legend was revived in 1830, when, it was said, a small oak coffin was found within the wall of Mary's apartments in the castle. It contained the body of an infant wrapped in an embroidered silk covering bearing the letter *J*. The substitution controversy still goes on, although the authenticity of this story is in some doubt.

Again, poor Mary. How often did she study the initials on the stone, and with what emotions? Had she no foreboding of what was to come? Mary fell on events and the intrigues of men who shape events. She has gone, but the stone stands still to remind us that a great but unhappy queen passed this way as we pass, and is worthy of a sigh.

Another link with royal days, the 'Honours of Scotland', are in the Crown Room of the castle. Here is the crown worn by Robert the Bruce, the sceptre and sword of state, far older than the English regalia. Many attempts were made to have them removed to London. All were foiled, and even a sharp command from Charles I was rejected by the Scots. Charles was forced to come to Holyrood to be crowned King of Scotland.

Cromwell was determined to get his hands on these symbols of royalty, and even laid siege to Dunottar Castle, in Angus, where he believed they were concealed. Cromwell was right, but the wife of the minister of Kineff outwitted him when she smuggled the 'Honours' out of the castle under the prying eyes of his soldiers.

Fancy is the best companion on any journey through history. It gives substance to shadows, solidity to wraiths, meaning to vagueness. How many untold tales are still trapped within these walls, how many heartaches?

Some of the old defenders still stand on guard; the iron cannon, muzzles pointing silently over the city that once shook to their anger. Mons Meg, the 'lass wi' the iron mou',' pride of the gunner in her day, takes star place. Born at Mollance in Galloway around 1468, Meg gave noisy and deadly service in various parts of the country. She could bite, blasting a five-hundredweight stone at a target more than a mile and a half away. Seized by the English after the Porteous riots, she languished in the Tower of London for nearly a century, before being allowed home again to retire. The warlike days of the old cannon are over, but they have one consolation. The slim, modern weapons which have ousted them from the Half Moon Battery, are condemned to a task that they would have scorned—telling Edinburgh each day that it is one o'clock and time for lunch.

Set on a ledge under Mons Meg is the pets' cemetery, tiny

tombstones rising to mark the animals who came to the castle voluntarily and shared the duties of the human garrison. At every turn there is a story worth hearing, worth preserving. But pass from the castle, under the portcullis and the state prison, where many great and honourable men lay miserably before being hustled to dishonourable death. The broad esplanade fronting the castle has been used as a drilling ground by the garrison since the beginning, the scene of many a spectacular and dramatic proclamation. The Edinburgh Military Tattoo revives some of its old glories for three weeks in the autumn of each year. Then the massed pipes and drums march and countermarch as of old, tartans streaming, kilts swinging, building up emotions that can only be relieved by roar after roar of enthusiastic applause from spectators from all nations.

It is a curious fact that part of the esplanade is Nova Scotia territory. Charles I decreed that the transfer be made so that newly created Scots Nova Scotian baronets could "tak seizin'" of their lands across the Atlantic. The decree has never been cancelled. The Prime Minister of Nova Scotia came to the castle in 1953, unveiled a plaque recording this odd fact, and ceremonially sprinkled some genuine Nova Scotian earth into the moat.

At the foot of the esplanade, on the left, stands Ramsay Garden. Allan Ramsay, the poet and writer, spent his retirement here, though the house has grown considerably since his day. He was at constant war with authority, and when he opened a theatre in Carrubber's Close in High Street in 1736, the magistrates, backed by the ministers, promptly closed it. Such frivolity could not be tolerated in Calvinistic society.

The move reacted against themselves. Alan opened a bookshop near the Mercat Cross. This attracted men of open mind and lively wit who liked convivial gatherings. The example was copied, and new clubs with some odd names sprang into existence. The most famous of these, the Crochallan Fencibles, met in Dawney Douglas's tavern in Anchor Close. Here came Robert Burns on occasions, to enliven some extremely lively meetings. A statue of Allan Ramsay stands beside the floral clock in Princes Street Gardens.

"Full many a shaft at random sent, finds mark the archer little meant," wrote Scott. So with the gunners in the Half Moon Battery. The two iron balls embedded in the wall of Cannonball House opposite Ramsay Garden were fired with deadly intent towards some kilted clansmen, who crashed up High Street in 1745 on the sole authority of Prince Charles Edward Stuart, and the dreaded claymores which had carved a red passage through Hawley's dragoons at Falkirk.

Castle Wynd, a popular path down to the Grassmarket in the old days, has been transformed into the stairway that drops steeply from Cannonball House to connect with an easier road to the old West Port. The White Hart Inn, visited by Burns and Wordsworth, is still in business in the Grassmarket, though most of the other historic buildings have gone. At the eastern end a walled enclosure in the roadway marks where the gallows stood and where more than one hundred Covenanters were executed for their religious beliefs.

Across the street from Cannonball House is a further reminder of dark days and shameful deeds. A bronze plaque fixed to the wall records that witches were burned near this spot over the years. The plaque marks more than that to thoughtful people, and emphasizes clearly the depths to which some men will sink to further their purpose. Witchcraft! What a weapon to put into the hands of ruthless, merciless authority, bent on bending or breaking others to their own warped will.

Superstition can excuse much, but nothing can excuse all that happened on Castlehill. Between 1479 and 1722 alone more than 300 terrified women, branded as witches, were dragged screaming to this spot, and cruelly done to death, while approving churchmen sat comfortably in front to ooze some form of distorted blessing into the horrifying spectacle.

No one was immune. Simply breathe the word 'witch', and the monster pounced. Lady Jane Douglas, acknowledged one of the fairest in the land, accused by a vindictive suitor she had rejected, was brought here after due 'examination' on the rack, and burned in front of husband and son. Few, if any, were impressed by the 'witch' tag. Lady Jane died because she was a Douglas, for political ends drive as savage a course as religious bigotry or blindness.

A modern glance at the evidence which condemned these unfortunate women, does more than suggest that they were foully, cruelly, and publicly murdered by men who, by the Grace of God or someone lesser, held 'honourable' rank and power over people who trusted them to deliver justice, not law, and humanity, not bigotry.

Down in the council chambers, the conferences went on, undisturbed by any thought of witches. Councillors had more important matters on their hands. From the beginning the half-mile ridge of houses named Edinburgh had grappled with an ever-growing problem. Water. Or rather the lack of it. The town had few wells within its walls, and these dried up far too often. Then drought struck, bringing disease swirling up the High Street closes to decimate the thirsty citizens.

In 1575, and again in 1582, the scarcity of water was so acute that the magistrates prohibited the brewers from taking water from the town wells, and ordered them "to fetch what they had occasion for from the South Loch". That loch lay where the Meadows are today. Taking the advice they gave to others, the officials stirred themselves at last, tapped the loch for the benefit of the town, and added new wells at the head of Liberton's Wynd, Blackfriars Wynd, and the Mercat Cross. Some of those wells stand in the streets to this day.

The search went on until in 1674 a desperate council turned to George Sinclair, a Leith schoolmaster, and besought him to "search out a well." He came to the castle to conduct his search, and turned his eyes towards Comiston Springs in the hills to the south, the tiny rivulets and burns called the Fox, Lapwing, Hare, Owl, Sandglass, and marked with their symbols.

"I made several observations with a most accurate level, but especially one from the highest ground in the castle, by the help of a light towards the fountain, on the evening of 29th May, 1674," he recorded later. "This gave infallible assurance to the magistrates that the source was 200 feet higher than the Weigh House, and gave great encouragement to the council to begin the work."

The city accounts for 1674 record that George Sinclair was paid "a gratiuite of £66 13s. 4d. for his attendance and advyce in the matter of water works." It was the best bargain Edinburgh ever made.

Much had to be done before the water could flow, but it was done, and in 1720 the Provost and Council, with a multitude of citizens, gathered at Castlehill to cheer the arrival of the first regular supply of good spring water, a meagre supply indeed, but certain. Dutchman Peter Bruschi had been contracted to bring out the water from Tod's Well at a fee of £2,900, but an airlock had formed in the pipe as the supply was turned on and Mr Bruschi, riding out to find the fault, became affrighted, and never returned. Almost at once, the great war for water opened in earnest. A now thoroughly roused council came to grips with a wide variety of interests, and found they would have to battle for every drop won for the growing town. They persevered, a spring was seized here, a burn acquired there, and reservoirs built to hold the gains.

Those old engineers carried out a magnificent job, judged even by modern standards. They skilfully set their aqueducts and pipes to flow the water over hill and dale to filter stations sited just as skilfully, using the height of the hills to overcome the resistance of the next hill. That first trickle slowly increased. They cut their way up through the Castle Rock, and created a vast tank under the esplanade near Ramsay Garden, designed to hold 1,700,000 gallons of piped and filtered water for the use of thirsty Edinburgh. The tank is still in use today.

In the fight for water the council has always had men of foresight and drive to lead the battle. The story of Edinburgh's water war over the centuries makes thrilling reading, and a tour of the victories is an education. Far to the south lie the hills that feed the springs that feed the burns that fill the deep lochs and reservoirs, No water—no Edinburgh. The age-old challenge has been met. The nagging worry was very much to the fore when housewives laid out their water vessels at the street wells, then waited for the welcome shout announcing that "the watter's on", never sure that it would still be on when their turn came. There stood the utensils—stoups, tubs, pails, pots, pans, kettles, jugs, pitchers, while the red-coated 'caddies' stamped impatiently, eager to get on with their job of pattering up and down the high stairs of the towering 'lands', to deliver small kegs of water at a halfpenny a 'rake'.

Most families owned a pair of stoups, a popular wedding gift of the time. These wooden vessels, 24 inches high and narrowing towards the top, were made by the coopers in Netherbow and the Pleasance, and sold in the High Street and Grassmarket on Wednesday and Saturday afternoons. A song of the time ran:

> They're naething but twae watter stoups,
> Ma mither sent tae me.

Stoups were easier to come by than water. The queues began to form around six in the evening—to wait. That wait often lasted till three in the morning, with nothing to show for it at the end if the wells ran dry, which they often did. But water they must have, and the disappointed ones were faced with a walk to the Powburn, or the Well-house tower at the foot of the Castle Rock, or a long trudge out to the Wells o' Wearie below Arthur's Seat. That well earned its name, but sentiment wins in Edinburgh's own old song, the plaintive, but lovely "Bonnie Wells o' Wearie".

Across a shallow valley to the south of the esplanade, stands George Heriot's School, where Cromwell set his cannon to bombard the castle, and sited a hospital. Heriot, a goldsmith and friend of kings—and queens, left a large sum of money to endow a school for boys who had the will but not the means to acquire an education. The school, dedicated in 1659, has grown over the years, as has its reputation, and still has foundation scholars.

Over the wall from the school stands Greyfriars Kirk, which rose from a convent established by Dutch friars in the thirteenth century. The kirk was opened in 1620, the first new church to be built in Edinburgh since the Reformation. All was uneasy peace until Charles I thrust in to declare that the Episcopal faith would rule in Scotland's capital whether the citizens liked it or not. A Royal Proclamation at the Mercat Cross emphasized the order, despite a strong protest from Scottish nobles, as well as people.

St Giles'

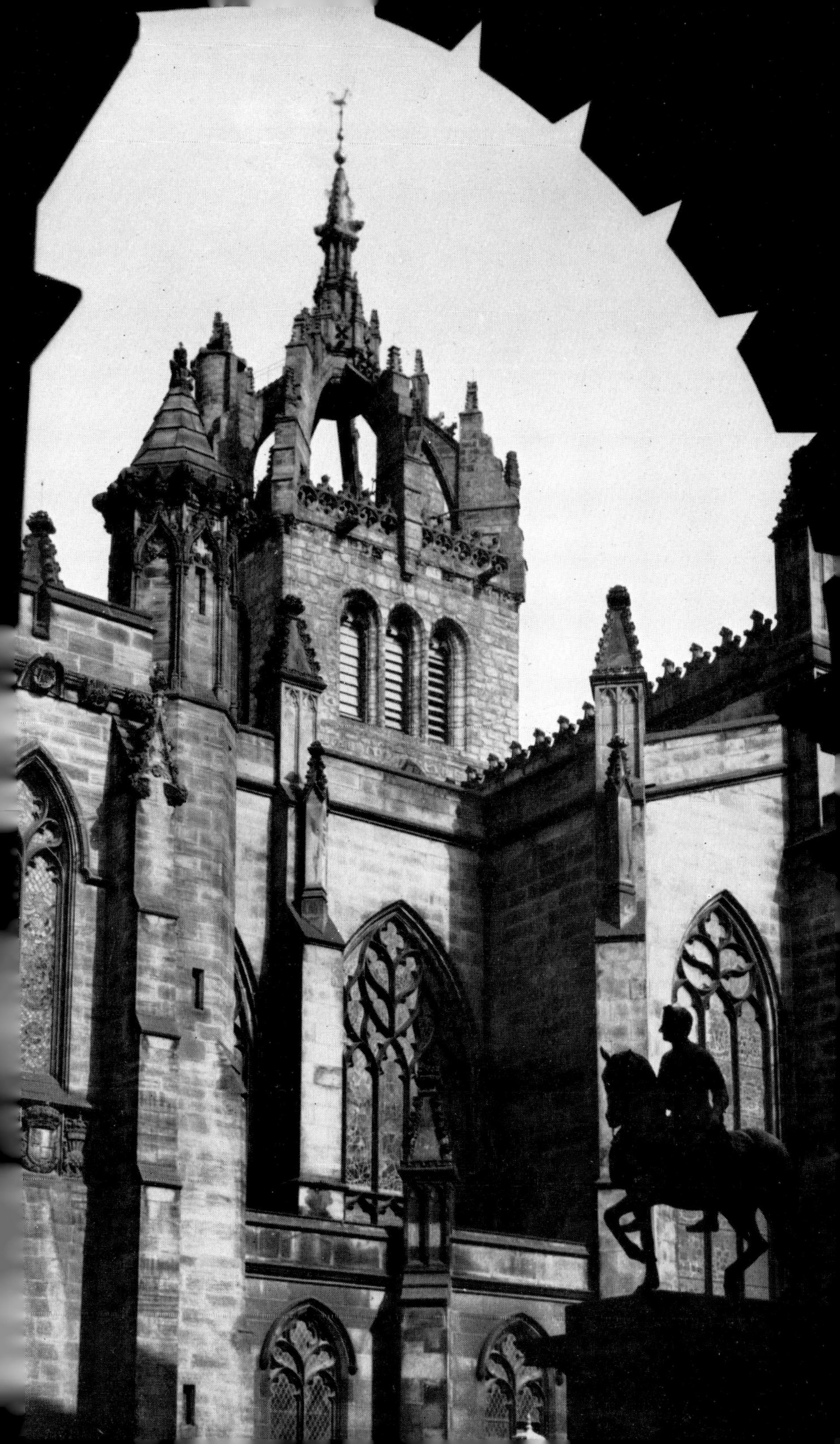

Protests having no effect, the National Covenant was drawn up, and thousands hurried to sign it in Greyfriars Kirkyard and around St Giles'.

The warning was ignored in the south. Charles and Cromwell passed, then Charles II came to the throne, and issued a new decree imposing Episcopal rule. Edinburgh exploded into religious strife, the Covenanters sprang to arms, only to fall on stronger arms. It became a sad, sordid story of torture and execution, the black deeds made all the blacker by being carried out in the name of God.

The 'Covenanters' Prison', exposed to wind and weather, still stands in Greyfriars Kirkyard, much the same as it was in the dark days, and a memorial in the Grassmarket gives sharp reminder of hidden evils, just like the plaque on the esplanade. The National Covenant is on view in Huntly House in the Canongate.

The old grey kirk sits in its walled enclosure today with the air of having stepped aside from the tumult to brood over its collection of bones, and its memories. Wisely, for the world it knew has gone, and the new world, which never heard of Greyfriars, grew very interested indeed when one of its lesser associations—a dog, trotted into public notice.

Fronting the gates at the head of Candlemakers' Row the bronze figure of Greyfriar's Bobby, a small Skye terrier, sits on his pedestal, wistfully surveying the passing throng. A figure familiar enough in Edinburgh, quite unknown beyond, till Walt Disney waved the wand of genius and passed the story of Bobby into hearts and homes throughout the world. A human story with a doggy hero. A tale of happy days on Border hills with auld Jock Gray, the shepherd; of hungry days in the poverty of the Grassmarket; of sad days haunting Jock's lonely grave in the quiet kirkyard. Disastrous days when Bobby was 'arrested' for not having a licence; triumphant days when his human street friends, who regarded the 'wee dug' as one of themselves, thrust in to brave the mighty Lord Provost in his own den, and found that great man was as human and warm-hearted as themselves. Bobby was given an engraved collar, complete with licence, and awarded the freedom of the city. He died in 1872, and on the

The City Chambers on the Royal Mile, once the Royal Exchange

suggestion of Queen Victoria, was buried in Greyfriars Kirkyard near his kind master and friend, auld Jock Gray.

Walk down Candlemakers' Row, past some aged buildings, meet the beginning of the Cowgate at the foot, and enter Grassmarket. The place of execution is marked, and a memorial is set to the Covenanters who died here for their faith. The old West Bow well, reminder of the waterless days, still stands, no longer wooed by housewives and their stoups. The White Hart Inn, visited by Burns and Wordsworth, is still in business, but the old market place is drabber and greyer since those days, now the home of many of Edinburgh's waifs and the homeless.

On the esplanade above, Castle Wynd, the popular road to the Grassmarket in the old days, has been transformed into a stone stairway, dropping steeply from Cannonball House to Johnston Terrace, the new and easier road. A few paces down Castlehill rises the Outlook Tower, with its camera obscura. Here one can see Edinburgh in a new and fascinating way, and pinpoint particular sections of the varied landscape. Further down, Tolbooth St John's Church points a long, slender finger to the heavens. Opposite is the south entrance to the Church of Scotland Assembly Hall, whose main entrance faces Princes Street. On this site stood the palace of Mary of Guise, mother of Queen Mary, built around 1544 after her Holyrood home had been destroyed by English invaders. The palace was demolished in 1861, but some of its carved stonework can still be seen in the National Museum of Antiquities in Queen Street. The West Bow, one of the routes into the city, came through its Port at this point. A busy enough highway on occasions, as the Bow led directly down to the Grassmarket, stage for public festivals—and executions.

Castlehill's short course ends at the Lawnmarket. Most of the old buildings have been swept away, but the atmosphere of former days still clings to the area, and some of the old dwellings are still there. Gladstones Land, conspicuous enough, was a very old house when bought by Thomas Gledstanes, a merchant, in 1617. It has survived the centuries, and is still in use 350 years later, for the years roll deceptively in Edinburgh.

Here in the Lawnmarket, just over 200 years ago, the 'gentry and nobility' promenaded in the evening to breathe the caller air, display their finery and draw envious and admiring glances. The fashions of the time were set by Lady Eleanor, wife of the Earl of Stair. In the closing years of her life she was a very familiar figure indeed, a dignified, respected old lady, out for a stroll in the Lawnmarket with her maid and negro pageboy. If Lady Eleanor were alive today, she would almost certainly be a student of the occult. She had some odd experiences in her lifetime, not to be explained by ordinary measures, and one of these was recorded by Sir Walter Scott in his tale, "My Aunt Margaret's Mirror". She was essentially feminine, and we have an entertaining glimpse of her, dressed as a servant lassie, features screened under a tartan shawl, slipping furtively down High Street with a friend, to consult a much-publicized fortune teller who had arrived in town.

What dark secrets of the future the seer unveiled for the two excited girls will never be known. But it is unlikely he gave a hint that more than 200 years after her death her name would shine prominently over the close mouth where she stayed, or that people from lands she and he never knew, would visit her home to look thoughtfully back into the past, as she was trying to peer through the mists that hid the future.

Lady Eleanor wed twice, her first marriage, to Viscount Primrose, being a disastrous affair. She died in 1759, and the dwelling bearing her name was presented to the council by the Fifth Earl of Rosebery in 1907. The house is now a museum, exhibiting many interesting relics of old Edinburgh, including the great clock taken from St Giles' many years ago. Scotland's national kirk still chimes the passing hours, but a well-kent face has vanished from the grey tower.

Blackie House, another survivor of the late seventeenth century, stands opposite Lady Stair's House. It was restored as a university hall, and named after the famous scholar, Professor John Stuart Blackie, who was born in 1809.

Robert Burns, the young Ayrshire farmer chasing fame as a poet, came clattering through the West Port in 1786 after a long, fêted ride from Mauchline, dismounted at Lady Stair's Close, and was greeted by his former crony, John Richmond, now working as a clerk in a law office. The two young bachelors shared John's humble lodgings for a time, fending for themselves, and drawing the water they needed from the street well outside. Burns, Richmond, and the house have gone, but a tablet at the close points the place.

Across the street is Riddle's Court and Close, associated with David Hume, the philosopher, and Bailie Macmorran, who was shot dead by a Royal High School student in 1595, when he intervened to break up a school strike over the denial of a holiday, surely one of the first ever protest sit-ins ever staged by students. The death shocked not only Edinburgh but King James himself, who had only recently granted the royal title to the old grammar school, whose roots reach almost beyond record.

A little way down from Riddle's is Brodie's Close, home of a real-life Jekyll and Hyde character, probably the original Jekyll and Hyde created by Robert Louis Stevenson. Deacon William Brodie was a respected member of the town council by day, an extremely clever housebreaker by night. He went once too often on the prowl, was recognized, arrested and hanged. If the Deacon's ghost ever flits through Lawnmarket, it must smile wryly, for a tavern bearing his name stands by the site of the gallows on which he hung.

Those same gallows ended the unholy alliance of two rogues who earned notoriety in a different fashion. Burke and Hare who lived in Tanners' Close, West Port, found that human bodies were needed for medical research, and had a ready sale. The infamous partners turned to grave robbing, then to murder. The inevitable slip-up came, and Burke went to the gallows, mainly on Hare's testimony. Hare escaped the rope—for a time. There were others in the grisly trade, however, and many of the devices installed to foil the body-snatchers can still be seen in some of the old churchyards.

Progress arrived to breach the solid line of the high tenements here. Bank Street dips to the north, and winds down to the Mound. On the south, George IV Bridge carries the highway towards Greyfriars Kirk, the University, and the Royal Infirmary.

The Cowgate passes under the bridge, considerably battered by time and the demolishers. The Magdalen Chapel still stands, however. It was erected in the sixteenth century, and its stained glass windows are rare specimens of pre-Reformation glass.

Step from the Lawnmarket into High Street, and into the Heart of Midlothian. The 'Kirk o' Sanct Geiles' dominates the scene, as it always did, the old 'Mercat Croce', the Market Cross, hard by. Here came the kings and queens, and all the pomp and pageantry of royal Scotland. Here came the provosts and magistrates to tell Edinburgh what was, and what would be. Here came the townspeople to cheer or jeer, and many noble heads forfeit to the headsman. A lively enough spot when Edinburgh was young. There was no room for shops, and traders set up stalls wherever they could squeeze in around St Giles'. They came with the dawn and went with the dark. Some were allowed to have lock-up stalls, and the 'Luckenbooths' stance is still marked. Housewives, rich and poor alike, pushed their way from stall to stall to buy bread, meat, milk and vegetables, while pigs, dogs and cats grubbed contentedly through the piles of garbage. Some of the inns here carried signs advertising eel pies and fresh trout straight from the Nor' Loch.

Fishwives trudged up from Newhaven and Musselburgh, creel on back, to sell oysters, mussels, and fish caught overnight by husband or son. They called their wares as they walked, and many years later Lady Nairne heard the familiar street cry, caught all the depth of sentiment behind it, and gave Scotland the enchanting song that is popular to this day.

> Wha'll buy my caller herrin'?
> They're bonnie fish an' halesome farin',
> Wha'll buy my caller herrin'
> New drawn frae the Forth?
>
> Wha'll buy my caller herrin'?
> O ye may ca' them vulgar farin'
> Wives an' mithers, maist despairin'
> Ca' them lives o' men. . . .

The Newhaven fishwives, now gone from the streets, have

retained their identity and spirit. Their choir is a reality as they appear in their distinctive costumes to sing the fine old songs of yester-year with warmth and feeling.

Congestion increased round St Giles' to the point of chaos. The magistrates struck at last and allocated places where the various trades could do business. It is an interesting pastime today to track down those old stances—Grassmarket, Lawnmarket, Fleshers' Close, Candlemakers' Row, Shoemakers' Land, Bakehouse Close, Playhouse Close, and many others.

Around St Giles' the centuries weigh heavily. Thistle and Rose united at last when Princess Margaret Tudor, daughter of Henry VII, came to Edinburgh in 1503, and wed James IV of Scotland. The golden age of the North had begun. The King had the palace in the castle repaired for his bride's reception, his monogram and emblems still decorate its walls. At the same time he ordered that a palace be built beside Holyrood Abbey, where Margaret would have the freedom denied by castle walls. The part built by James is still in use.

Margaret was a fine queen, and pushed the cause of her adopted country with all the wisdom and foresight shown by that earlier Margaret more than 400 years before. James granted a charter to the Royal College of Surgeons, and drove the necessity of education, even for the poorest. A Scottish fleet was created, led by the *Great Michael,* largest ship afloat, built down at Newhaven on the Forth. Walter Chepman and Andrew Myllar combined to introduce the new art of printing, and royal authority was obtained to establish a press in the Cowgate. Peace and prosperity arrived with Margaret, Scotland and England walked hand in hand, and Edinburgh flourished. If Margaret's father had lived just a few years longer, what a different history might have been written.

It was not to be. He died, and the new king, Henry VIII, strong-willed and dominant, clashed with the French, Scotland's old allies. The Queen of France appealed to the Scottish King for help, and peace and prosperity departed abruptly. James, with all the quixotic chivalry of the Stuarts, gathered his army, the largest ever to take the field in Scotland.

Scottish army indeed. Came the yeomen from the towns, the

shepherd from the hills, the hardy Borderer, the men of Fife, of Ayrshire, of Perth. Scotland's manhood poured to war. The 'fiery cross' flamed along the valleys of the North, and the clansmen, halting internal feuds, seized targe and claymore, then hurried south to strike a blow for Scotland.

That magic name—Scotland—worked the miracle. The country united in common cause. Discords charmed to harmony, foes changed to friends. The tartan columns streamed towards Edinburgh, drums beating, pipes challenging.

So Scotland's fighting men massed on the Burghmuir before marching on to one of the greatest disasters ever to strike the country—Flodden Field. James, twenty-five nobles, fifty knights, and ten thousand men fell in that red reckoning. Lady Nairne recorded the aftermath, and the pipes wail of it to this day:

I've heard them a'liltin', at the yowe milkin',
Lassies a'liltin' afore dawn o' day,
But noo they are moanin', on ilka green loanin',
The floo'ers o' the forest are a' wede awae....

Something uncanny happened in Edinburgh the night before the army marched. There are many variations of the legend. Sir Walter Scott recorded the most popular, terrifying indeed to a superstitious people.

He describes, in *Marmion,* how unearthly figures were seen over Edinburgh, before a dreadful voice rang out from the Mercat Cross naming those doomed to die in the coming battle. The foreboding created by the ghostly prophecy, superstitious or not, were fully realized. Rumours of deadly battle came, then a lone rider arrived, man and horse sorely stained and wearied. Under the eyes of a silent crowd, he spurred slowly through the Netherbow Port, and broke the news of disaster.

The magistrates hastened to the Mercat Cross and summoned all men who could bear arms to stand ready to defend their town—all women to pray for aid in a desperate hour. The people toiled, and the Flodden Wall rose, but the days and nights passed tensely and no invader came. Parts of the wall cling to the old town to this day.

Bishops and lesser mortals clashed, and Castlehill glowed redly as 'witches' and 'heretics' were hurried to the stake and burned. The fires blacked out suddenly when the grim, austere figure of John Knox strode into the troubled scene to take his place as minister of the Parish Kirk of St Giles'. There were no half measures, he preached the love that stirs hatred, the peace that sparks war, the faith that breaks or makes a people.

Not even Knox could escape the wear of the years, but his spirit soared above infirmity. In the closing months of his life he had to be lifted into the pulpit, but as his sermon heated the faith within the frail body, generating the same fires within those who listened, he became "so vigorous that he was like tae ding the pulpit in blads, an' flee oot o' it."

"The voice of this one man, John Knox, is able, in one hour, to put more life in us than 500 trumpets continually blustering in our ears," reported Thomas Randolph, England's Ambassador, in 1561. Strange that the body of the man who gave Scotland her faith should lie in an unknown grave. Until a few years ago a brass plate, engraved "J.K.1572", was set in the earth of Parliament Square under the chill, leaden eye of Charles II, the arch enemy of all that Knox believed in, but where the reformer actually rests no one knows with certainty. Today, a statue of John Knox stands in the quadrangle of New College.

The drama of royal Scotland was played out in the Heart of Midlothian. Crafty men, honest men, sincere men, weak men behind the scenes that brought it to an end, and the curtain fell with a crash that shook Edinburgh for a very long time, and was to agitate Scots for all time. It was the year 1707. Rumours of an impending 'great betrayal' had been whispering through the wynds and closes, and riots and demonstrations of protest had flared in the streets. Troops were hurried in to keep the uneasy crowds in check while, all unknown, the 'betrayers' did their worst in a cellar opposite the Tron Kirk, signing away Scotland's independence.

The beat of drums on May Day announced an important proclamation. All Edinburgh crowded at the Mercat Cross as the trumpets rang out. Then the fact emerged, and the roar of rage that burst from the multitude blotted out the sentence of doom. Royal free Scotland was no more, and the miserable tatters of her parliament were already heading for the Border and London. The infuriated citizens broke loose, and more troops were rushed in to hold the streets and curb the tempers.

With Scotland stripped of her independence, Edinburgh drooped. The life went out of her, beautiful still, but old suddenly, and helpless. No point in looking south for aid, her future was now in the hands of those whose vision was little more than the length of a London street. North and South are poles apart, so with their views. The South had a sharp reminder of this in 1736. In that year a crowd assembled round the Lawnmarket gallows to witness the execution of a smuggler, Andrew Wilson. The rough treatment meted out to the condemned man by Captain Porteous and his soldiers on the short walk from the Tolbooth angered the crowd. They made no trouble, however, until Wilson was dead, then moved forward to claim the body. Porteous, enraged, ordered his troops to open fire, and snatching up a rifle, set the example. Six spectators were killed and many injured.

Porteous was tried on a murder charge, found guilty and sentenced to death. London, almost automatically, and certainly unwisely, issued a reprieve. The reply came swiftly and violently. A crowd gathered, it was no mob. Quiet, disciplined, but dangerous. They attacked the Tolbooth, seized Porteous, dragged him to the Grassmarket, and hanged him from a Dyer's pole. London fury availed nothing. The leaders, men of standing, were never traced, but the city had to pay a heavy fine, and the unfortunate provost was removed from his post and penalized.

So the withering years passed until 1745 arrived bringing a steadily growing rumour that the war pipes were skirling in the north, and that Prince Charles Edward Stuart, the 'Young Pretender', and his fighting clansmen had burst from their mountains and were striking rapidly towards Edinburgh, a Stuart throne, and an independent Scotland. Then came the news that the Highland army was across the Forth, and had smashed the government force at Falkirk. The sight of panic-stricken dragoons fleeing along the far bank of the Nor' Loch, well ahead of the dreaded claymores, was effective confirmation. The town council also noted, beat to arms, and hastily despatched a representative to treat with the Prince and plead for delay. "No delay," said Charles, and demanded the immediate surrender of his Capital.

The alarmed messenger hastened back to report, the Netherbow Port swung open to let his carriage through, and the unseen Lochiel, approaching with his Camerons, seized the opportunity, rushed the gate and carried High Street without a blow. Much has been written about the 'cowardice' of the Town Guard on this occasion. There was no cowardice. Events proved that most of the townsfolk in sentiment at least were Jacobite.

The people woke to find kilted clansmen at every point of vantage, although the defiant boom of the cannon up in the Castle as it fired down the length of the old town, told that at least it was uncaptured. Prince Charlie rode down the Royal Mile through milling crowds pressing in to shout the Gaelic words already learned from the 'invaders'—*Ceud mille failte,* a hundred thousand welcomes. It was gala time in every street, every close. Pipes lilted, flags snapped in the breeze, white cockades appeared everywhere. Edinburgh was Jacobite, and down in the valley, grey Holyrood awoke and blazed into the splendours of a Royal Levée. Scotland's Prince had come home.

The pipes skirled with double fervour when Charles and his clan chieftains stood in front of a great crowd gathered at the Mercat Cross, to hear a royal proclamation: "Charles, Prince of Wales, Regent of Scotland, England, France, Ireland, and the Dominions thereunto belonging . . ." Down at Dunbar General Cope set his army into motion to march north and end the Stuart illusion. Cope's own illusions were shattered on the battlefield of Prestonpans, a few miles from Edinburgh. A new song was born, and the pipes of some Scottish regiments still play the tune at reveille.

Hey, Johnny Cope are ye waukin' yet,
Or are your drums a'beatin' yet?

"The saddest words of tongue or pen, the saddest are these, 'It might have been'." What a short jump separates triumph and despair. Charles gauged it. Derby chilled the hope, Carlisle destroyed it, Culloden underlined in red the end of a high and heroic adventure. The malice written even more redly along the lonely glens of the north, showed again at the Mercat Cross when the hangman publicly burned the standards of the Jacobite chieftains.

The Heart of Midlothian, what a stage, what a cast. And old St Giles', who watched it all unfold, still looks greyly down upon the passing show. And the play goes on, ourselves the actors now, with never a chance of rehearsing anything, even if we knew our parts.

The history of the old kirk would fill many books, its secrets many more. Old when Richard II arrived with his army in 1385 to sack and burn both church and town. But a new St Giles' rose from the ashes, fortified against the further shocks that would come with the centuries. If stones had a voice, what a tale would be told here. Of human deeds, and inhuman deeds; of courage, of cowardice, of loyalty, of treachery. Above all, of faith. And yet the reek of human blood taints the incense in too many chapters, the contradictions strike too sharply—a Bible placed upon the altar for the congregation, a dismantled gallows tossed into a corner to await the next doomed wretch. The story of St Giles', thrilling, degrading, inspiring, a serial that can never have an end.

Another institution rooted deeply in the past—Scottish Law—is very much in evidence around the kirk. Opposite the spot where the Lawnmarket gallows once did its grisly work stands the Sheriff Court. The man who selected that site must have had a grim sense of humour. Figures loitering uneasily near the entrance show that the court is sitting. These are the witnesses and men on minor charges waiting the summons that will set them squarely under the unemotional eyes of the Sheriff. Across the square is the Court of Session, Scotland's highest tribunal, dreaded by the hardened criminals. Here, not so long ago, came Peter Manuel, the multiple murderer from Glasgow, to plead for the life many times forfeit. He made his plea, the learned judges judged, and Manuel passed to the hangman.

Manuel was but one of a long, long list. Step behind the Grecian front of Parliament House, and find Parliament Hall, almost as it was when built in 1632 for the Scottish parliament. The Union swept away both King and parliament, but the Hall is still here and still imposing. An ornate window commemorates the College of Justice established by James V in 1532. James is shown presenting the charter to Alexander Mylne, Abbot of Cambuskenneth, the first Lord President. Nobles and Officers of State watch the presentation. The statues placed in the Hall mark famous men, famous days: Lord Melville, Lord President Blair, Lord Advocate Dundas, Duncan Forbes of Culloden, Lord President Boyle, Lord Jeffrey, and, among many others, Sir Walter Scott, who was Clerk of the Court for twenty-five years. They passed this way. Stand for a moment, let fancy run, and you may still hear the rustle of their passing.

At the other end of Parliament Square is the Burgh Court, where the criminal small fry are hauled before the bailies to answer for their misdemeanours. Appropriately enough, the Burgh police headquarters stands handy.

Across the street the City Chambers sits well back from its arched entrance, the town war memorial in front. This is where the Lord Provost and his council guide the destinies of the ever-growing town. Erected in 1753, it was intended to be the Royal Exchange. The building, taken over by the council, has spread considerably, swallowing up some famous old closes in the process.

Not even here is the past evaded. A few steps down from the noise and bustle of modern times, Mary King's Close, the street of sorrows, stands much the same as it was when life deserted it more than 300 years ago. It is a narrow highway that once dropped down from High Street to the old road that led round the Nor' Loch. The council chambers hide its entrance now, but the exit gate can be seen in nearby Cockburn Street. The close was typical of its time. Children laughed and played round the entrance, men toiled, and women endured to keep the laughter ringing. In 1645 plague came to Edinburgh, struck venomously along High Street, and slipped silently into Mary King's Close. Then sorrow sat in every home, and death was the least of it. Daily came the cart, rumbling dully over the cobblestones, and the dreadful cry, "Bring out your dead," fell lifelessly upon the lifeless atmosphere. With the cart came the partings, child from parent, babe from mother, husband from wife, and the next day—the wife.

Day after hopeless day, night after sorrowing night, the invisible killer struck and slew. Human endurance crumbled under the curse. The few still with life fled, never to return, and left their homes to the horror of it all—and the silence. Fear took over, people avoided Mary King's Close, and tales were told of wraiths, and ghosts, and heart-rending wailings from long-dead homes. Came the builders, and the accursed close was hidden from view to sink deeper into the silence.

Now, more than three hundred years later, you may walk down the street of sorrow, although permission is required as there is some danger from decay, and see it almost as it was left in those tragic days so long ago. The paving, worn by countless feet; the hearths, chill and blackened; the empty cupboards; the iron hooks hanging in the butcher's shop; the horse shoe nailed to the door for luck.

Memories of another kind are stirred a few yards further along High Street. A medallion on the wall at No. 231 marks where James Gillespie had his snuff shop, and a business that brought him a fortune. Gillespie, who died in 1797, used some of that fortune to found a school and a hospital. A famous girls' school carries his name today.

Anchor Close, where Robert Burns caroused in Dawney Douglas's tavern with the Crochallan Fencibles, is in this area. Johnnie Dowie's, in Liberton's Wynd, also stood high in Rabbie's favour. It was a drinking age, and a gentleman of the time relates how he went to Dowie's one morning, opened the door, and found a heap of drunk bank clerks sleeping it off on the floor. The Crochallan Fencibles got their name from a lilting Gaelic air, "Crodh Chailein", 'Colin's cattle', while 'Fencibles' was no more than a skit at the regiments of foot soldiers being raised all over the country at that time. The members of this famous club, all men of talent and humour, assumed some military rank or title, and mock trials were quite regular occurrences after some breach of club regulations. Then followed a fine rough and tumble, until the accused was finally passed to the deputed 'hangman'. Burns's verses on "Rattlin' Roarin' Willie" presented an excellent portrait of the 'Colonel' of the Crochallans, William Dunbar, W.S.

There was no lack of interest on the Royal Mile of those days. All sorts of freak clubs were formed, an evening of rehabilitation after the long day's darg, and many of the well-to-do and professional men threw themselves into the frolics with the wild abandon of a beatnik. The Hell Fire Club, with its blasphemous toasts; the Sweating Club was a gathering of fashionable young thugs who terrorized those out for an evening stroll; the Dirty Club ruled that no gentleman should appear in clean linen; the Boar Club met in a tavern which they called their sty, each member being obliged to grunt like a pig for a few minutes; the Spendrift Club dedicated themselves to spending no more than 4½d. a night; the Odd Fellows wrote their names upside down.

There were, of course, more innocent pleasures. For 3d. there was the chance of viewing a "great beast calit ane drummondary, cleven futted like unto a kow". The Craig's Close spectacle was a sensation. In 1784 a Princes Street hairdresser exhibited his grotesque twin brothers under the title of the 'Irish Giants' at 1s. a peep. At least 8 feet in height, broad and handsome, the girls of the period were queueing to see them. Weir's Natural History Museum was situated at 16 Princes Street, and at 4 St Andrew Square Count Barrowlaski, or Count Barrel o' Whisky as he was more commonly called, played the guitar, admission by ticket only at 3s. 6d. each. The Count was about 3 feet high. There was the occasional organized street fight, and cock-fighting drew the crowds to Leith Links and the Grassmarket.

Remaining names recall lost links. Old Stamp Office Close housed the office of the Scottish Inland Revenue, and held the home of the Earl of Eglinton and his fair Countess, where heroine

Fiona MacDonald received part of her education. Here too was Fortune's Tavern, the most fashionable in town, which staged the receptions of the Lord High Commissioner to the Church of Scotland. Fleshmarket Close nearby proclaims its business. A butcher in England is a flesher in Scotland. A plaque is set at the corner of Cockburn Street said to mark the home of Provost Sir Simon Preston, where unhappy Mary Stuart spent her last night in Edinburgh after the defeat of her supporters at Carberry Hill in 1567. What Mary's thoughts were that dreary night only she could tell. The street is named after Lord Cockburn (1779–1854), the great Scottish judge who took a keen interest in the welfare of the city. The Cockburn Association, formed in 1875, guards the town's interests to this day.

Old Fishmarket Close is on the south side of High Street. It was here that George Heriot came to set up home after his marriage. A short distance away is Old Assembly Close, where fashionable Edinburgh once danced. Oliver Goldsmith visited the 'assemblies' in 1753. Hard by is Bell's Wynd, at the head of which once stood the 'Black Turnpike', a mansion which came into the hands of the Earl of Home. The Earl entertained Mary and Darnley here when they came back from Dunbar, even while the city was still buzzing with the news of Rizzio's murder.

The Tron Church, built in 1637, is prominent enough. It took its name from the 'tron', the public weighing machine set in the roadway near where the vegetable sellers sat around the kirk. The kirk lost its wooden steeple in the great fire of 1824, and is now council property. Before the age of television, this was the gathering point for Edinburgh folk on Hogmanay, to welcome in the New Year with music and song, but with the advent of Kenneth McKellar and Andy Stewart the crowds grew less, although there have been moves to revive the tradition in recent years.

The bridges drive across High Street at this point; North Bridge on the left, sloping down to the east end of Princes Street, Register House and the General Post Office. On the right, South Bridge carries the highway towards Newington and on to the Borders. High Street dips more steeply from the Tron, famous closes on both sides. Niddry Street, formerly Niddry's Wynd, holds St Cecilia's Hall, once acclaimed for its concerts in the long ago, but now a University museum. Carrubber's Close, where Allan Ramsay opened his short-lived theatre in 1736, is nearby. The Episcopalians carried on worship in this close when ejected from St Giles' in the upheaval of 1688.

A carving above the entrance to Paisley Close recalls the collapse of a tenement here in 1861. Thirty-five people died in the crash. One young man, trapped in the ruins, kept calling cheerfully to the rescuers, "Heave awa' lads, I'm no' dead yet," and his words are recorded on the stone. Blackfriars Street, once Blackfriars Wynd, held the residence of the "high and mighty Lord St Clair", Archbishop and Cardinal Beaton, and the Regent Morton. The carved lintel in Morton's home bears the date 1564.

Many noble families also lived in South Gray's Close, at the foot of which stood the Scottish Mint until the Union in 1707. The Museum of Childhood, with the toys of yester-year gathered from all over the world is in Hyndford's Close. An old stone well stands in the street opposite Fountain Close, to recall waterless days and weary vigils. A few yards from the well stands what is believed to be John Knox's House, jutting out from Moubray House, which dates from the fifteenth century, and is probably the oldest dwelling in Edinburgh. It is still in business. Knox's house is distinctive. James Mossman, goldsmith to Mary, Queen of Scots, was Knox's immediate predecessor and it carries his initials. His advice, "Lufe God abufe al and thi nychbours as thi self," is set prominently across the wall. Knox is said to have lived here during the latter years of his life, and until his death in 1572. Ever ready to 'spread the word' and denounce the 'excesses' of Queen and Court, he often harangued the crowd from the stone stairway outside his home.

Edinburgh ended here, the bulky Netherbow Port blocking the highway, with members of the Town Guard watching over the comings and goings. The old reformer must have been wakened at times by the sharp command ringing through the darkness, "Who comes?" He must have listened to the creak of

The Canongate Tolbooth still plays its part in history as a museum

the ponderous gate, the jingle of a sword scabbard, a joke, a laugh, and the clippety-clop of hooves dying away up High Street. But time marches on. The port was demolished in 1764, its clock removed to Dean College, where it still records the march. The site of the port is easily traced, and brass studs are set in the roadway to mark where the Flodden Wall rose after the news of battle disaster. World's End Close is the last in the old town. Just outside the wall in the old days, St Mary's Wynd, now Street, was the track down to the Cowgate and on to the south. To the left, Jeffrey Street, formerly Leith Wynd, led and still leads to the north-west.

Canongate takes over, reaching down to Holyrood, enough of its old buildings left to produce the atmosphere of the days when high-born nobles and their supporters, proud, warlike, crowded the street. One word out of place, one insult, real or fancied, set the swords flashing too, too often. Easy to imagine the colour and glitter of the royal parties riding up towards the castle or back to Holyrood, an almost daily street scene.

High Street grew downwards from the Castle, Canongate upwards from the abbey. As the name suggests, this was a favourite walk of churchmen when Holyrood Abbey sat on the edge of the great Drumsheugh forest, a hunter's paradise, and grassy fields lay between the abbey and Edinburgh's Netherbow Port. The years blotted out the fields as the palace took shape and the noble families established their town residences as near to the Court as they could get. Many of those homes are still in use, the carved monograms and texts quite prominent. Many, unfortunately, are gone. Morocco Land fell to the demolishers in 1950, but left the stone figure of a Moor to mark the site, and recall a love story that goes back more than 300 years, but is still told.

The Master of Grey, says the tale, led an attack on the home of the Provost, then fled to Morocco to escape execution. He returned in 1645, disguised as a Moor, and found the old town sorely stricken by plague, only sixty-five men being left fit enough to bear arms. The 'Moor' demanded a ransom and the provost's daughter, to save the town from immediate attack. The

6

One of the ornate gateways to the Palace of Holyrood, with Arthur's Seat in the background

girl was seriously ill with plague, and the 'Moor' agreed that if he failed to cure her illness, he would forfeit the ransom. He nursed her back to health, they fell in love—and wed.

New Street, where Lords Kames and Hailes once lived, has acquired a more modern newness, the red-brick bus depot, adding little to it. Opposite is newly renovated Old Playhouse Close, site of the Canongate Theatre, which opened in 1747. David Beatt, the man who read out Charles Edward's proclamation at the Mercat Cross, became manager. The management must have been fighters, for the theatre weathered many an attack by the unco guid, which was perhaps their greatest performance.

Further down a ring of stones marks the old position of St John's Cross, the Canongate Burgh Cross, now standing beside the Canongate Kirk. Tobias Smollet and his sister, Mrs Telfer, lived in nearby St John Street. The Canongate Kilwinning Lodge of Freemasons, to which Robert Burns was affiliated, is located here. It is claimed that their St John's Chapel is the oldest masonic chapel in the world.

Moray House, built in 1628 by Mary, Countess of Home, was twice occupied by Cromwell when his forces invaded the city. Now a teachers' training college, it is a house of memories, one of the more poignant created by the Argyll wedding party crowding on to the balcony to watch the condemned Montrose, weary but dignified, seated on a sled, being dragged to the Mercat Cross and execution. The great Montrose, defeated in battle, rose above his misfortune, and the people lining the street, urged by the ministers to torment the doomed man, were touched by his demeanour, and remained silent. It was left to the Duchess of Argyll on the balcony to deliver a final public insult. The see-saw of time swung and Argyll, his son, and some of the guests followed Montrose to the same destination and the same end.

Shoemakers' Land, sometimes called Bible Land, is opposite. Further down, the Canongate Tolbooth still stands in history as it has stood since 1591. Time was, time is, and time goes on; the big suspended clock ticking it off, second by second, over what was once council chamber, courtroom, jail, all under one roof.

This is where the Canongate rogues came face to face with the Canongate bailies, and met swift and rough justice. Today some of the memories are preserved, for the old building continues to function as a museum.

Huntly House, the city museum, is just across the street, where a copy of the National Covenant is kept along with other relics of the past. The house was acquired by the Incorporation of Hammermen of the Canongate in 1647, and was held by them for over a century. It became the home of the Gordons of Huntly for a time. A pend leads through it into Bakehouse Close and to Acheson House, which carries the date 1633 and the Acheson crest, a cock standing on a trumpet, which in turn rests on a midden, hence the saying—"Crawing ower yer ain midden heap".

Canongate Kirk rears back from the hubbub in a green oasis of peace, dignified, time-worn, as if withdrawing from the clamour of an uncouth modern world, in which it must still play its part. A collection of grey stones marks where many famous Scottish sons found rest. The kirk fairly bristles with them, for it was built by James VII in 1688, to take the congregation he ousted from the Abbey Church. It carries the arms of the Burgh of Canongate.

Robert Burns visited the cemetery here when he came to Edinburgh, and sought out the grave of Robert Fergusson, the brilliant, tragic young poet who had so inspired the Ayrshire bard. The neglected grave, unmarked, unnoticed, angered Burns. He commissioned and paid for the stone that now rises to point where poor Fergusson lies, greatness torn from him in the mad house.

Step round the kirk to another grave bearing the one word, 'Clarinda'. When Burns was angling for an excise post, he made friends with John Nimmo, an Edinburgh revenue officer who lived with his sister in Alison Square. Nimmo invited Burns to a tea party, and at the party Miss Nimmo introduced him to Mrs Agnes McLehose, a familiar figure in Edinburgh society. A few tongues have wagged since that meeting. Agnes, known to her friends as Nancy, had made a most unhappy marriage. Her husband had gone to Jamaica, leaving Nancy with two children. She was lonely, emotional, poetical. So was Burns, and the friendship grew. They wrote to each other continually. Burns took on the guise of Sylvander, Nancy became Clarinda. So they walked and talked through the Arcadian hours, dreamed, and woke to dream again.

> Had we never lov'd sae kindly,
> Had we never lov'd sae blindly,
> Never met or never parted,
> We had ne'er been broken hearted.

It had to end—and ended. But that is the message he left her, the story of love itself. Burns died in Dumfries in 1796, and Mrs McLehose was left in Edinburgh to mourn her lost love, which she did for many years. Then she too died, and passed to Canongate kirkyard, around which the fair Clarinda and her Sylvander had wandered so often. And in Nancy's drawer back home were found all the letters that Burns had sent to her, the writing worn and faded. Clarinda. A name on a stone, flowers on a grave to show that she is remembered, as well as the poet.

The old associations crowd thickly. Reid's Court and the restored Manse of the Canongate are here. Queensberry House, home of the Duke who was Lord High Commissioner when he took the leading part in signing away Scotland's independence in 1707, is now a hospital. Whitefoord House, where the Earl of Winton lived, and where 'my Lord Seton' had his lodging, was described in Scott's *The Abbot*. Near too lived Professor Dugald Stewart, friend and benefactor to Robert Burns. The house is now a haven for old soldiers, wearied by long-ago campaigns in foreign fields.

Golfers Land conjures up a perfect example of Edinburgh democracy—a duke and a shoemaker partnering each other at a game of golf. But what a game! The story tells how two English nobles teased James, Duke of York, who was to become James VII of Scotland and II of England, on the Scottish fondness for 'the gowf', and threw down a challenge. James, stung, took it up and laid a wager on the result. He then sent out runners to find the best golfer in Edinburgh. They returned with John Patersone, a shoemaker.

The day dawned, the entire Court and much of Edinburgh trooped down to Leith Links to witness the first ever Scottish-English golf international championship. Scotland won and James generously handed over half the wager to his partner, who built Golfers Land with the money. Easy come, easy go. Patersone later became bankrupt.

White Horse Inn, famous from the sixteenth century, still stands in White Horse Close, named after a white palfrey owned by Queen Mary. Here came the steaming, muddied horses, dragging the lumbering stage coaches, an assembly point for the London coach. The council has given the old inn a new lease of life, but not as an inn. It has become one of the best examples of modern restoration work in the country, £65,000 worth, where Edinburgh citizens who can afford the rents can have history with modern comfort.

Across the roadway the letter *S* is set at intervals to mark the old sanctuary line of Holyrood Abbey. Many a tense race was run down the Canongate when an unfortunate debtor fled just ahead of a pursuing bailiff. Once beyond that line and the debtor was safe—the bailiff knew that also. But so, too, did the folk in the street, and the odds were on the hunted man, for the bailiff was never a popular figure.

On the right stands the old Guard House of the palace, the arms of King James V still blazing from the wall. In front, beyond the great gates, is Holyrood Palace, and all that ruthless invaders left of the abbey.

Holyrood! Mystic name to Scotland. Never had palace a more perfect setting; in the green of the great King's Park, the dark cliffs of Salisbury Crags high above, the mighty cone of Arthur's Seat towering behind.

The castle is stern, the atmosphere of Holyrood peaceful. Yet who can say which of the two worked the greater mischief; the fortress, with its eternal clang of swords, or the cloisters, with its intrigues, plots and murders. The palace is stately, flanked by two towers that look twins, though separated by more than 150 years. Those years wrote some of the most bitter pages of Scotland's history.

Back in the days of the first Margaret the great Drumsheugh forest swept across this area, a hunter's paradise. Here came Margaret's son, David I, to a miraculous adventure. In an encounter with a stag he was unhorsed, but even as he clutched at the goring antlers, the stag vanished, leaving a cross in the bewildered King's hands—the Holy Rood.

In thanksgiving for his escape, he ordered the creation of an abbey on the spot of the encounter. Here, in front, is what is left of that abbey.

The building had a guest house, giving shelter to the various Kings who supported and protected it. James II was born here, crowned in due time, and wed. James was killed at Roxburgh, but his body was brought here for ceremonial burial. His son, James III married Margaret of Denmark here, and here also Margaret was crowned.

The first great change came with James IV. In 1501 he started to raise a palace over against the abbey, fit home for a queen. So grew the North-west Tower, and with its completion came the bride, Margaret Tudor, daughter of Henry VII of England. James visualized the palace much as it is today, but he was killed at Flodden before the work of extension could be started from his solitary tower.

Henry VIII was furious when a demand for the surrender of the infant Mary Queen of Scots was refused, and an army was sent to Scotland under the Earl of Hertford, with orders to burn and destroy Edinburgh. Hertford followed his instructions thoroughly indeed. Palace and abbey went up in flames, only the thick, solid stonework preventing complete destruction. The English marched south, and the great abbeys of Melrose, Kelso and Jedburgh blazed behind them.

Barely had work started on the restoration of Holyrood than Hertford appeared again, with a new title, the Protector Somerset, but with the same intentions. From the Forth to the Borders the land was in ruins.

Strange that such a man should bear such a title as Protector, but Somerset's deeds did more to unite Scotland than all the preachings of the factions. Restoration continued. James V added a little to the palace, and it rose again with all the life and colour that comes with royal living.

In 1603, Elizabeth of England died, and the life and colour drained to the south. Cromwell arrived forty-seven years later, and chose it to quarter his dragoons. Then fire consumed much of the building, and restoration had to begin anew. In 1671 Charles I gave the order, and William Bruce of Kinross, with Robert Mylne, added the second tower and completed the palace.

Almost a century later, in 1758, an effort was made to re-roof and restore the wrecked abbey. The breed of builder had deteriorated, however, and the 'modern' roof collapsed a bare ten years later. Since then, the ancient, long-suffering building has grown that much greyer and more tattered, but the examples of workmanship throughout the ruins stand as a challenge to modern architects.

Some say that the abbey could have been rebuilt at the turn of the century, but Queen Victoria did not want it altered, and succeeding royal names have seen fit to preserve her wishes.

More interesting than the stones by far are the people whose voices rang through the rooms and corridors. The people, and the emotions of the people.

What were the thoughts and feelings of young Margaret Tudor, for instance, when she arrived before the city in 1503 after a long, tiring journey from her more gentle southern home. Just fourteen years old, she would have scanned the landscape, wilder and ruder than she had known, and the Scottish nobles drawn up to accord her a welcome. How intently she must have scrutinized the two figures riding out from the main body, the Earl of Bothwell, bearing the sword of State, and behind—the King, the man she was to wed.

Margaret was lifted on to the King's saddle, and the cavalcade entered the city, passing Greyfriars where the friars exhibited sacred relics, down High Street, wine flowing from the fountain at the Mercat Cross, through the grim Netherbow, and so to Holyrood, and the palace built to be her home.

An observant English noble was in Margaret's retinue, and recorded all he saw. Margaret was welcome, the town in festive mood impressed the little princess with that fact. Not even the observant noble could guess at her innermost thoughts.

Margaret was destined to be happy. The golden age of Scotland arrived with her, and the name of Flodden was unknown. The gold passed with the years, and in 1538 Mary of Guise came from France to wed James V. Here again pomp and pageantry took over and ran merrily under the expert guidance of Sir David Lindsay of the Mount, Lyon Herald. In due time Mary came to Holyrood to be crowned and take over her Scottish home. Her short reign was troubled. The Church was corrupt, the nobles were split. Came the invaders, and Mary fled to the castle while her palace burned. James died in December 1542, shortly after hearing that a daughter had been born to him at Linlithgow.

"It cam' wi' a lass, it will gang wi' a lass," said James, forecasting the end of the great Stuart race. The 'lass', one week old, was Mary Stuart, the future Queen of Scots, and the most famous resident of Holyrood Palace. Her story was to spread across the world, and grow through the centuries. It was Mary's name which featured on the Greenwich treaty the following year, a treaty that brought disaster to Scotland. Luckless babe, then seven months old; fate was to weave the very pattern all through her lifetime.

Even at that age she was queen, and her nobles and fighting men closed around her. She was taken into the castle and held there while the invaders battered in vain at the massive walls. For better security she was carried to France, and there, while still a child, she married the heir to the throne. At seventeen, Mary Stuart was Queen of France.

Fate struck again. One year later her husband died, and she came home to Edinburgh as Queen of Scots, taking up residence in Holyrood Palace. Never did a girl of eighteen come to a more troubled scene. A young queen of great beauty, with all Scotland in her hand, meant power, and there were many who sought it.

Came Henry Stuart, Lord Darnley, tall, handsome. Mary, freed from official marriage orders, fell in love, made her own decision, which was disastrous. They married in 1565, and in a matter of months she saw with clear sight just how disastrous. Darnley was vain, callous, drunken, weak in character, and that character stamped itself into history one dreadful night on 9th March, 1566.

Mary had an Italian secretary, David Rizzio. Smooth, genteel, and something of a musician, Rizzio was far removed from the coarser, rougher pattern of the warlike Scots. Here again, Mary was indiscreet. Reared in the refined atmosphere of the French court, she could never grasp the savagery and roughness surrounding her. She confided in Rizzio more than she should have done, and the wily secretary made full use of the confidences to further his own ends.

The emotions that eluded Mary, did not elude Rizzio. But the Queen had power, and stood behind him. That, and the immensely thick walls of Holyrood House were sufficient protection. Rizzio should have known that in a land of violence, the sword is all-powerful.

So the grey day of 9th March blinked in and died away into darkness. The scene and the weather have never changed. The black clouds shrouded Arthur's Seat, and the gales of March tore at the towers and screamed through the roofless abbey. The Queen was seated in her supper room with the Countess of Argyll. Arthur Erskine, Captain of the Guard, and Lord Robert Stuart, stood by the wall, all absorbed by the melody conjured from Rizzio's harp. Then above the gale, above the music, the jingle of spurred boots, and the clank of sword scabbards from the winding stone stairway below. For Rizzio there was no escape.

Darnley had plotted and plotted well. At a given signal the Earl of Morton positioned his men to bar all doors and passages. Darnley with the Earl of Ruthven, their men behind them, crept up the stairway that led to the Queen's bedroom, and burst in.

The harp was silenced. Rizzio's acute brain saw what was intended and panicked, clinging to the Queen's skirts. Ruthven, ill and showing it in the pallor of his face, demanded the dismissal of Rizzio. Words rang high, then Morton's men stamped into the room, seized the screaming Italian, and dragged him out. The

Countess of Argyll, horrified, snatched up a candlestick and held it aloft. The screaming was ended suddenly as the daggers struck home. . . .

No stage drama ever produced such a scene. Mary, upright, shocked, but every inch a queen; the Countess, motionless, back against a wall, candlestick held aloft; Erskine and Stuart circled by drawn swords; Ruthven, pale, staring blindly at the drawn dagger in his hand; Darnley, frightened into soberness by the realization of the deed that was done. Then the ghastly sound of the body being dragged across a floor—and the stamp of feet dying away down an echoing stairway. Ruthven went out, then came back and asked for a glass of wine. . . .

Murderers, but foolish murderers. Mary was young, she was lovely, she recoiled from the weakness to which she was bound. A strong man could fall in love with her without a thought of power. One man did, the Earl of Bothwell, and woman-like Mary turned towards his strength, again drawing the venom of all around her. Not all, Bothwell had his own following, fierce, loyal, warlike. So the weeks passed, then fate struck again.

Darnley became ill, and was taken to Kirk o' Field to recover. Came April 1567, a tremendous flash, and a thud that brought startled Edinburgh folk from their beds. Kirk o' Field was no more, and Darnley was dead. What really happened is still argued over, and the historians of the day worked well at creating confusion.

Bothwell was blamed. That was inevitable. But Bothwell was strong, determined, and in love. There was the dramatic scene when he produced his extraordinary document naming himself as the Queen's suitor. The Lords signed, unwillingly indeed, but a ring of armed men around them left no option. Then the marriage in her own council chamber, the wild ride to Dunbar, and a honeymoon that lasted just ten days.

The arrival of armed nobles ended the dream, and husband and wife rode forth together to meet them at Carberry Hill. Bothwell offered to fight any man of equal rank to prevent bloodshed, but his challenge was rejected, Mary being the most vehement in forbidding the conflict. The lovers parted with many kisses,

Bothwell and his men galloped back to his castle, and Mary, surrounded by mounted men, returned to Edinburgh, to be held prisoner in the Provost's home in High Street.

We have a heart-aching glimpse of her here, a tearful face at a window, hair dishevelled, appealing to her people to help. She was escorted down to Holyrood, and really believed that her nobles had relented at last . . . she was going home.

They were pitiless times. Late that night she was warned for a journey, and in the grey dawn she set out once more, tired, wearied. Mary was leaving her Holyrood home for the last time. The journey ended on the shores of Lochleven, and she was rowed over to the tiny island castle where for eleven months she endured captivity—and worse. All forms of communication were forbidden, and the world beyond was a vague silence. That silence was broken once when the Laird came to her, and told her that the bonfires blazing on the hills were celebrating the crowning of her son, James VI.

Yet beyond the silence were men who remembered. An odd whisper came filtering through to Mary via Willie Douglas, a sixteen-year-old poor relation of the Laird. Came reports also, of mysterious bands of armed horsemen, riding along the banks of the loch and looking towards the island. Mary's hopes beat higher . . . and higher. . . .

On 2nd May 1568 the horsemen came boldly into the open near Kinross, and were seen instantly by old Lady Douglas, Mary's custodian. Ever suspicious, she asked for a messenger to speak their business, but was diverted. That night Willie Douglas, heart in mouth, lifted the castle keys from where they were hung, slipped down to the water's edge, busied himself with the boats moored there, and made certain there would be no pursuit.

So Mary and Willie walked openly across the crowded courtyard, passed through the doorway, and Willie instantly slammed the door shut, locking it. Then they were in the boat, rowing madly for shore. There was only one pause, halfway across, when Willie Douglas stood up and with an exultant yell sent the castle keys spinning into the water.

The boat touched shore, and they leapt to land, tears of joy streaming down the Queen's face. A horse was ready, Mary mounted, the armed men closed round, and the cavalcade moved off. They crossed the Forth the same night, Willie Douglas riding with them. Men of brave and high principle, alas, woefully weak in numbers.

Eleven days later they came to Langside, and the decisive battle. Mary's supporters were routed, but with a devoted little band she eluded her enemies and fled to the south, riding sixty miles to the Solway. On the other side lay England. A fishing boat took her there—to nineteen years of captivity, and death.

Various rooms in Holyrood still carry her initials, various signs show that Mary Stuart lived here. O Holyrood! Her story still lives in the heart of Scotland.

Mary's son, James VI, lived at Stirling as a boy, but came to his mother's palace in 1578, at the age of twelve. But was he her son, this man who made little effort to free his mother? That matter is touched upon in another part of this record. Twelve years later, James brought his bride, Anne of Denmark, to be crowned in Holyrood.

On the night of 26th March 1603 came the clatter of hooves in the courtyard below, and Sir Richard Carey roused James from his bed to tell him he was king of England. The King passed south, returning for a few weeks fourteen years later. He never came back. Holyrood's days as a royal residence were numbered.

Eight years after his accession, Charles I came to Holyrood in June 1633 to wear the Scottish crown. The Duke of York, who became James VII and II, lived in the palace as Lord High Commissioner. He came to the throne in 1685, and decreed that the abbey church should become the Chapel Royal—a Roman Catholic chapel. As a result abbey and palace were sacked by Protestant mobs, following the landing of William of Orange.

The Union of Parliaments came in 1707, and Holyrood sank into quiet slumber. For one brief moment it blazed into life again when Charles Edward Stuart and his Highlanders came clanging south in 1745, then slept once more, and still sleeps, stirring slightly each May as the General Assembly opens, or when the Queen comes to her northern Capital, which is seldom.

Step over the soft green turf towards tiny Dunsapie Loch, turn, and study the scene. Abbey and palace, and the Royal Mile behind, reaching up to the castle through the most absorbing tale ever told. If the centuries could produce their ghosts, what a pageant would march down that highway. No other city in the world has crammed so much drama into such small compass. Never did name ring more fittingly—The Royal Mile.

IV

. . . SUNDAY MORNING

AT 9 a.m. on Sunday there are more seagulls along Portobello Prom than people, and more people queuing for Alec Robertson's hot rolls in Bath Street than seagulls. There are more parked cars than drivers in the city streets, more empty yachts bobbing at Cramond than yachtsmen, more grazing sheep on Arthur's Seat than young lovers, more children than adults, more silence than noise. Sunday morning in Edinburgh is the scrape of Saturday night chip pokes on Leith Walk, the screech as *L* drivers emergency brake in the Durhams, the rattle of Corstorphine lawnmowers, the drone of Turnhouse early flyers, the solemn tolling of church bells over the city—slow and soulful at St Giles', deep and dignified at St John's in Brighton Place, modulated sombreness from Abbeyhill, steady baritone from Tolbooth St John's atop the Royal Mile, fast falsetto from St Michael and All Saints Episcopal at Brougham Street, a tuneful enjoining of the faithful to ancient St Andrew's and St George's.

Sunday morning is drawn curtains, blue chins, lazy-lies, garden toils, humping newspaper boys, husbands washing cars, husbands pushing prams, bacon sizzling, grilled kippers tempting. Sunday morning is for everyone.

By 10.30 Edinburgh begins to put on its Sunday braw. Kilts from where they were hung the week before, trousers razor-edged, creaky shoes from the finery cupboard, precious hats from their boxes. On Sunday morning Edinburgh's pride goes to its head. Hats! They are flaunting flags of righteousness. Thou shalt not be without hat for kirk on the Sabbath, and unswervingly Capital females follow the commandment. But what hats! And style! And nerve! And kilts, too. More of them on Sunday than on all the weekdays of the year put together, and Edinburgh males know how to wear them. Above kilts and below hats faces are befittingly solemn, disciplined into tranquil expression. "Good mornings" are an economy of face muscles, but with a gallantry and graciousness not normally noticeable. Sunday children are a diminutive race of paragons, unrecognizable after ordinary Saturday, faces burnished, angelically radiant. Sunday people are transcended.

Now here comes a No. 45 bus airting for distant Juniper Green by way of a few top-ten kirk attractions. Three small boys, sartorially straight from and Aitken & Niven's window, bound for Restalrig Church of Scotland, but with furtive whispers and ducked heads they wait two stops and make for Dunsapie Loch instead; two elderly ladies, bristling with Bibles and hymn books for the Canongate; an enormous puce-faced matron with matching purple sunshade hat struggles off at St Giles', where she is greeted by morning-coated ushers; two young boys in kilts with their kilted father ask for the top of the High Street with the lilt of the Islands in the vowels, then step into Edinburgh's towering Highland Kirk; a mixed gathering for the intermediate stations before Morningside's Holy Corner, where the bus almost empties of faithful. It contains now a severe-looking gentleman with bushy hair and eyebrows, his wife coney-coated; five sinisterly quiet children; two maroon-blazered George Watson's teenagers, replaying yesterday's rugby; four middle-aged ladies discussing an operation on a fifth who is sadly absent. There is also a man with three paint-pots, a lady with a small dog which cowers under the seat, and a young couple with a sound-asleep baby. Apart from such chance travellers, the church-time buses have their own regulars, tight little communities of their own, total strangers to each other, nameless, identities known only by observations over the months or years—the nurse, the banker, the coalman, or simply the girl with the cough, the lady with the squint, the man with boils. Yet should one of the accustomed faces be absent there is an interest, often concern, sometimes even voiced.

As the severe gentleman steps from the bus, his foot slips and he almost falls on the pavement. He fixes the driver with an un-Sabbath look. The bus moves away and the conductor innocently remarks in glorious repartee to nobody in particular, "He gets his eyebrows on the cheap from Cyril Lord."

By 11.30 with the churches in session, Edinburgh's religious apathetics show face on the streets and on other buses. They appear happily unrepentant. For them Sunday is a communion between club and ball at Dalmahoy golf course or a breaking of bread with the ducks at Duddingston Loch; it is meditation with rod and line out Harperrig way or on the other reservoirs, lochs and burns in the Lothians; it is the triumphal hymning of the wind in the pines on the way up Turnhouse Hill to Carnethy in the Pentlands; deep contemplation on the tramp over Scald Law, East Kip and Black Hill, with a delve into rucksack for lunch above Habbie's Howe, grouse exploding from the heather, whaups skirling and the white specks of eider on the loch below.

Sunday morning in darkest Niddrie is wastepaper by the ton, children by the regiment, shadowy cats and dogs by the score. Dead beer bottles, stockingless women, curlers, blaring transistors, sick, gusty laughter. Crying children, shouting children, fighting children, happy children, playing children, mostly in the gutter. More big dogs than little dogs, Alsatians, Labradors, mixter-maxters, dusty dogs, snarling dogs, friendly dogs, sniffing dogs, over-amorous dogs. Boys playing bools, cowboys, spacemen, baddies, goodies. Pseudo-mother little girls, sadly impatient for entry into the adult world, hobble on high-heels behind their tattered prams and battered dolls. Sadly, because in Niddrie children grow up fast.

For the down-and-outs and homeless, the inmates of the Castle Trades Hotel in the Grassmarket, Sunday morning is an extra hour in bed, the luxury of lazing all day, of wandering up and down the stairs as they please. Some go for a walk; some, with a shave and wash, have even made it to church; some sun themselves beside the gents' toilet and policebox, watching the world go by. A to-ing and fro-ing outside the Trades and Greyfriars' Hotels; two little girls hopping peevers, happy innocence and the wisdom of years on their smudgy faces; now here is a dog carrying the Sunday papers; the St Cuthbert's milk horse, harness brasses glinting, pulling his red-painted cart with a jingle; a surreptitious idling figure trying car doors, but no one shouts; there go two straying tourists with their cameras, peching up the hill to George IV Bridge as a policeman passes them on the way down. Above their heads the grey castle soars as it has always done, the heads of an early bus party poking over the ramparts like a defending force from the old days.

Down by the Firth a new skyline, perhaps the shape of Edinburgh to come, the vast Pilton Development, rearing up like . . . what? A hospital? A factory? A school? A prison? No, of course, it's a huge ugly battleship, Sunday-cleared for action, minus guns, ready for launching into the Forth below, with tiered superstructures, decks, television antennae, window portholes, blue-painted glass walkways as ship's rails and, with half a glance, five ship's cats ready to sail. It is incredible. It is a pretence in glass and concrete, a masquerade, a monster—or is it a marvel? It is peopled desolation, a nightmare from an architect's bedlam—or is it planning genius? From somewhere on an upper starboard deck sounds proof at least of human habitation. A radio is tuned to a Service. Abruptly on the stroke of twelve the hymn and booming organ dies into nothingness. It is time for 'Family Favourites'. The first record is a Rolling Stone number. It is fitting.

But the view! Like swans the yachts are out on the estuary, the sun catches glitteringly at the Fife townships half a world away, reflecting in spears from the white and dayglow orange of Oxcars lighthouse, dazzling a hundred constitutionals along Cramond Esplanade, where even more cars are parked, windows shut tight against fresh air, while the occupants devour the Sunday paper juicies. To the left the golfers are scurrying like ants across the green of Silverknowes—swipe, scurry, swipe—as the crew of a No. 8 bus enjoy a little peace at the terminus.

Sunday afternoon is a gallop in the woods around Penicuik and Gogar; a blether of mothers in the suntrap backcourts off the High Street, with washing dangling above. It is a picnic on the sands at Gullane or Arthur's Seat, or prodding below the big stones for crabs at North Berwick; a ring-a-ding of tills in the johnny-a-thing shops where papers, pins, sugar, balloons, hairpins, tatties and cheese all mixed up together have ready sale while the other shops are closed; a window-shopping expedition for antiques down the Royal Mile, while elder Canongaters sit on the benches by the kirk and watch with knowing winks. It is a game of football in the street with jerseys for goalposts and a lookout for the bobby; a cycle dirt-track by Granton; an adventure up the Water of Leith; it is mountaineering in the Zoo, a stroll over the Forth or the Radical Road; casting a sea-line from Newhaven's West Breakwater.

There is a small boy entering the Botanic Gardens, his hand in his father's fist, his face a tremulous wonderment of anticipation. Then off he goes into the world of little boys, plunging through mysterious jungles, secret bowers, exotic blooms, dark leafy caves, tall tiger and elephant grasses, green sinister pools, a riot of imagination that conjures black panthers from the squirrels and man-eating sharks from the goldfish, gloriously unaware of real-life hideous monsters lurking close by in the Gallery of Modern Art.

There are two pensioners, man and woman, entering Saughton Park at the pace of age, a white stick tapping. Slowly over the bridge, along the path and into their own private forget-the-present land, an explosion of roses, air heavy with fragrance, colours drained from the rainbow. But they search for something beyond the roses. On they go through the sunken Italian Garden with its shaped hedges, fine statuary and beckoning seats; and still on, but only a little farther—and then there is understanding. The Garden of the Blind. A tumult of flowers and herbs and shrubs whose scent is the quintessence of ecstasy. Honeysuckle, lavender, mignonette, heliotrope. An invasion on the sense of smell, immediate capitulation. The old folk stand for a time allowing the sensations to wash over them. Then they make their way along the guiding rails, where the names of the flowers are set out in Braille on little hanging plaques. It is a simple pleasure. As they smile to each other their faces reflect it.

Down at the Mound the soapboxes are out, tongues sharpened, the crowd lively. The barter of the rostrum is heckle, debate, jeers, and invective. Silence is an insult, abuse a triumph. On the steps of the National Gallery the star of Protestant Action is in the ascendancy. His bellow is inaudible. As eye and ear survey the scene, the Pope's name is taken in vain five times. There are growls of protest and jostling shoulders of support. Beside the railings the Young Communists are in need of rescue.

Dramatically the crowd's arch-provoker feigns conversion. With over-acted sincerity he asserts with a wink that at last he has been won over. Indeed he wants to join the Party. The crowd senses further diversion. They wait expectantly. Flamboyantly he takes a ten-shilling note from his breast pocket. He hands it to a suspicious Red Tie with exaggerated camaraderie. He lifts a large bundle of *Morning Stars* and distributes them to the gathering. He retains one. Suddenly with an oath he tears it into little pieces and shrieks at the others to do the same.

The National Secular Society has an audience of long-haired men and short-skirted girls, but there is much movement from one group to another; a coloured gentleman finds an interest in Black Power among a handful of noisy students; an elderly woman earnestly warns of the peril of strong drink to three sceptical amused soldiers; a young woman hoarse from shouting, predicts gloom, horror, nuclear extinction, and a continuance of the disgusting weather if there are any more irresponsible nuclear explosions. A wandering voice from the rear interjects to say that at least the last part is the fault of the Pope.

Because the Sabbath is a holiday the evening tries to steal it. Inexorably the hours melt away, thoughts turn to tea and television, baths and bedtime stories, homework, the evening out, the rounding-off of the day. Already the bells again call out over the city as Sunday wanes, and a new week approaches.

V

NEW TOWN

GIANT cranes are now an accepted part of the city's skyline during these days of almost overnight demolitions and sprint builds. Their long Meccano jibs hang over the development sites like huge *T*s, hoisting up the new Edinburgh with dramatic swiftness, or razing the walls of the old order to clear the way for the future with a grumble and a cloud of slow-settling dust. Higher and higher they soar, so that now Edinburgh has gone full cycle, tiering up again its skyscraper flats in Leith and Liberton, Comiston and Morningside, just as they stood once as the tenement high Lands of the Old Town's Royal Mile.

The expansion of the city since those days when it was an infant in size though a noble capital of distinguished longevity is a story of achievement and pride, where the creation of classic Edinburgh is concerned, a triumph of architectural planning, that in the space of some seventy years fashioned one of the most beautiful cities in the world. Unfortunately, and it is only too obvious today, the building of modern Edinburgh has also seen some of the worst forms of urban development malpractised upon it.

The need to expand the cramped old city pressed urgently in the middle of the eighteenth century. Then, like an eager, able artist with an empty canvas, the planners of Edinburgh Town Council set about the task of producing their new town.

For centuries Scotland's capital had occupied the fine defensive position on the ridge running from the foot of Arthur's Seat up to the castle on its rock, and, although a certain amount of new building and replacement work had been done before this time, the Old Town was still excessively overcrowded and even dangerously dilapidated in parts. That nothing had been done before was just one of the results of a strange state of pernicious cultural lethargy that seemed to have the whole of Scottish thought and action in its dulling grip. Then suddenly came the enlightening.

The Forty-Five uprising was over, Prince Charlie's final fling to restore the Stuarts to the throne had ended in disaster, and though some romantics may still grue the day, at last peace sneaked back into Scotland. Peace! It was something that the country hardly knew. Torn for centuries by bitter religious strife and civil war, the people of Scotland had conditioned themselves to think of little more than keeping alive, shutting their eyes and minds to the doubts in an uncertain future. Charlie's boat headed back over the sea to France, and after King George II's forces had extracted their due amount of vengeance, the country waited for more war as it was so accustomed, and there was no war. Slowly came the realization that Scotland had been plunged into a state of wondrous tranquillity.

With peace came the first glimmerings of revival as a nation, this in spite of the fact that already her parliament had been consumed by that of England in 1707, not entirely without success, but it still rankled in many places in the Capital—and, for that matter, it still does today. Yet it was this rekindling of national conceit that became one of the most potent factors in the extraordinary blossoming of Scottish culture after 1745, and because Edinburgh was the capital of Scotland, it was in this city that it reached full bloom.

Scotland's story had certainly not been bereft of famous sons before this date: fiery John Knox, gentle Allan Ramsay, erudite George Buchanan, inventive John Napier and many others had all left their marks on our history. There had also been a building programme of sorts in Edinburgh, and the town council could point with justified pride to the new sides of Parliament Square, earlier ruined by fire, the stately James's Court and a few more landmarks of distinction. Progress was not limited to the construction of new buildings. The Royal Infirmary was winning acclaim for its work from all over the country, and received its charter as early as 1736. Even in those days when sleepy Edinburgh was just stirring to wakefulness, it had all the look and feel of a capital city, and this was something remarked upon by foreign visitors who viewed the Royal Mile for the first time with consternation.

But as the second half of the eighteenth century began to unfold, there was suddenly almost a queueing up of native talent of far-ranging genius: David Hume and Adam Smith assumed the roles of philosophers of European reputation; James Watt tinkered with his water system and produced the steam engine, even if he had to go to England for the birth; John Rennie and Thomas Telford won fame as engineers of outstanding ability; John and William Hunter were two of the best-known surgeons of their century; Sir Henry Raeburn became a celebrated painter; riding up from Ayrshire on his borrowed pony, lauded and fêted, came Robert Burns, with romantic Sir Walter Scott following close behind; and James Craig and Robert Adam began to wrestle with the problems of Edinburgh's new town for the new age.

The first direct steps to extend the city—and they were by no means faltering ones—were taken in 1752 when the "Proposals for carrying on certain Public Works in the city of Edinburgh" were published. This document was almost unknown and certainly unappreciated until Professor J. A. Youngson of the economic science department of Edinburgh University brought it to general notice in his book on the makings of classical Edinburgh. 'The Proposals', as Professor Youngson made clear, were more than a mere blueprint for the creation of a new town, they were the blueprint for one of the finest and most classic cities in Europe, giving the impetus that set Scotland's cultural revolutionary ball spinning and bouncing, a lasting testimonial to the far-sighted town council, who saw Edinburgh not just as the Scottish capital, but in relation to the outstanding cities of the world.

'The Proposals' set out in detail the reasons for extending the Capital and the need for expediency. They took advantage of the fact that part of an old six-storey block had recently collapsed, and others had to be demolished for safety, leaving piles of unsightly rubble in some of the most noticeable parts of the town. They went on to draw attention to the natural beauty of the city's position, to its poor comparison with London in terms of town planning and industry, to the resultant stimulation of the arts. They took to task Edinburgh's reputation for meanness, and cunningly inserted the hint that much of London's development had been aided by 'private gentlemen'. In short, 'The Proposals' were an odd mixture of endeavour, hope, and daydreams, with a solid core of hard-headed realism—and a definite suggestion of determination. Finally came the action; the city proposed to build an exchange, a building to house the law courts, the town council, the advocates' library etc., and to win through parliament an act to "extend the royalty, to enlarge and beautify the town, by opening new streets to the north and south, removing the markets and shambles, and turning the North Loch into a canal, with walks and terraces on each side". It also called for a national contribution to help meet the cost.

The situation was ripe, and, as happens so often when history is in the delicate embryo stage, the strong man of personality was revealed to implement the plan. George Drummond, the Lord Provost, was a juggernaut when it came to clearing a way for furthering the interests of his city, his by adoption only, for beetle-browed Drummond was a Perthshire man, a Whig and a devout member of the kirk, who had done some sprinting with General Johnnie Cope after Prestonpans. It was not the only time he saw action, for he was at Sheriffmuir too, although perhaps his greatest battles were still to come as he set his shoulder behind the idea of a new town. It was Drummond who was largely the inspiration for bringing the Royal Infirmary into being, his clarity and scope of thought were very much part of 'The Proposals', and, as a doer of deeds, he was impatient to see the translation of thought into fact.

Think what this meant. Think of the vision behind the plan and the enormity of the task as Drummond stood on the castle ramparts with his councillors and painted an imaginary picture of their fine new town as they surveyed the hills, the cliffs, the ravines, the Nor' Loch and its swamps, the rough-hewn road stretching northwards down to Leith, and the sail-speckled Forth with the Fife hills humping up beyond.

As they looked over the grey Old Town with its multi smells and decaying tenements, and over the fields and country houses to the south, Lord Provost Drummond must have been in convincing form as he talked of noble buildings, stately Grecian pillars, domes and spires finer even than those in Berlin, Paris, Turin, or that other well-known city 373 miles to the south. After 'The Proposals' were published, he did not dream his dreams for long. A year later the workmen were clearing the site for the first part of his plan—and the Exchange, now the centre of the City Chambers, was under way.

Of course, as could be expected, the building of the new Edinburgh was hardly a story of triumphal progress with never so much as a set-back. In fact a frustrating assault course of problems was to be negotiated at almost every stage, and right from the outset finance was the major hurdle. Ready money was in short supply, even though a subscription cast widely had yielded a fairly fat purse, with donations coming from all over the country, from small burghs, the professional classes, merchants, traders, those with titles. To ensure that there would be sufficient funds, £10,000 was borrowed from local banks, which proved a mammoth underestimate by the time the Exchange was completed.

Yet despite a few burned fingers and flat wallets, this was not enough to prove a deterrent against further development. Architect John Adam's handsome structure pleased the city, although the chattering, hard-driving merchants never used it for their business, preferring to do their bartering in the streets, following the tradition that had been their way of life for centuries.

It was the start. But bigger, more important projects clamoured for action. Tall-masted ships came beating up the Forth under full sail to unload at Edinburgh's Port of Leith, ships from many lands with rich, heavy cargoes; and their hazardous journeyings across the sea could hardly have been more tiresome than trying to transport those cargoes up the hill to the Old Town. Clearly easier access to Leith was priority, and if Edinburgh was to

Randolph Place below the dome of St George's Church
(overleaf) Edinburgh from the Castle ramparts

ORATORY
OF
SAINT ANNE

MACKIE'S
EDINBURGH SHORTBREAD
TIMPSON SHOES

extend to the north some method of negotiating the Nor' Loch was urgent.

A bridge was the obvious answer. In spite of snipings from landowners, the uncertainty of capital, and a fine haggling over plans, Lord Provost Drummond pushed ahead with the idea, gave the contract to William Mylne, and laid the foundation stone himself in 1763, three years after drainage had begun on the unsavoury, high-reeking Nor' Loch.

But as the North Bridge began to grow, plagued by money problems and, at one point, even having part of it collapse on five workmen, it became obvious to the planners of Edinburgh that the time was ready to exert control, and discipline the growth of the city to conform to the lines set out in 'The Proposals'. In 1766 out went the call for the master plan, the all-important blueprint that would decide the future look of Edinburgh, the document that would make Edinburgh Town Council, with all their high-flown, pretentious plans for their city, either eulogized and venerated by ensuing generations of citizens—or the laughing stocks of Europe.

Six entered for the competition, and the man who won the historic award was young city architect, James Craig, son of an Edinburgh merchant. For Craig it was like a fairytale that slowly and painfully turned into a nightmare. The acceptance of his plans, altered and redrawn though they were, catapulted him from the cosy obscurity of life among the great anonymous of Edinburgh to national eminence. Then came the slide from public gaze while his plan, the head-in-hand grindings of his brain, grew into stone and mortar substance. At the last of it came poverty and death, almost unnoticed. Such is the reality of life, as many found before and have found since—of those who go unrecognized while they live.

James Craig's ability has been the matter of considerable argument over the years. Some praise rapturously, others denigrate with scornful contempt; yet his true worth as a planner is obvious to all who first step out of Waverley Station—the quite splendid use of Edinburgh's natural position. The concept of having buildings on one side only of Princes Street and Queen

Coates Crescent, typical of New Town architecture

Street, the two parallel extremes of Craig's plan, immediately give the impression of space, grace and grandeur, and succeeding generations of Edinburgh town councillors have wisely seen fit to leave well almost alone.

The basic design of the New Town followed a well-tried pattern; two spacious and elegant squares—St Andrew Square and Charlotte Square (then St George's Square)—linked by the wide, straight thoroughfare of George Street, with other parallel but lesser streets on either side, Rose Street and Thistle Street, named after the emblems of England and Scotland. It had been done before in some other cities, not always successfully, but where Edinburgh won was in its splendid use of its natural position, its spaciousness, and the harmony of its frontages. Unfortunately, later town councillors have looked the other way under the pressures of commercialism, and today the battle for preservation is a hard-fought, depressing affair, with the trends of recent years giving little confidence in the statements that emit from time to time from the High Street when the subject reaches the point of conflagration.

As the years slipped by, the New Town began to take shape, restrained or perhaps protected by Craig's grand design, and, as the new buildings flowered, the people of Edinburgh saw that indeed it was to be a city of great beauty. The city was lucky in that there was a ready supply of handsome, light-coloured, calciferous sandstone from the quarries of Craigleith, Barnton, Ravelston and Hailes that gave the city an added distinction. Craigleith stone was particularly attractive, and much was sent south to build Buckingham Palace and the British Museum. Most of the paving stones came from Hailes, while the other quarries supplied the large building blocks.

The first major undertaking after the North Bridge was Register House, planned to hold the public records of Scotland, which were in poor condition, rotting and worm-eaten. Robert Adam and his brother James were appointed architects, an imaginative choice, for Robert's reputation was well-earned; and although the new building proved a headache to erect due to lack of funds—work halted for six years at one stage when it was labelled the most magnificent pigeon house in Europe—Register House, even with a curtailed design, eventually set the tone and gave a superb example for the New Town to follow.

Robert Adam was to Edinburgh architecture what Burns, Scott, and Stevenson were to native literature. It was Adam who first fitted the fair face to Craig's grand design, a perfect double-act, as he studied and considered the mould with understanding, then introduced the dignity and refinement required of a capital city with such skill, taste, and restraint that his activities in Edinburgh became the talk of Europe. Gay, shrewd, ambitious, Kirkcaldy-born Adam was the son of an architect who gave his talented offspring the opportunity to travel and study on the Continent, where he imbued the very spirit of his profession, polishing and improving himself so that he could take his place as a master among the London sophisticates, friend of nobility and men of power, certainly the most highly regarded architect of his day in Britain.

The publication of his book, after he had been inspired by the wonders of the Palace of Diocletian of Spalato, made him the pride of the Metropolis, and as a result much of his work was undertaken south of the Border. At his funeral to Westminster in 1792 some of the best-known dignitaries in the country paid their respects, with the Duke of Buccleuch as one of the pall-bearers. It is not the amount of new building achieved by Adam that leaves Edinburgh so much in his debt, but the standard he set for the city right from the beginning which was the challenge to others to emulate or even try to surpass.

Up went the much-needed South Bridge as the Capital over-spilled on to the other side of the Old Town, demolishing some of the historic wynds and closes in its path, clearing away the Black Turnpike, with sad memories for a tearful Mary, Queen of Scots. The bridge was to the design of Alexander Laing, although there was a certain amount of bad feeling here, for Robert Adam had also prepared a number of detailed plans for the development, which were declared by many to be much superior if more costly. Already there had been some building completed on the south side. Adam Square and Brown Square were at opposite ends of

Chambers Street; Argyll Square has been replaced by the Royal Scottish Museum; Nicolson Square is still there. The most magnificent square of all on this side of the Royal Mile was George Square, built by James Brown on ground which the town had refused to buy, recently the scene of an Edinburgh controversy as the elegant houses fell before the demolishers' bulldozers.

Up too, but more slowly, went the university, as part of the southern approach, its magnificence largely lost today in the narrowness of its surrounding streets, and the snarling mad-ant traffic. It is not all Adam, but his genius is obvious throughout the design. Yet the university, apart from the annoyance of alterations to his plans, would have brought him little pleasure. Caught up in the general financial depression during the wars with Napoleon, it stood for years an unfinished, desolate shell, like a battle scene from the conflict which had ended its growth.

Whether it was the challenge, the inspiration of the Georgian age or a matter of chance, there was no shortage of architects of skill to continue the work of creating classic Edinburgh. In fact, the man who won the contract to complete Adam's university project was an architect of rare ability. It is a pity that nature and circumstances could not have been kinder, and spread William Playfair and his contemporaries a little more evenly through the centuries, especially into the twentieth.

To Playfair's design some of the country's real masterpieces were dotted about the growing city. We tend to remember Playfair—another son of a Scots architect—for his superbly classical National Gallery at the Mound, his finest achievement; yet Edinburgh owes perhaps more to him than to any of the other city-makers, not just for the accomplishment of such splendid legacies as Donaldson's Hospital, the Royal Scottish Academy, formerly the Royal Institution, the Royal College of Surgeons, as well as many other public and private houses, but also for the considerable role he played in planning parts of the city itself.

Another of the architects to come to the fore at that time was William Burn. Although his part in the rise of Edinburgh was less effective, he still produced some quite outstanding work.

St John's Episcopal Church on Princes Street was his creation; the soaring Melville monument at St Andrew's Square, Edinburgh Academy, the Merchant Maiden's Hospital, John Watson's Hospital at Belford, are all part of the Burn contribution. There was Thomas Hamilton with his Royal High School, the Dean Orphanage, The Burns Monument, and Physicians' Hall in Queen Street; and quixotic Robert Reid, the King's architect, who seemed to fail with his perspectives in St George's Church in relation to exquisite Charlotte Square, and who drew the wrath of the town for the facelift he gave their revered Parliament Square—yet he was also responsible for the splendid Heriot Row, and, with the help of William Sibbald, planned the extension of the New Town on the opposite side of Queen Street across the gardens.

There was James Gillespie, the poor Dunblane boy who married into a fortune and added his wife's name to his own to win a considerable reputation as Gillespie Graham. Later, in Victorian times, came David Bryce and David Rhind, responsible for many of the great banks and commercial offices in the centre of the town; and Bryce was mainly behind the Scottish baronial style which found favour all over Scotland, while the Edinburgh Royal Infirmary with its giant clock-tower was also his inspiration. Sir Robert Rowand Anderson was the outstanding architect of the late nineteenth century. But indeed there are many who played their part in the creation of classic Edinburgh, to remember with pride and gratitude, and perhaps, because their genius is lost to us now in an architecturally sterile age, with wistfulness, too: Mylne, Nasmyth, Lissels, Elliot, Stark, Pugin, Bryce, Lorimer, Browne, their names mean little now, but their works are all around us, a memorial to themselves and to the council who gave them the opportunity, and a reminder—or a twinge of conscience—to today's councillors of what architecture really is, and of the city's heritage that is in their trust to gloriously enhance, or thoughtlessly debase. . . .

As the new Edinburgh spread itself, so the stories unfolded; the small, seemingly unimportant and almost unrecorded events that were still of enough significance to alter the history of the town. Take, for example, the story of Princes Street, Edinburgh's main thoroughfare, as famous round the world as Fifth Avenue, Regent Street or the Champs-Elysées. While green grass still grew there, it appeared on Craig's plan as South Street, cutting across what was then called Bearford's Parks, where the stone for the North Bridge had been quarried. Later South Street became St Giles' Street, after the great church of the Old Town which looked down with all the dignity of age on the agitation of the rising young city. One day King George himself came to see the progress of his northern capital. His eye fell on 'St Giles' Street', the same unfortunate, displeasing name borne by one of the most squalid parts of London. It would never do, said the King. It must be altered. So with due deference to the Prince Regent and perhaps with an eye to a royal subscription, St Giles' Street was restyled Prince's Street. Not quite the end, for in 1848 the apostrophe was dropped, and at last it took the title that we know today—Princes Street, which over the years has now changed its face and character even more times than its name.

In those beginning days the venture was new and uncertain, and builders were breaking no legs in the wild rush to stake a site on the street so many people now consider is the very symbol of Edinburgh. Interest was so slow that at one stage the town council had to offer an incentive, a premium of £20 to the first person willing to take the plunge. So eager were the council to see the street completed that they carelessly offered a position to city plumber John Graham, in exchange for some of his ground on Multrees Hill, later the elegant St James' Square, later still levelled as a slum clearance, and now under development again. The offer included the terms of payment set at one penny Scots a year, and Mr Graham was excused rates. It was with chagrin that the council then discovered that the quarter-acre site took in part of the proposed Princes Street development. A long, bitter legal battle followed and finally, after Graham's death, a coach-builder offered to give the family an area at the other end of Princes Street, which they accepted. But the council paid dearly for their oversight. The new owner, John Home, who acquired 162 feet of Princes Street frontage, insisted on the original contract being met—and for the next 156 years did not pay a penny of rates.

There were indeed squabbles a-plenty during the making of Princes Street. Probably the most important was the fight to preserve the south side from development. Craig's original plan had been altered to allow for a poky little lane called St Anne's Street, which led off the west end of North Bridge in a steep gradient to what is today Waverley Station. Craig had intended that the whole of the south side should be clear of buildings so that it could be used as a pleasure ground. The council, however, gave permission to John Home, the man who had avoided paying his rates for so long, to build a workshop on the site, provided it did not rise higher than the level of Princes Street. That started the battle. Some of the city's leading citizens objected vehemently, and after wordy legal hostilities the matter was taken to the House of Lords, who decided that Craig's original idea should be strictly adhered to. It meant that Princes Street would retain its character for a little longer, and explains, of course, the south-side position of the great Edwardian baroque pile of the North British Hotel, which creates its own particular effect, and why the roof of Waverley Market is sawn-off at Princes Street level.

The erection of the north side of Princes Street was a haphazard affair at first, with little control of where and how the houses were built. The street was widened on two occasions, and at one stage the east end took on the appearance of a slum, with swarms of dealers, street traders, hawkers, and johnny-a'thing men scuttling about their business amid all the smells, cries and colour of an eastern bazaar. The Mound came into being in 1781, when the rubble which had been cleared from the foundations of the new houses was heaved into one huge central dump opposite Hanover Street, splitting the marshy Nor' Loch area in two. Legend has it that a Mr George Boyd, a Lawnmarket clothier, was the first man to use the dump, and this short-cut between Old and New towns became known as 'Geordie Boyd's Mud Brig'. When work was at its height more than 1,800 cartloads of rubble were deposited each day. The castle end of the Nor' Loch was eventually drained by 1821 and turned into a nursery, while the east end was given to the Princes Street Proprietors to be developed at their discretion, which should have made attractive gardens indeed, for at that time they were for their eyes only.

The Proprietors were a private body of householders who had feued[1] homes on Princes Street, between Hanover and Hope Streets. They first appeared around 1811, and set about improving their 'estate', unstintingly, for they spent about £7,000 on drainage, landscaping, providing paths and secluded walks under the castle rock, tree-planting, and introducing shrubs and flowers to transform the valley into a delightful private promenading ground for the city's leading citizens, who were quite willing to pay the three guineas for the privilege of owning an access-giving key.

Imagine the howl of protest when it was first suggested that a railway line linking Edinburgh and Glasgow should pass through the centre of this little Eden. The Proprietors, men of money and influence, attacked the proposals as if the railway had been routed through their homes. They fought with every tactic available, cleverly preparing their case for Parliament, and were successful at first, limiting the speed that the railway was laid, and keeping their precious gardens inviolate by insisting that the terminus should be at Haymarket.

But a spider-web of lines had been creeping northwards from London, public imagination was fired with the new idea, and the financial success of the railways was enough to silence most protesters. So the determined men of the railway board returned, persuasive, reasoning, cajoling, pointing the benefits that would flow if their plan was approved, arguing that the line from Berwick to a station at the east end of Princes Street would be a natural link with Glasgow, and illustrating how it could best be achieved through the gardens, with minimum inconvenience and despoliation. The Proprietors wavered. Opinion and the mood of the times were against them. They agreed at last, at a price, and, preserving their haughty dignity to the end, so long as the offensive, noisy trains could not be seen from their drawing-room windows.

[1] Houses held in return for homage and service to an overlord.

Whitehorse Close, one of the finest examples of restoration work in Britain

Chessel's Court, another Royal Mile restoration triumph

THE BOOK-HUNTER'S STALL.

The days of exclusiveness were almost over, and when that organization bearing the daunting title of the 'Scottish Association for the Suppression of Drunkenness' came on the scene, the Proprietors gave up. This austere, impassioned body of do-gooders, dedicated to the extinction of the Devil of Drink, began to campaign that the gardens be opened to the public on Christmas and Hogmanay, so that citizens would have somewhere to go other than the city's clubs and pubs. The fire of the Suppressors could not be extinguished. They did their work well. The gardens became no mere receptacle for those with a seasonal hangover, but a fine fashion parade that was enjoyed by everyone in the city, eventually on every day of the week.

One of the other Princes Street landmarks was built about this time—the Scott Monument, that 200-foot tower of monstrous Gothic magnificence that looks like a giant space rocket waiting for the blue touch paper to be ignited. Here is yet another Edinburgh controversy. Its merits and faults have been argued over since the foundation stone was laid in 1840. Right from the start there was contention, for the designer, Mr George Kemp, a carpenter by trade and self-taught amateur architect and stonemason, won the open competition and fifty-guinea prize against fifty-four other entries in a city rife with architectural talent. Kemp had presented his plan under the name of John Morvo, and there was considerable shock among some of the committee when it was discovered that the fine-sounding John Morvo was in fact the son of a Peeblesshire shepherd, and only a student of drawing and perspective. But who now is to say that this extraordinary structure has not fulfilled its purpose? The romantic story of George Kemp would alone have been enough to sway Sir Walter. And who would dare suggest it be swept away with confidence that something more suitable and distinctive could take its place?

Princes Street, of course, although part of the New Town, was never one of the great Georgian showpieces. Architecturally it was a hotch-potch that grew up without system. Only a handful of buildings on its north side have any real merit these days, and they seem to become fewer every other year. Yet visitors to

8

Greyfriars Bobby on his stance on George IV Bridge

the Capital have the image that Princes Street *is* Edinburgh, and as more and more of them arrive—for Edinburgh plays an ever-increasing part in the tourist stakes, as well as being a favourite conference centre—they see poor old Princes Street probably at its lowest ebb, with the eroding tide fast gnawing at the last of its splendours. Which just goes to show that good town planning can often compensate for inferior or shoddy architecture—because Princes Street still retains a quality that is unique in Britain, a noble grandeur that springs from that dramatic sense of space, and how it has been used to such advantage against the magnificent backcloth of the castle, the trees and greenery of the gardens, the fine siting of the Mound, and the towers and spires of the Old Town. This is the real quality of Princes Street. It sets the character of the whole city, and above all this is what must be preserved.

Not that today's planners have an easy task. To keep faith with the past in an age when architecture in general is nondescript and indifferent is problem enough; but to preserve the virtue and the dignity of a single building in a changing street is something with which the New Town planners were not faced. Wisely, Edinburgh Corporation have taken action to control and safeguard the architectural future of Princes Street in the long term. The aim is to restore order and unity by bringing discipline to bear on the future height and materials used in new buildings. But perhaps it is already too late. There is little left now worth preserving, and it will indeed be a very long time before we see the effect of the council's measures, for the controls will only come into use as old buildings are demolished and new ones take their place. At least it is a step in the right direction, a holding policy that may preserve something to please the eye of future generations—so long as the stipulations are adhered to (which certainly did not always happen in the building of the New Town), and if agreement can be reached by the experts on what architectural merit really means.

So where in Edinburgh do we look for those fine examples of the old days, the gracious Georgian days when it would seem that a task, whether painting a picture, building a house or merely writing a chatty letter, was hardly contemplated unless the result was to be a small masterpiece. Here I must make it clear that I am no expert on architecture. Yet it would be impossible to remain long in Edinburgh without taking an interest in its fine buildings and the people who created them. For me the eye is my guide. I know when I like a building, and I know when I do not. I can also, to some extent, analyse these thoughts. Nevertheless, my views on the Edinburgh scene must be personal in the extreme, although there is so much architectural worth in the city which enjoys universal praise.

If there is one outstanding example to serve as the epitome of that glorious age it is the easy grace of Robert Adam's north side of Charlotte Square. Here he took Craig's concept of unit planning, and with his own touch of genius produced a block of houses that in harmony and excellence of design are outstanding by any standards, fitting for the most splendid European capital, yet somehow individualistic of Edinburgh, reflecting the very character of the city.

Elegant, with classical Corinthian pillars, balustrades, circular panels and windows, the ornamentation is never overdone, although the temptation must have been strong, for the other houses at that stage of the New Town's development were poor, drab affairs in comparison. Restrained, with never a hint of monotony in the unity of the frontage, this north side of Charlotte Square, with its silver-cream stonework facing the trees and flowers of its circular gardens, now almost a race track for Edinburgh's locust traffic, was hailed as a wondrous achievement when it was built, and it still is. Deviations from the original plans were allowed by the Town Council, the results not being particularly fortunate on the east and west sides. Adam's design for the proposed church was virtually discarded, and although Robert Reid's replacement has many merits, the overall architecture is of a lower standard, the tall Ionic pillars at the front being somewhat disproportionate.

Charlotte Square is the remaining gem of the original New Town, for the rest has suffered not a little over the years from the inevitable changes of time and the jingling tills of commercialism.

Remembering that one of the aims of creating an elegant New Town was to attract back to Edinburgh some of the former wealthier residents and aristocracy who had found it more pleasant to set up house in London, it was indeed successful for a time, although today the move is in the opposite direction. George Street, the very vertebrae of Craig's plan, is still a handsome-looking highway, but now only parts of the top flats and attics remain residential, and as the big stores expand, the multi-storey office blocks reach skywards, the pressure is on to change it into another Princes Street of shop fronts. Yet perhaps the move is hardly as negative as some purists maintain. It is a natural progression. If there is a demand for more shops centrally, then more shops will arise, and they will take over whatever buildings are available to contain them, for where the economics of business are concerned no frontier or tradition is recognized. But, after all, in how many cities in Britain can you escort wide-eyed tourists on the trail of the city sights and point out to them with pride—along with the splendour of the castle, aged St Giles', historic Holyrood Palace—the architectural excellence and beauty of the local post office?

Apart from the gradual erosion of its architecture in recent times, which if properly tackled is controllable to a certain extent, George Street remains a street of distinction, spacious and dignified, just as James Craig intended it to be, stretched in ramrod line of symmetry atop the last rolling ridge below the castle rock before the sloping fall-away down to Forth. How many people have stopped, surprised, at the intersections to find themselves suddenly confronted with a dramatic vista sweeping over the shimmering roofs of lower Edinburgh, out across the slate-grey firth to Fife's green fields? It is the superb siting of George Street which gives it atmosphere and a certain grandeur still, albeit evocative of another, older and more gracious age.

Douce Queen Street, a better-preserved George Street with a Sunday face, looks sedately out across its gardens to the north. Here in sound condition are many of the original New Town houses, a little severe and matronly for some, but a splendid example of the high ideals of those town planners of old. Queen

Street is the least interfered with street in the New Town and demonstrates clearly the success of integrating individual houses into a set pattern. In 1770 Robert Adam built No. 8 for Lord Chief Baron Orde, and though it is now an office, many of its exquisite plaster ceilings are still intact, a reminder of Adam's skill at interiors as well as his genius for exterior design. Some of the famous people who lived in the street liked to have their names inset into the pavement outside their front doors. A number are still there, and a walk along Queen Street recalls them to mind out of the pages of the history books.

St Andrew Square, planned to balance the New Town with Charlotte Square at the other end of George Street, still retains a goodly portion of grandeur, with the centrepiece of statesman Viscount Melville perched aloft with the pigeons on top of a mighty fluted column, sprouting from circular padlocked gardens, crocus-dotted in spring. But today, as the Viscount surveys the passing scene, there is a pained expression on his sad stone features as he frowns down on the twentieth century's terrible duo—glass and concrete, the veneer outer crust of the modern office block, the great common denominator of present day architecture, on the very spot where thinker David Hume spent his last years—and he would certainly have plenty to contemplate today; a nod of satisfaction for the Royal Bank of Scotland, securely nestled in Sir Laurence Dundas's splendid town house, designed for him by Sir William Chambers in 1772, with its elegant partners on either side (what swaggering assurance must its clients have to know their money is in such safe magnificence); a sniff of disgust as the fumes from the bus station float up the Viscount's rocky nostrils, and cast a smear of oily dust across the windows of some of the last remaining original frontages on the north side.

St Andrew Square, with its banks, insurance and business houses, has been called the richest square in Britain. The changes wrought by the years have altered many things, but not the refined, invigorating air of opulence. The combination of Georgian and Victorian architecture in George Street and St Andrew Square provides a few contrasting shocks in scale and appearance, but are certainly not so incongruous as to be incompatible. Some of the outstanding eighteenth-century buildings are still prominent, and those that followed in the nineteenth century, like David Rhynd's majestic, six-pillared National Commercial Bank, have a splendour all their own.

The backbone of the second New Town is Great King Street, wide, handsome, and little touched by redevelopments. Built in a style for greater days than eventually became its lot, a pervading wistfulness seems to hang over its uncrowded, echoing pavements as the rest of the city passes it by.

Heriot Row to the south and Fettes Row to the north are the flanking streets that correspond with Princes Street and Queen Street. Like their more famous counterparts both are one-sided, and although Fettes Row is both inferior in architecture and aspect to Queen Street, Heriot Row, the home of fashionable Edinburgh for more than a hundred years, is most pleasing, in spite of a certain amount of meddling and tinkering with the original in the name of improvement.

At the end of Great King Street is perhaps the best complete example of the New Town style, the gracious and spacious Drummond Place, which survived the Victorian period in one piece, and looks extremely fit and healthy today. Its position in the unfashionable east end, the terminus of the second New Town, perhaps accounts for the mercy of being left virtually intact. Drummond Place goes unappreciated in Edinburgh nowadays, but in the fullness of time, and with encroachments continuing on central private housing, it may well come into its own, especially if the Capital is to continue with the distinction of being a city where it is possible to work as well as to live with some degree of sophistication, which is something not easily achieved elsewhere.

Royal Circus, Bellevue Crescent, Gloucester Place, Royal Crescent all bear the stamp of the New Town planners on the north side. Abercromby Place, extending on from Heriot Row, was the first Edinburgh street to be built with a curve, which was a major development at that time. It was designed by Reid and Sibbald in 1804.

The completion of the first and second New Towns was by no means the end of architectural good taste in Edinburgh. Craig and Adam had set the pattern, and it continued to recur as the city waxed in size, although indiscriminately, sprinkled here and there, without the benefit of the grand design. This was surely the spoliation of the new Edinburgh; it robbed the city of the chance to grow under the discipline of a carefully schemed master plan, either modelled on what had gone before, or even something excitingly original. Certainly Edinburgh remains a city of outstanding attraction, but what heights might it have attained if the same thought and direction that went into the New Town had been brought to bear on the fast-growing young city.

One of the first to extemporize on the theme of the New Town was the Earl of Moray on his estate just west of Heriot Row. The result was the great and grandiose mass of Moray Place, without doubt an experiment which ended in success, although not strictly in line with the other New Town buildings. Imposing, perhaps just a little too majestic, it nonetheless seems the very epitome of the determination abroad at the time to build with glory at any cost, although the Earl went to some lengths to avoid paying for much himself. It is a magnificent prospect indeed to a plan by Gillespie Graham, and is certainly the finest piece of private building in the city, on a difficult, sloping site. Its smaller neighbour, Ainslie Place, another outstanding work, is more delicate in comparison.

Towards the west, the New Town style appeared in Melville Street, Atholl Crescent, Rothesay Terrace, a later development, Alva, Maitland and Walker Streets, and suddenly without warning among the hildiegeleerie around Haymarket. It is there again at the railway station, the first to be built in the city, and a much better looking building altogether than those of the Victorian style which the trains seemed to bring from London with them.

Some of the random speculative building emulating the New Town style was extremely successful, some fell on hard times. Picardy Place and Forth Street, designed on spec by Robert Burn, did well; poor time-saddened Gardner's Crescent, off Morrison

Street, became a discredited failure. Set amid the industry and hubbub around Tollcross, it must have broken some poor architect's heart, as he saw the growth of the fashionable city swing away to the north, segregating his stately but forlorn half circle that still retains a modicum of dignity among its tatty surroundings.

The New Town style pops up again in Morningside, in Portobello at East Brighton Crescent, Brighton Place, Sandford Gardens, and down Stockbridge way it fairly blossoms on what was once the ground of Henry Raeburn, the painter. His estate had been considerably enlarged through marriage, and the most attractive of his developments is leafy Ann Street, named after his wife. Here is one of the most attractive little streets in Edinburgh, with all the dignified good looks of the New Town, but in miniature, two rows of doll's houses set in landscaped gardens, in summer an exotic city oasis of colour-splashed greenery, a-twitter with birdlife. St Bernard's Crescent, Raeburn Place, Saxe-Coburg Place are all in the New Town theme.

The Calton Hill area was a site which attracted the planners; perhaps it received over-much attention in the beginning, for it was seldom out of financial worries, and the hill is crowned by the greatest, classiest white elephant of all, the chaste, impressive ruin of what was to be the National Monument, "Edinburgh's Disgrace" as it is known to city children, although their parents now tend to look on the folly with something approaching affection. It was to have been a church on the grand scale, the exterior designed by William Playfair and C. R. Cockerell as an exact copy of the Parthenon in Athens to stand as a national memorial of the Napoleonic Wars. Perhaps it is now even more reminiscent of the Parthenon, for after the king laid the foundation stone in a fine ceremony in 1822, it progressed at the near non-rate of twelve columns in eight years, when funds eventually ran dust dry, and it has been left like that, a glorious pantomine set, an everlasting source of material for visiting music-hall jokers, and one of the truly great sights that gives character to the Capital.

At that stage of the New Town's development, Edinburgh began to look on herself as having something of the attraction of ancient Athens, and what better idea than to make the Calton Hill a kind of latter day Acropolis, they thought. The Nelson Monument was the first of these buildings, like a long, extended, telescopic battlement tower beside the little observatory, built by Craig to look like a fortress in miniature. At one time Nelson dinners were held in the monument, while his admirers recounted the great man's prowess in battle, and today the sound of cannon still has significance, for when the one o'clock gun lets fly from the castle ramparts, giving half of Edinburgh minor heart seizures, a time-ball drops from the top of the monument as if it had been expertly shot down by those castle artillerymen, a reminder of days when it was a clock-check for Edinburgh folk, especially for the mariners in Leith.

A new observatory was started in 1818 under Playfair's direction, again with an eye on the splendour of Greece. It was cruciform, with four porticoes in a Roman Doric manner, with a Greek Doric monument to his Uncle John in a corner of the boundary wall. One of the outstanding legacies of the Greek period is the old Royal High School, begun in 1825 in a basic Grecian Doric style but with much more fluidity about its classic lines as could be expected with Thomas Hamilton as architect; he was also responsible for the circular Corinthian temple of the Burns Monument, a little farther down the hill. It looks over to the graves of fellow poet Robert Fergusson, and the fair Clarinda, Burns's Edinburgh love, as they sleep in the peace of the Canongate Kirk in the heart of the Old Town.

Calton Hill was not the only corner where the Edinburgh Grecians found an outlet, and traces of the Greek revival can be found all over the city. Around the Botanic Gardens there are examples. Inverleith Row marks the beginning of the innovation of the semi-detached villa, definitely Greek, with variations of Doric and Ionic porches. In tiny Middleby Street in Newington it reaches an exquisite delicacy apparently in miniature, a delightful effect produced by the houses being built on a gradient so that only the top floors are visible from the front. Salisbury Road, Duncan Street and Arniston Place are Newington streets built in the early part of the nineteenth century, although much of the south-side development was governed by the opening of the South Bridge. Nicolson Street and Square (after Lady Nicolson) were well advanced by the end of the 1880s, and an Act of Parliament in 1794 directed that Nicolson Street should be extended to form the main approach from the south.

The Calton Hill area is the site of the largest single block in the city, William Playfair's regal-looking Royal Terrace, almost a quarter of a mile in length, using four Ionic and three Corinthian colonnades along the frontage, which has been divided into seventeen segments. Regent Terrace, on the other side of the hill, presents a pleasing face of Greek Doric porches and unusual iron balconies at first floor level, useful attractions for the host of small hotels and such incongruities as the American Consulate and Madame Ada's School of Dancing. The Calton Hill plan, once with pretensions of being the biggest development in the New Town, stretching as far as Leith Links, includes the architecturally interesting Windsor Street, Blenheim Place, Brunswick Street, and Leopold Place.

There are few cities with so many magnificent churches, their spires almost forest-like on the skyline. Edinburgh, the scene of many a religious clash and row, a holy firing range for centuries, has profited greatly in churches by being the capital city, a stage for impression with mammoth splendour. Those stately churches are now a show of religious force, wealth and power, an understanding of beauty, demonstrating the ineffectuality of the De'il against the Capital's formidable front of righteousness.

It has been said more than once by the uninitiated that Edinburgh must be a very evil place indeed to require so many places of worship. Today the city has a surfeit, and a dearth of congregations to fill them. One church has been changed into an electricity generating station, to outward appearances ready for worship, but the low throb and hum of transformers is the deception; another has become a bingo hall, the caller like some heathen priest of the dark ages mouthing his booby numbers from the pulpit in an incantation bordering blasphemy; yet another church is now a Woolworth's store; another a paper depot; another a betting office.

The style of the churches, of course, varied to the taste of the denominations who built them and their financial resources. The Church of Scotland had a predilection for well-disciplined classic adornment; the splinter groups and dissenting bodies, always short of money, generally leaned towards classical simplicity; while the Romans and Episcopalians had a special liking for the Gothic. The whole aim of the old churches was to seat a large congregation in such a way that they could easily hear their preacher.

Basically, churches are of the same pattern, but the architect, after he had tiered the flock into galleries and placed the minister at one end of a rectangular interior, set himself about the task of planning the exterior with the money available to grace the city. This is where Edinburgh won.

Many of Edinburgh's most elegant and best known churches were built during the eighteenth century, those golden Georgian days, and in the Victorian era. The towering New Greyfriars was completed in 1721, ironically from money gathered from a duty on ale. It was added to the west side of Old Greyfriars, which dates back to 1614, the site of that remarkable protest of the National Covenant, drawn up among the gravestones.

St Andrew's Church, which became St Andrew's and St George's a few years ago, was the first to be built in Craig's New Town, and still lends much character to George Street. It was completed in 1784 after Major Frazer of the Engineers had won the open competition for the project. There was some controversy at the time, for the steeple was given a six-bell peel after the English style, and many thought that such an important church should have remained traditional.

It is believed that the full eight bells were installed when William Sibbald added a steeple in 1789. The bells were fixed after it was found that their swinging threatened the structure of the steeple, but the eight cords operating the clapper all lead to one frame, and a small team of elders, pulling one rope at a time, have learned to play hymn and psalm tunes on them. There is a tradition that the sound of the bells of St Andrew's inspired the music of "Wha'll buy my caller herrin'?"

St George's Church in Charlotte Square, now taken over by the Record Office; the Old Tron Steeple; St Mary's Church in Bellevue Crescent; Playfair's unusual St Stephen's; St Cuthbert's Steeple in Lothian Road, apart from the castle's St Margaret's Chapel, one of the oldest religious buildings in the city, still with its tiny battlemented tower which gave protection to the night watchmen when the body-snatchers were on the prowl; St James' Church, Leith, for long also with a full eight-bell peel ringing out on Sunday; the impressive Highland Church of Tolbooth St John's, atop the Royal Mile, once the home of the General Assembly, now the only church in the city providing a sermon in Gaelic; the twin-towered New College at the Mound, a famous part of the Old Town skyline: all are part of the wonderful heritage of the Church of Scotland and Edinburgh.

For many years there were several penal laws practised against the Roman Catholics and Episcopalians in Scotland, and it was almost the nineteenth century before their churches bore much in the way of architectural merit in Edinburgh. Delicate St John's Episcopal Church on Princes Street was to a William Burn design and in use in 1818, unusual in that it had no gallery. At the same time St Paul's, York Place, was built by Archibald Elliot, bearing a distinct reflection of King's College Chapel, Cambridge; three-spired St Mary's Cathedral at the end of Melville Street, the work of Sir George Scott, is the second largest church in Scotland, the smaller twin spires at the front are called after the Walker sisters—the Mary and Barbara spires; the Roman Catholic St Mary's Metropolitan Cathedral in Broughton Street, designed by Gillespie Graham in 1813, was an unusual Gothic development.

Slowly, as it expanded, Edinburgh began to eat up the villages and hamlets in its path, places that today we take for granted as mere suburbs, yet at one time were separated from the city by green fields and moorlands, each with its own individual character; and although their identities tend to be lost nowadays, except where local clubs and associations keep the old community spirit and loyalties alive, Edinburgh suburbia has still a fascinating tale or two to tell.

Stand on the castle ramparts and look around; the great city is spread out below, a million stories in its ghost-crowded streets, the stages of its esculent development not immediately obvious in the centre of the town, but clamouringly distinctive on the outskirts. Edinburgh crooks its finger towards Balerno at the foot of the Pentlands, with Currie and Juniper Green already within its clasp; out towards the huge twin bridges of the Forth, with Barnton and Clermiston consumed; seaward through Portobello to Musselburgh with the cone of Berwick Law as the guide line; south up the hill with Gilmerton and Liberton long absorbed; new schemes constantly tentacling on the city fringes, with fifth-column—or are they refugee?—Edinburgh citizens settling in the satellite dormitory villages and townships on the perimeter; while in the city itself surveyors and builders glean their maps, searching, ever searching, for vacant, forgotten plots that might support just one more house, or better still, a scheme, even of pigmy size.

Focus the attention more closely. People go about their business, dodging the traffic in crowded streets where sheep and cattle grazed. The central population of Edinburgh is being spilled out into what were formerly villages and farms. The once teeming Cowgate is now half empty. The High Street and Canongate are being restored, but not their populations. As every citizen of Edinburgh knows, the Heart of Midlothian is situated just outside St Giles', but the heart of the city of Edinburgh is much more difficult to pinpoint, or even to find, and thrombosis conditions are becoming increasingly detectable. Edinburgh folk, until now limpet-like in their resistance to change, are being wrenched out of their old haunts and deposited farther and farther from what used to be their homes. The community life of their neighbourhood is largely over, the rich fellowship that once typified the life of Leith and the centre of the city is almost a thing of the past, and no real effort has been made to revive or replace it. Yet community life and local affiliation and loyalties should continue to be at the core of a great city like Edinburgh. And it was so until recent years: Murrayfield, Stockbridge, Newington, Haymarket, Gorgie—all individual communities at one time with their own character, yet now all as much a part of Edinburgh as the Royal Mile or the Grassmarket. Today they are losing their identity in the great population exodus, and in a few years' time it will be a difficult task indeed to specify what really is the true Leither, the Merchistonian, or the man from Broughton.

Look down the Firth till the eye is suitably affronted by the red-brick, sore-thumb chimney of Portobello power station, erected like a gaunt, distasteful tombstone to what lies below. That is the eyesore gateway to what was once the Queen of the Forth. Portobello! How hath the mighty fallen! At last there is a plan, the residents are told, a tale that has been told many times, and with each passing year poor Portobello has become a little more run down, more drab, more dreary.

It is difficult to believe that within the memory of some of the older folk Portobello held more holiday attractions than many of the heavily publicized Continental highspots do today. From near the foot of Bath Street a fine pier struck out into the sea for 1,250 feet with a splendid concert hall and restaurant at the tip. The Forth steamers called there to take trippers off to Fife. There was no lack of passengers. Each day seventy special trains headed for the Brighton of the North, while fleets of private buses and crammed trams shoogled their way to the beach. The Portobello Marine Gardens were opened in 1910 behind King's Road, with the vast Empress Ballroom as the centrepiece, flanked by a concert hall, a cinema, and a roller skating rink. All-day variety shows, musical comedy, and opera with the top artistes entertained the throng. There was an amusement court, complete with scenic railway, river caves, the joy wheel, and the mountain slide, all for a 7d. entrance fee, or 2s. for a fortnightly ticket.

Each day dare-devil Diving Cormack plunged 70 feet into a small pond. Captain Spence and his sister made "sudden ascents into the heavens" in a balloon, with equally sudden descents by parachute to splash into the sea before the startled eyes of the crowds. In 1912 'Scotland's Greatest Aviator', Mr W. R. Ewan, brought his flying machine to Portobello sands to shock them even more as he coaxed his contraption into the air and flew, yes actually flew, for almost a quarter of a mile at some 30 feet above the ground, while 5,000 disbelieving watchers stood agog. Those were the days! There was a Punch-and-Judy show at the Mound then, Punch doing his stuff in classic Billingsgate:

Isabeller, Isabeller,
Bring aht yer umbreller,
We're goin' away
For a 'oliday
Dahn ter Porterbeller.

Unfortunately, there is little to go to Portobello for nowadays. No passenger trains stop, a bus depot stands where the Gardens spread their glitter. Even the sand is disappearing and the Glasgow folk, who for many years made it a kind of pilgrimage for their annual dook, are deserting it fast. Age and change they understand, but in the fastidious tastes of modern holidaymakers, neglect is never tolerated. Today Portobello's adornment for the holiday atmosphere takes the shape of a short metal arm fixed to the top of lamp standards along the promenade. On each arm there are a few coloured, low-powered bulbs. No one can ever remember seeing them all alight at the one time. And the Portobello folk, surely the most friendly people on the East Coast, sadly accept the downfall.

Thankfully the stories of Edinburgh's kickshaws in the newer town as it gobbled up its surrounds are hardly as sad as Portobello's lingering death. There is Canonmills down below the symmetrical lines of the New Town, once the very gateway to the Capital. The origin of that name is not hard to guess. Since the twelfth century the Augustine Canons of Holyrood had tapped the Water of Leith to turn the wheels that ground their grain.

Some of the mill buildings are still there, rickety and decayed, and a few of the village greybeards can even remember them in use. Surrounded by Georgian respectability and elegance, certainly Canonmills had its growing pains as the city engulfed it, then spread beyond. But, of course, there were moments and memories too . . . like the time Queen Victoria sailed up the Forth to pay a visit to the city. The handsome archway over the Water of Leith at Canonmills was chosen as the spot where the

Lord Provost and his council would welcome the Queen. The signal that the royal ship was in sight was to be a flag hoisted to the top of the Nelson Monument on Calton Hill. Based on the 'fiery cross' system of older days, the castle gunners would then fire a salvo warning Edinburgh—and the town council in particular—that the Queen was approaching. There was only one snag. No one could find a flag. By the time word had circulated and the councillors had reached their post, Queen Victoria was in the centre of the city, with a scarlet-faced Lord Provost and retinue of harassed, portly city officers scurrying in her wake trying to preserve a modicum of dignity at full sprint.

Robert Louis Stevenson was born nearby, at No. 8 Howard Place; the musician Chopin lived for a time at No. 10; in Tanfield Hall the fiery Free Kirk of Scotland was constituted in 1843.

Changed days! Gone is the Happy Land, that euphemistic title for one of the toughest, most squalid slums in Scotland; there are few baggies and beardies to be caught by bare-legged laddies with their jeely jars in Water of Leith's Puddocky; even Jessie King, the last woman to be hanged in Calton Jail in 1889, is almost forgotten for her baby murders, although her name was once on the lips of every citizen in the city, and her house has been swept away.

Out towards the humped Pentlands another rich viand of a village gulped,—douce, respectable Morningside. Morningside, Edinburgh's 'pan loaf' district, where they all speak with mouthfulls of silver marbles, or so the comics of the old Lyceum, King's and Palladium theatres would tell their patrons. "What, ladies and gents, is a c–r–e–c–h–e?" they would inquire from their audience. Then, amid expectant sniggers; "A creche is a collision between two cars in Morningside . . . and a saik is something they haud their tatties in," and the theatres would rock. Morningside at one time held the city's main assemblage of power and influence, the home of professional men, of bankers, wealthy merchants, judges, professors, and men of rank and title, living in their great, stately stone houses set in sweeping grounds. Many still remain, but there has been a scattering over the years, a gradual running down, and those same theatre jesters now cast

The Duke of Wellington outside Register House

their jibes in the direction of affluent, prestige-growing Barnton. Unfairly they ring a premature death knell over the glory that was once fair Morningside, forgetting that much of that glory is still there. They look at it as if here, among the supposed toffee noses in their house-castles, is the very epitome of Edinburgh's reputation of east windy, west endy, the city of pride and poverty or, as those jokers have already put it—"curtains at the windows and nae sheets on the bed". After all, funny men have to earn a living, and Morningside will laugh to help them along.

I have my own prejudices. Having lived there, and married at Holy Corner, where four churches meet, with others in close attendance, Morningside will always reflect its name for me. A suburb of character and characters, with a sniff of justified superiority, a pervasion of staid righteousness in its profusion of churches and Bible-sounding streets—Jordan and Canaan Lanes, Nile Grove, Little Egypt; and, in spite of the changes (even multi-storey flats now, luxury ones, of course), there is a dignified, steady-as-you-go timelessness about Morningside—like the clock on the old village school opposite Falcon Avenue, whose hands have stood at 3.40 for more than a hundred years. And even the school is now a place of worship.

On the western side of the town is Corstorphine, with an ancient, colourful history of its own long before the zoo and its penguins, the largest colony in captivity outside Antarctica, brought a different kind of fame. Here is one community that really is trying to do something to keep the links with the past and give its parishioners a sense of history. And that name? It catches the imagination of visitors. They roll it round their tongues and take it home with them. Gorgie, Joppa, Burdiehouse, Craigentinny, Dumbiedykes, Corstorphine. Perhaps there is a touch of the exotic in the long vowels and rolling *R*s. Some will tell you that it has connections with Torphin, the great Saxon hero, others believe that its meaning is literal—'The white mist that lies in the hollow', and certainly, in the grey of the morning before the sun puts it to flight, a wispy, clammy vapour clings to the ground just to the south, for this was boggy marshland at one time, the home of the swamp birds, the long-winged harrier and

9

Children playing in St James Court

heron. Corstorphine has a ghost, too, a misty White Lady, the unhappy wraith of Christine Nimmo, who stabbed Lord James Forrester with his own sword for making impolite fun of her down at Corstorphine's old, hard-swilling Black Bull Inn in the High Street. It was under the aged sycamore at the junction of Dovecot Road and Sycamore Terrace, their secret meeting place, that the scandalized Miss Nimmo took vengeance on her uncle, and from time to time over the last 200 years, her ghostly figure has been seen sadly surveying the spot that brought her to the gallows.

Up in Liberton there still stand the remains—well cared-for and tended—of the original village that was devoured by the land-hungry city .The old kirk is still there, its neo-Gothic square tower a distinctive landmark and headstone to the old order, the mill and the neatly restored cottages a breath of older days. Very old days, for the story of Liberton goes back to the rough-and-ready times of Malcolm Canmore, and possibly even before him. There is a tale of how water or holy oil from St Katherine's grave on Mount Sinai was spilled at Liberton on its way to Queen Margaret, and immediately a healing spring gushed from the spot, now St Katherine's Well in the grounds of the children's home. Liberton always had connections with the church, and the first parish church goes back to 1279, when King David established a chapel of St Cuthbert's. Today the church is still well attended, and so it should be, for Liberton has swollen many times from its former size, an increase of more than 15,000 between 1951 and 1961. It is still growing as those peregrinating Edinburgh citizens try to put down roots in new territory, not now in the peaceful shadow of Liberton Kirk's tower as in other days, but below tall, oblong skyscraper flats, up there among the seagulls, with long views right across the city, of a carpet of rooftops down to Forth, of green fields and hills, yet with no peewits or whaups at their feet.

Rich, evocative histories all: Craigentinny with its 'Marbles', the beautifully ornate tomb of the extraordinary William Henry Miller, who erected it at a cost of £30,000, for years a majestic landmark, now a detection job to find it, a distinguished aristocrat of a monument, set in a monotony of modern villas and bungalows; Craigmillar with its ancient castle where the foul murder of Darnley was plotted, a scene of dark deeds still; Grange where the monks of St Giles' farmed in sequestered contentment; Colinton the childhood home of Robert Louis Stevenson, much of the original village atmosphere remaining; like the villages of Dean and Swanston, peaceful oases in the garrulous throb of the city; Merchiston where Napier invented his logarithms in the baronial castle, later part of a famous boys' school, now the centre-piece of the Napier Technical College; Duddingston and its thousand ducks in the nature reserve, the encampment of Prince Charlie and his Highlanders, who doubtless quaffed a draught or two at the Sheep Heid Inn, the oldest licensed premises in Scotland; Blackford Hill where Marmion surveyed the spires of the Old Town below, where now the Astronomer Royal in his Observatory surveys the stars above.

And so the scene changes. In Glasgow the mood is to erase and build anew. Glasgow folk never quite understand why even the moving of a lamp-post in Edinburgh is an operation viewed with suspicion by half a dozen preservation societies. Yet even with those alert watchdogs to safeguard the Capital's distinctive qualities, Edinburgh has changed; slowly in terms of individual years, dramatically over half a century, with agonizing velocity in the last two decades.

Architecturally we live in the Utilitarian Age, and until now, because of the inhibitions of money, time and materials, it seems that architects have sought some kind of self-expression in grotesqueness of shape, something that has been thrust increasingly into the wide-open eye of Edinburgh. Set against the genius of Adam and Playfair, many appear tawdry and undeserving of the Capital city. The architectural language of Adam and Playfair is long dead, and no worthy successor has yet appeared. Now a new language is required which is of our time, but sensitive and grateful for those past glories.

The problems that defeat Edinburgh as a city—population disposal, traffic volume, the efficiency of public services—have long baffled other cities throughout the world with distinguished reputations for advanced thinking. But Edinburgh is not any other city. Unfairly or not, we expect more from the Capital, and most of all we expect leadership. Perhaps it is particularly unfair, for reshaping a city as ancient as Edinburgh is a much harder task than starting from scratch on a new town like Glenrothes or Cumbernauld.

It is not, however, necessarily good planning to create a social revolution at the same time as a renovation. It is not especially an improvement to have advocates, professors, business tycoons or literati who have a predilection for living in history and an ability to pay for it, setting up home in the restored sections of the Royal Mile, not when it means evacuating the folk who have lived there for years, and preventing their return by setting rents beyond their means. The character of old Edinburgh is as much a part of its people as its fine buildings, and to shuffle them around the city, willy nilly, erodes that character. Let the Canongaters return to the Canongate, the Highstreeters to the High Street, and let the folk who live in peace in Abbeyhill, Stockbridge, Blackhall, Pilton or Inverleith remain there. There is a reactionary sentiment! Easily said, but with a thousand attendant problems to implement.

An outsider may criticize Edinburgh only in fear of swift retribution; an insider only if of long standing and a devotee. There I stake my claim. There *is* no other city like Edinburgh. It is unique in the world. A great, beautiful, romantic, astonishing, feminine, haughty, sublime city. It will change. Of course, it will change. It has and must change. The New Town of Edinburgh—that vision of dynamic fire-eater Provost Drummond, James Craig and those far-seeing city fathers—is 200 years old. Let the wisdom and the lessons learned from that age guide our present city elders and their successors over the booby-trapped gulf of the next two centuries.

VI

SEATS OF LEARNING

JANUARY brings to Edinburgh a remarkable phenomenon. Like hares in March, a certain responsible section of the Edinburgh public begin to demonstrate acute disturbance symptoms, sometimes agitation, even emotional distress. It is an unusual condition unique in its proportions in Britain. It is the time fond parents toss their tremulous four-year-olds into the snarling competition jungle of the great big unsheltered world, when with honeyed word and promised joys they drag their unsuspecting offspring around the city's famous fee-paying schools to sit their entry tests, make calculated cosy chat with discerning headmasters that sets the nerve-ends twanging, then wait a month of fears for the results.

In Edinburgh acceptance by one of the city's multitude of fee-paying schools is an accolade of honour. Among some of the higher income brackets the worries of non-acceptance is almost syndromatic; among those financially struggling to keep a child in attendance it is a glorious agony. The pupils attending such schools are counted by the battalion, at least 14,000 of them involved in the city, for Edinburgh has more fee-paying schools than the rest of Scotland put together. More than 20 per cent of the Capital's children go to them, compared with about 7 per cent in Glasgow, and 6·5 per cent in the remainder of the country.

The competition is daunting—300 tiny applicants for sixty places in some schools. Parents recognize the odds, for even being an 'old boy', or having an elder brother or sister at the school of their choice is no guarantee of acceptance. There is only one course open to them—a grand parade of the innocents around all the schools. That means, if he is a boy: George Watson's College,

Daniel Stewart's College, Edinburgh Academy, Melville College, the Royal High School, George Heriot's School; or if the predilection is to follow English public school lines then Fettes School, Merchiston Castle, and Loretto School are the choices, while Scotus Academy is for Roman Catholics. For girls there are St Margaret's, St Denis', St Hilary's, the Mary Erskine, George Watson's Ladies College (planned to go co-educational with the boys' college), James Gillespie's, Lansdowne House, Cranley, St George's, St Serf's, and a number of others. There are also some excellent co-educational schools, and a few private preparatory schools like Cargilfield.

So winds the route taken by that extraordinary January safari of tender small fry, led by the chubby hand, bribed with sweets, threatened with punishments if they do not behave and show themselves off to advantage, guiltless baby doves all, although probably enjoying every misunderstood moment of the tilting, while their more worldly spectator parents display all the gesticulations of neurotics.

Why do they do it? In a city famous for its advanced educational thinking, with some of the most modern and advanced state schools in Britain, why should a parent scrimp and scrape to pay to educate his son or daughter out of his own pocket?

Of course, snobbery, the cliché argument, is relevant, but only up to a point. As Labourites have indicated so often, fee-paying schools are quite inconsistent with comprehensive education, the old warring talk of cloth caps versus bowler hats reflected in the words. And that may well be the case in some cities and a golden goal to reach some day. But in Edinburgh the reasons are deeper and more simple to understand. Basically, children are sent to fee-paying schools in the Capital to fulfil a desire to find the best education possible, which is human and right and part of the great tradition in Scottish education. The city's fee-paying schools, subsidized or not, are now an established tradition in themselves.

What are the benefits of a private school education in Edinburgh? Most of the children come from like backgrounds, where parents care enough about schooling to pay for it, which is an incentive to the child in itself, especially if his family find it a struggle. The classes are smaller, providing more individual tuition, and there is the stimulation to spur on the really bright children. They also attract some of the best-qualified teachers. Much emphasis is placed on sport, particularly rugby, and some of the schools boast the finest playing-fields in Scotland, with stadia worthy of football league teams.

The term 'fee-paying' has quite irrelevant side-meanings to be misconstrued by the emotional or axe-grinder. There is an overriding classlessness about the city schools that almost debunks snobbery. Edinburgh is a centre of professional people who have kept the city's thinking vigorous for years with a constant promulgation of ideas, suggestions, demands, and innuendoes for improvement that have spread and influenced every level of society. Their thirst for good, healthy education has had special appeal to Edinburgh people as a whole, and today, bus drivers, coal heavers and dockers conjure up the money—and it costs anything from £30 to £500 a session—to share the tradition and privilege. It is a tradition that should be respected. Today the aim is for greater social equality, and the existence of fee-paying schools makes its achievement more difficult.

As a city, Edinburgh is not typical, for besides its proliferation of private schools, the standard of the State schools is probably higher than anywhere else in Britain. If those parents who may suffer any twinge of political conscience or principle were to martyr themselves and their children by rejecting private and adopting state school education in the hope that others would follow the example, they would be disappointed. There are no such signs. The only way an integration will be achieved in the foreseeable future, unless by some dramatic and meantime hidden social change in society, is by government measure. Edinburgh has long since resisted the pressures to have the system altered, for as long as there is a demand for such schools, and while there yet remains some freedom of choice for the individual, no matter how limited it has become in recent years, then the demand should be met.

Some years ago, an American psychologist researching into genius found its characteristics most common among Jews and

Scots. He explained it was because of the importance they placed on schooling. Certainly the compulsive craving for learning through the years in Edinburgh has had an effect ranging far beyond the confines of the classroom. It has visibly permeated throughout the city. Besides such long-respected seats of learning as Edinburgh's ancient university and the renown of the city's pioneers and teachers in the fields of medicine, there is a vast industrious army of part-time students, at least 26,000 involved in all kinds of technical, vocational and extra-mural studies, many of them attending day-release classes, others nocturnals, coming out in the dark winter evenings to take advantage of 200 different subjects, swotting for 'Highers', mechanical, management, secretarial skills, languages, the arts, local history, and such fascinations as criminology, ornithology, archaeology, astronomy or even the intricacies of baking a cake, or tying a fishing fly. In many ways the humble evening class studies done by two-thirds of the fifteen to eighteen-nineteen-year-old boys and girls, one, two and three nights a week to improve their work-a-day qualifications, should be symbolic of today's young people. This is the side of their lives that we seldom read about, yet it is a more realistic commentary on our much-maligned modern youth than the headlines that are so often forced into the newspapers. Perhaps their young enthusiasm is still not sufficiently encouraged, and surely the time is not so far distant when more employers will give them the benefit of day-release or more.

The story of education in Edinburgh follows very much the history of education in Scotland. It is a tale of proud achievement and the envy of other nations until comparatively recent years. Now other countries have moved ahead in educational thinking and implementation, at the very time there is doubt and confusion about the future among teachers themselves, a division among educationists. Many are over-impatient for radical innovation, others entrenched in the ways of the past.

The task of planning for the future is indeed perplexing—and urgent. Some of the great shadows over humanity in a world ridden with fear of nuclear extinction may be partly removed through education. Yet education today is a shifting quicksand of movement, a struggle to cling to tradition, yet not too fiercely, for this is the age of change, fast and dramatic, and the challenge in education is to understand and come to terms with it.

It was back in the seventeenth century when the seeds of education in Scotland took firm root. The Act of 1696 planned to have a school in every parish. The Book of Discipline of 1561 had already shown the way. Children should remain at school, it said, until—"their talents have been discovered and developed so that the common wealth might have some comfort by them". Even then there were those in Edinburgh conscious of the need for education. In the twelfth century school lessons were regularly given in the Abbey of Holyrood, and the monks of St Anthony's in Leith scattered some of their wisdom in organized classes. The town council records indicate that there were at least half a dozen schools by the end of the sixteenth century engaged in teaching the two important *R*s of that age—reading and writing. The Royal High School, one of the corporation's prides, reaches back to the days of David I, when it was under the care of Holyrood Abbey, and a procession of celebrated scholars have issued from it through the centuries.

Today in Edinburgh 65,000 children slothfully fight the clock each morning on the way to their local authority schools. This figure includes toddlers at the city's nurseries, and about 1,000 unfortunates attending classes for the handicapped. And trying to set an example of punctuality are some 3,000 teachers, who with about 2,000 janitors and cleaners, a few hundred clerks, kitchen and administrative staffs, supply the schools' labour force. To keep this vast assemblage efficient, it costs at least £7½ million a year, teachers' salaries using up more than £3 million of it, with bursaries and grants to enable senior pupils to remain at school without undue hardship showing through the years the most precipitous increase.

The responsibility for local authority education in Edinburgh rests with the Education Committee, comprised of twenty elected members of the town council, and nine others including the University Court, the Educational Institute of Scotland, and the churches. The Committee is advised by the Director of Education, who has a ready ear for news and views throughout the teaching strata, as well as useful links with parents and employers. Edinburgh has been fortunate in its education executives. For many years they have been in the van of new thought and techniques. Edinburgh was the first city in Scotland to use push-button teaching aids; a pioneer of educational cruises; one of the leaders to experiment successfully with tutorial classes in the primary schools; to introduce the Cuisenaire system of teaching mathematics; elementary science using simple apparatus for the very young; probing into how early the teaching of languages can begin, so that many teachers in the city are hailed each morning from their primary classes with a merry "Bonjour, Mademoiselle!"

Edinburgh's far-sighted policy of school building, especially timing replacement of old and obsolescent schools and their programme for the big new housing schemes is in advance of the rest of Britain, like the introduction of language laboratories to perfect oral approach in language training in secondary schools and in the evening for use by business men. New school planning and equipment is of a standard unsurpassed in this country, and give such schools as Craigroyston, Firrhill, Forrester and Liberton an immediate respect. Behind the glass and concrete exterior wedge of the new Portobello Secondary dominating the eastern seaward skyline are thirteen science rooms, lifts to transport forty pupils at a time, a swimming pool and a theatre for school productions. It is a herald of the schools of the future. Yet it is not so long ago that many Edinburgh children went to school barefoot during the summer, rich and poor alike, for the 'barie' season knew no social barriers.

There is many a dignitary in the city today who wore shoes only when weather, convention or promotion to higher grade made it obligatory. Now their children sail the seas to foreign lands as part of their school education, they make exciting visits to the outdoor wonders of the Cairngorms at Glenmore Lodge, the National Sports Centre at Inverclyde, the ardours of the Moray Sea School, camps at Broomlea, Abington, Middleton, Aberfoyle, the artificial ski slope at Hillend, or day-trips and excursions to the multitude of interests in the city itself. School has evolved to become doctor, dentist, nutritionist, sociologist, mentor and shielding extending arm of the all-encompassing Welfare State. It is the new concept for the new age, and perhaps —but only perhaps—the brave new world.

The distinguished educationists who have strived over the years to sight the target and create the standards must not go unsung. They have left Edinburgh the most glorious legacy of all—the right to the finest education in the country. Edinburgh's children have been given the advantage and privilege of an education unequalled in Scotland. It is a distinction they should never forget, nor forget the story of the men who made it possible. It should be a compulsory lesson for senior pupils.

For fifty years Simon Somerville Laurie set the pattern back in the nineteenth century, and his pupil, Alexander Darroch, one of the outstanding administrators, continued the work, placing emphasis on teacher training as a priority. Viscount Haldane did much to establish the principles, rules and framework of modern education; J. B. Frizell, Director of Education for twenty-eight years, steered the course over the difficult transition years to present times; and Dr George Reith continues the tradition. There are many more, past and present, who have influenced the course, for such a charge as the education of a city is essentially the work of a team. Edinburgh owes them much.

Apart from the new Heriot Watt University, the teacher and youth community leader training work done in Moray House College of Education, the training of young technicians at the ambitious Napier Technical College, those craftsmen at the machines who are the vital link between scientist and technologist, equal to one seventh of the total supply for the industries of the central belt of Scotland, the senior seat of wisdom is, of course, the University of Edinburgh, its importance and influence felt throughout the world, the close association with the city of Edinburgh one of its features. It was as a 'tounis college' that the University began its career in the quickly-erected buildings at Kirk o' Field in 1583, on the spot where Darnley, husband of Mary, Queen of Scots was murdered. A much smaller affair then, just Robert Rollock, the university's first regent, and about eighty students.

The launching of a university was then a bold step on the part of the town council, imaginative and hopeful, for the country was still bedevilled by political unrest, religious feuding and intrigue. But hope was created on realism, and the town council reserved the right to wield the disciplinary cudgel if need be on any scholars who "if they enter not to wark . . . with diligence, the gift granted be the King's Majesty to the guid town will expyre the XV of April nixt". The study course then lasted four years, teaching was mostly in Latin, and students were limited to reading only for Divinity and Arts. A 'tounis' college it has remained, despite the long battle for self-government in the eighteenth and nineteenth centuries, first by the Regents, later by the Professors, and won eventually in the 1858 Universities (Scotland) Act. But Edinburgh and its university, the town and the gown, foils for each other, today act as reciprocal agents in prestige and achievement, the university neither overbearing with its pride in accomplishments nor servile in its dealings with the city fathers, and the town council are certainly not obsequious sycophantic yes-men touching forelocks to the greatness of the university, as happens in such places as Oxbridge. They wisely understand that the city of Edinburgh is bigger than both.

The impressive university building begun by Robert Adam, completed and adapted by Playfair in the grand manner and now called the Old College—or Surgeons' Hall by those taking the bus—is still recognized by many as the university. (One history lecturer is frequently heard to say that bodies were once wheeled about here but now they walk in themselves.) Yet in recent years there has been an amazing growth of the university all over the city, new and reshuffled departments, new buildings, new styles, much of it, unfortunately, hardly in keeping with the ideals of the first New Town planners who built the Old College. Many of the new erections have the design and attraction of piled fish-boxes from Newhaven, an affront to both Edinburgh and the university, although no one with a dash of sensitivity in his soul or an eye for dramatic architectural effect can fail to appreciate the perspective and symbolism in the soaring Hume and Appleton Towers and the complex that has sprouted from the razed Georgian splendour that was once recognizably George Square.

The controversy over the appropriateness and legality of the George Square scheme, which thundered and groaned for years, city traditionalists versus sanguine university visionaries, and ended with the implementation of the development plan, gave the university a confidence and freedom of action that was hardly thought possible little more than a hundred years ago when it first broke from the tutelage of the town. Now the development plan when completed will see the growth of a university township within the city, a kind of culture island, complete with shops, businesses, lecture halls, quadrangles, traffic and pedestrians on different levels, in the city but not of it, with its own rules, regulations and laws for its scholarly inhabitants, perhaps even part of it becoming a type of free-trade area of cut-price, sponsored goods for penniless students, that will see it become a tourist curiosity like Shannon Airport, New York's Greenwich Village or London's Soho.

If the money is forthcoming, the university is not short of far-reaching plans for the future, apart from a number of internal reorganizations, streamlinings and improvements. Like all universities it has its problems, finance being a major one, and such concerns as the ever-increasing student numbers, their admission, and wastage, their administration and government, all common worries for universities throughout the country. But in spite of modern pressures on it, today the University of Edinburgh's renown is as widespread as ever, its names as famous and revered as those in the past: Ritchie-Calder in international relations, Carstairs in psychiatry, Waddington in genetics, Mathew in architecture.

Those first eighty students of 1583 have swollen to 8,000 with the university itself becoming increasingly bigger business, now with an income topping £4 million, 80 per cent of which comes from government grants. Rollock's first course of 'Philosophy' has grown to embrace six faculties—divinity, law, medicine, arts, science and music. It has become one of Britain's great cosmopolitan universities, a move which began during the years when England's establishments of learning welcomed only those of the Anglican persuasion. Now at least a fifth of the students at Edinburgh University come from outside the United Kingdom, the links with Africa particularly close now with a Centre of African Studies, and a number of Edinburgh-Africans have found their own fame as the leaders of their countries.

The university, of course, is already in one sense a tight community within the city, with the University Court as its governing body, corporate, with perpetual succession and a Common Seal. It has fourteen members representing the university lecturers, the graduates, the students and the town. The court is responsible for the university's property and finance. It can make appointments to almost all the university posts, the most important exception being the principal, who is selected by the Curators. The main academic body is the Senatus Acadamicus, which includes all the professors, and some members of the lecturing staff. It supervises all teaching and the reins of discipline. The appointment of chancellor is carried out by the General Council, comprising the chancellor himself, the court, the professors, graduates, readers and lecturers of more than one year's experience. The most important point is that the system works and that the university's thinking keeps abreast of the times. There is a tendency among academics to be cut off from reality, yet some of the refinements to degree courses and the introduction of new degrees are stimulating in that they demonstrate that at least in Edinburgh thinking is very much of the world and the moment.

It is in the field of medical wisdom and skill that Edinburgh has perhaps won her greatest fame as a city of learning. The story of the Royal Infirmary alone is an epic of non-stop drama, with all the ingredients of a best-seller. Startling medical discoveries and breakthroughs, heroes and heroines by the score, set against the background of incredible dedication and toil to push forward by the merest fraction the frontiers of man's knowledge of life and how to save it. The goings on of the television doctors' adventures seem puny and dull in comparison.

The story goes back to the days when that extraordinary Lord

Provost, George Drummond, was stomping around Edinburgh doing more for the Capital than has been done since by one man. The idea of an infirmary was first put forward by John Munro, who had already won considerable prestige for the city as Deacon of the Incorporation of Surgeons. The idea was supported and developed by the Royal College of Physicians, and Drummond was fascinated. Quickly he launched the fund that gave the infirmary life in Robertson's Close in 1729.

The first patient was Elizabeth Sinclair from Caithness, suffering from anaemia. Three months later she was discharged, recovered. Two years after receiving its Royal Charter the foundation stone of a new Royal Infirmary was laid in 1738 in what became Infirmary Street, with beds for 228 patients, and an operating theatre to seat 200 medical students. Today the Royal is almost Scotland's national hospital, recognized as one of the world's great medical teaching centres, with beds for more than 1,000 general patients. The need for still more modern accommodation will be met in the new Royal Infirmary of Edinburgh, the plans for which are already well laid.

The celebrities and characters who emerged through the centuries in Edinburgh's world of medicine make an astonishing list, almost tracing the history of the profession. Dr David Clerk and Dr Colin Drummond were the Infirmary's first full-time physicians, attending every day for a princely annual £30 sterling. There was Dr Gregory of the mixture fame, a concoction of rhubarb and ginger, that was not wholly responsible for making him a Professor of Institutes of Medicine in 1776, for he thoroughly believed in the principles of all-out attack on disease, especially "by free blood-letting, the cold effusion, brisk purging, frequent blisters and vomits of tartar emetic". Surgeon Robert Liston would arrive at the operating theatre, scalpel in hand and ready for business, in the sartorial splendour of a dark bottle-green velvet coat, double-breasted shawl vest, grey close-fitting trousers and a pair of large Wellington boots. William Gairdner soon discovered that drumming feet running over a certain Infirmary stair made exactly the same sound as the amphoric echo from the lungs heard through a stethoscope. Gairdner's Corner soon reverberated to the thumps of students' boots as they were ordered to remember the exact note and pitch. Those were the misty beginning days of modern medical study, when the body-snatcher's grisly trade was rife, when Burke and Hare roamed the streets with gruesome intent, when Dr Knox, the anatomist, was reviled in the public glare for buying murdered bodies for his lectures.

There were less tragic occasions, less humorous, though tragedy and humour are never far apart. There were moments of highest drama like the scene at 52 Queen Street, the residence of Dr James Young Simpson, when he brushed his long hair aside and with a last look at the sun and trees outside his dining-room window, inhaled deeply from a sinister little phial containing a rather frightening liquid that Dr Simpson called chloroform, while his wide-eyed assistants bravely did likewise, wondrously falling into deep and total oblivion. Or the scene at the Royal Infirmary as a result of that experiment when he placed his chloroform-soaked handkerchief over the nose and mouth of a little Highland lad, terrified and in agonies with an infected arm, and watched him quiet and still as he removed a section of bone, while the distinguished doctors, who had gathered to watch the result of Dr Simpson's personal war on pain, had to wait to have history confirmed until a Gaelic-speaking student could be found to translate the boy's incredulity at feeling and remembering nothing of the ordeal.

There was Joseph Lister who came as a house surgeon and returned to develop his campaign against post-operative sepsis, which took fearful toll of life even after an operation had been successful. Lister's long laborious hours of research, trial and error, despair and hope, laid the foundation of modern hygiene and antiseptic measures that today would be equivalent to a cure for cancer.

The quest for medical knowledge and learning in Edinburgh still goes on. In recent years Professor Norman Dott has received world recognition for his work in neuro-surgery, Dr D. H. Bowie gave the lead in high speed vacuum sterilization, and Professor M. F. A. Woodruff has been acclaimed for his kidney transplant

Almost a symbol of Edinburgh, a line-out of schoolboy rugby jerseys below the Salisbury Crags

operation. Today, over at the Western General Hospital, strides are being taken in what until now has been the tottering process of rehabilitation after serious injury or illness. There have been remarkable results with those who have suffered dysphasia, a disorder of the language function that makes it difficult to formulate thoughts or express them to others, or even understand what is being said. Then there is the work for the severely handicapped, pitiful cases, some with only the power of breathing, like the man whose body had been useless for thirty years, speechless, helpless, a vegetable human, who had movement in only one foot. A hopeful new world was revealed by a tailor-made machine that enabled him to communicate by using a taped vocabulary mounted on synchronized drums, and operated by a foot-control that let him say what he wanted at the rate of forty words a minute. There are other machines (many of them displayed from time to time at the Scottish Hospital Centre) that can control a television set, change the channel, the volume, the brightness, manipulate a typewriter, switch on a light all by puff of the breath.

Edinburgh has always led the field in research into rheumatoid arthritis, and a team from the city was the first to isolate a bacteria from the joints of patients with the complaint, while the Northern General Hospital gives them the best attention in the country. The Simpson Memorial Maternity Pavilion has an international reputation for mother and child care, and pioneered much of the way in eliminating the risk to a mother's life as her child is born. The Royal Infirmary continues specialized work with coronary thrombosis cases, Scotland's curse, the highest figures in the world, but their intensive care unit, the largest in Britain, has had an outstanding success in saving lives. Strides are also being made in preventive medicine, for such is the doctor's dedication to preserve health and life that it is now not enough for them merely to cure or alleviate pain and sickness, he must seek to stop it occurring at all. There will be even greater emphasis on preventive medicine in the future, and in the new reconstructed Royal Infirmary it will play a prominent part of the work.

The university itself has many research projects in hand, one of

The whale bones at the entrance of Jaw Bone Walk across the Meadows

the most fascinating is their work in phonetics, which has long been studied in Edinburgh, and now one of their developments is the refinement of a speaking machine, the locquacious Pat—short for Parametric Artificial Talker—who can even sing a song or shout encouragement to the Hibs. Pat the chatterbox, a sexless but trim complex of wires and knobs, speaks by electrical circuits operating in much the same way as the human vocal tract, with eight control signals representing a number of elements in human speech, emitting a voice loud and clear but with the disembodied unearthly quality of a Dalek. And what is the use of learning about how we speak? What business man would not welcome a device that typed as he spoke, or a computer that could discuss a problem, or more knowledge of what prevents some people from speaking, or a device to make it easier for those suffering from speech defects? They are possibilities for the future, and perhaps Edinburgh will supply some of the answers.

So the research work goes on, probing, checking, waiting, observing, treating, hoping, ageing, month after month, year in year out. This is the story of Edinburgh's achievement in medical knowledge, the tradition, the white, disinfected corridors of learning, passing the wisdom won to those who want it for the benefit of the world, a story of firsts all the way: one of the first X-ray departments in the world (granted £500 and the hospital plumber's shop to do the job); first to establish a laboratory to bring experimental physiological work to bear on the wards; first dietetic department in Britain, first to develop the Presterilized Trolley Top Tray System, saving vital moments in a surgeon's time at operations; first health centre in Britain, which the rest of the world copied. And still the work goes on: breakthroughs in mental health at Morningside's Royal Edinburgh Hospital; research into medical computers to prevent the possibility of doctors making emergency decisions on insufficient information; research into electronic signals in the circulatory system to give the surgeon a continuous indication of his patient's condition; research into suffering caused by genetic abnormalities.

There are more, many many more that will only come to light one day when they leap at us from the newspaper headlines and we marvel at a new wonder and realize, as we read down the column, that it all began in Edinburgh. Perhaps it really began in one of the city schools, in Heriot's or Stewart's, Broughton or the Portobello High, or perhaps by the fireside at home, the influence of that Edinburgh yearning for knowledge, conscious or not. Certainly if every city in Britain cared as much about learning as Edinburgh, a great and wonderful educational revolution would sweep the country. If. . . .

VII

SEATS OF WISDOM

YOU see them in deep reminiscence at the foot of Leith Walk, grey heads nodding wisely; or seated along Portobello Prom watching the waves roll in like years; or up at Bruntsfield spectating the putting in summer; or down at Newhaven scanning the ships plying the Forth. They are the older generation, the pensioner sages. They sit on their favourite seats and talk of the old days. They are worth listening to for their wisdom is hard won from experience. They share their thoughts and memories with each other or whoever will listen, and stay silent, for theirs is a selective fraternity, age the virtue, and those of another later era are not always understanding. Their talk is of thirty years ago. A short span after all, not even half the lifetime of a man, a blink in the life of a city. Just yesterday, in fact. Yet glancing back on Edinburgh's yesterdays they glimpse an age already remote, and a style of living that has gone. This is the conversation from one such seat of wisdom. . . .

Thirty years ago much of the horsepower did, indeed, come from horses. Television was not yet born; the motor car monster was still not strong enough to devour our streets; hospitals were maintained by voluntary contributions; churches had full congregations, and Sundays were peaceful affairs. Men worked willingly for under £3 a week, glad to get the job.

Transport in the city was supplied by tram-cars. Edinburgh trams were unique in Scotland—hauled through the streets by an underground cable. "Yon man is like an Embro' caur," said an old minister of the time, commenting on a local doubtful character, "directed frae above, but powered frae below."

But they got you there—cheaply. You could go down to Leith

or Portobello for a penny, almost as quickly as you can go today in the modern buses, for one shilling and a penny.

For entertainment, Edinburgh was supreme. Theatres and cinemas galore, top London stars drawing the crowds each week. Jack Hulbert and Cicely Courtneidge were certain successes. If they returned today they would still be successes—but where are the theatres? Where for that matter have the cinemas gone? Those old 'picture houses' were institutions, building up a society of supporters as loyal as the football fans who back Hibs or Hearts each week. Saturday night was joy night, when you could step into a magic world flickering on the screen. More. Even the small fry could sit round the show, demand—and get—a cup of tea and two biscuits for a threepence admission. Adults paid extra—sixpence.

If you were to ask you would probably be told that the first 'talkie' to come to Edinburgh was *The Singing Fool,* which opened in the New Picture House in Princes Street on 10th June, 1929. Starring Al Jolson, presenting five shows a day for three weeks, each show decanting one more crowd of weeping women on to the pavement almost opposite the Mound, for this was the sobbie to end all sobbies.

The first 'talkie' in the city, in fact, was a Scottish production, *Till the Bells Ring,* a comedy, featuring Graham Moffat's Company. It went on at Poole's Synod Hall on 11th October, 1926, almost three years before Jolson had been heard of.

Those masters of the entertainment world, the Poole family, have kept Edinburgh amused for more than a century. As early as 1897, the Poole's of the day was experimenting with the new-fangled 'moving pictures', and began to arrange shows of this great marvel. To one of his shows, came the first 'fake' film ever made, *The Dispatch Bearer.* Produced by a circus company in Wales, it purported to be an episode in the Boer War, much in the news at the time. It ran for exactly four minutes.

In 1902 came the first 'talking picture' experiment—Harry Lauder singing "I Love a Lassie"—a squeaky phonograph behind the screen supplying Harry's voice. The boom started. The Operetta House opened in Chambers Street in 1902, followed by the Cinema House in Nicolson Street. The Albert Hall went up in Shandwick Place, then came Pringle's Picture Palace. The rush was on.

The Albert was known locally as the B.B. The door 'barker' was a Mr Denholm, tall, brilliantly uniformed, a familiar sight to all in the district, most of all to the small boys. They delighted in parading past the doorman, just out of reach, chanting:

Here lies the body o' Harry Denholm,
If ye saw him noo, ye widna' ken 'im.

What Harry said is not recorded.

By 1911, the Princes Street cinemas had a man behind the screen, giving a running commentary—"As you see, ladies and gents, the hero is about to overtake the villain...", and the applause rang out. Cowboys and Indians arrived with much galloping about and firing of revolvers. Boy ushers were trained to carry canes and watch the screen. On the pointing of a gun down came the cane on a hard wooden seat, and it sounded like a real shot.

The Singing Fool brought the new era that ousted an old. The husband and wife Punch and Judy show, so long established on the Mound almost opposite the cinema, vanished, never to return. Stars rose, glittered, faded, but left many happy memories. Janet Gaynor and Charles Farrell in *Sunny Side Up*; Eddie Cantor living down his *Roman Scandals*; Norma Shearer, Maurice Chevalier, Colin Clive; and the first of the crooners, Rudy Vallee in *The Vagabond Lover*.

Down in London, a young Scot named Baird was striving to cast animated pictures through space on to a glass screen, while in various parts of the world groups of soldiers were sitting down at odd times to play a game called 'Housie'. The two big enemies of the silver screen were on their way.

There were other forces at work. The city birthplace of *The Singing Fool* passed to Marks and Spencer in May 1930. Two years later, the Palace, built in six months to give its first show on Christmas Eve, 1913, was acquired by Woolworth.

The rot set in. The Alhambra, down in Leith Walk, stuck out

till March 1958, and left its memories. Famous names had walked across the Alhambra stage to stardom—Gracie Fields, Bud Flanagan, Tommy Lorne, Harry Gordon, Dave Willis, Jack Anthony, and many more.

But life went on—or ended. James Ingles Ker, of Dunfermline, died suddenly in Edinburgh in September 1936, and left a feeling of loss all over Scotland. He was a fighter. From the moment it became obvious that road transport would challenge the might of the railways one day, the old problem of the Forth crossing, solved by the railway bridge so long ago, had arrived again. James Ingles Ker stepped forward with the solution. A Forth road bridge.

He drove his dream with such vehemence and sincerity, that all Scotland rallied behind him to battle with stubborn London officialdom for the right to go ahead with a project of the utmost necessity for Scotland. That battle was to last for more than thirty years. He never saw his dream come true, but the Bridge, the Glencoe road, and many other Scottish undertakings stand as a memorial to him.

They look back and revive an unforgettable impression of Edinburgh, the memory of a great city struck into instant immobility and silence at a given signal. That memory takes them back to the closing week of January 1936. King George had died. Seventy guns had boomed from the castle that morning to proclaim the fact. When a king dies, something dies with him, and Edinburgh—all Scotland—mourned the passing in their own way.

Came 28th January. In London the king was being buried. The day dawned in Edinburgh, dull and rainy. Schools and shops were closed, flags drooped half-mast and forlorn.

An hour after noon the bells tolled, and people went their ways strangely subdued. At half past the hour a single gun crashed out. All Edinburgh stopped in her tracks, and a great hush fell upon the city.

The crowds moving in the streets halted as if petrified. A tram-car edging around the G.P.O. jerked to an abrupt stop half-way across Princes Street. Down in the Waverley, engine crews stood back from their controls. For two long minutes, the silence, the unreality, the sheer incredibility of it was awesome. Then the bells rang out, and Edinburgh came to life again. People moved once more, and that frozen tram rattled round on to the main line. But Edinburgh had stamped a memory never to be forgotten by those who experienced the wonder.

Joy and sorrow run hand in hand. A king had gone, a king arrived. Pomp and pageantry came into its own again, and the crowds moved solidly to the Mercat Cross, Holyrood, and The Shore at Leith. Lord Provost Louis Gumley faced 50,000 townsfolk at the Mercat Cross, and proclaimed the new king—Edward VIII.

Edward was liked, acknowledged to be "the most popular figure in the world today". That 'VIII', however, struck a discordant note in Scottish ears, and indignant letters appeared in the papers about 'an insult to Scotland', and pointing out that it should have been 'Edward II', as far as Scotland was concerned. The same breeze blew many years later when Elizabeth came to the throne.

As it turned out, Edward's reign was brief. "We heard him on the radio explaining to his people why he had abdicated. We, who did not know what was going on behind the scenes, could guess, and regretted his going."

Poverty and misery were widespread that year. Scotland had 255,300 unemployed, and there was no welfare state. Hunger marchers from all parts converged on London, unaware that dug-in officialdom is hard to dig out. That officialdom had just announced its 'higher' scale of unemployment relief—£1 4s. a week for a married couple; a single householder got 16s. if a man, 15s. if a woman. Allowance for one child—one only—"must be not less than four shillings a week". Some miserly local authorities were already slashing at even that starvation 'dole'.

Coming events cast their shadows before. The front pages of the papers began to carry startling reports: Hitler in Germany had threatened this, Mussollini in Italy, had said that. All talk. The shock came in March 1936. Pages of pictures showing long columns of steel-helmeted German soldiers marching into

Cologne, Frankfurt, Mainz, Coblenz, guns rolling behind, war planes roaring above.

It was clearly an act of war. France screamed hate and fury, and rushed to man her fortresses. But it takes two to make a war. The League of Nations talked on in Geneva, and the politicians of the allied nations followed the example. No one could see that the shape of things to come—had come.

The groups were in the streets to drive the fact. Black Shirts, Brown Shirts, Red Shirts, White, Blue, Green—marching and counter-marching in the cause of idealism—blind to the fact that their kind of idealism is always decided on bloodstained battlefields. Plenty of ex-soldiers about to point a truth, but old soldiers' views were never very popular in political circles. One quoted a cynical French comrade in that earlier war, "I go to fight for general disarmament and to end the war to end war."

"Westminster improved on that one," said the quoter drily, but without bitterness, "by adding that that particular war would make Britain a land fit for heroes to live in."

Advertisements were appearing; one inserted by a new firm, Scottish Aviation, publicized the opening of a new flying school at a place called Prestwick, in Ayrshire, prophesying that "this airfield will one day be the largest and best in the country." The men behind the scheme had indeed long vision. They were true prophets—so got the usual reception of prophets.

Another prophet spoke that year, the Right Rev Dr H. S. Reid, Episcopal Bishop of the diocese, speaking in St John's, Jedburgh: "It is not easy to be a minister of God these days. It is a disturbed and troubled world—politics without principle, diplomacy without honour, promise without fulfilment, wealth without work." But don't we still hear the same groans?

Another slice of old Edinburgh was wiped out by council decree—Grange House, in Grange Loan. How long it had been there no one really knew. It was the home of the vicar of St Giles' at one time, and it was said that an underground passage ran from the house to the church. Prince Charlie visited it in 1745; Walter Scott played in it as a boy. It had three ghosts, a Cowled Monk, a Green Lady, and a Miser. The miser amused himself on occasions by rolling a barrel of gold through the echoing corridors. Many people had heard him. House and spectres were quickly wiped from the Edinburgh scene.

There were occasional parades in the streets not seen nowadays. The missions were very busy, with more need for their services than the more popular 'darkest Africa'. The Grassmarket and Carrubbers Close missions were always to the front. Big-hearted people reaching down to where no one else would reach, and distributing an immense amount of pleasure—and hope.

Periodically, there was a glimpse of a tiny part of their work, long processions of happy children crocodiling through the streets on their way to Waverley or the bus station, and a day on the green grass on the borders of the city. Pathetic little people, poorly dressed mostly, some in bare feet, 'tinny'—a tin mug—suspended round the neck by thankful mothers. Even the short trip in the bus or train was an adventure, and the grass was green and fragrant and free.

So the closing months of an old era slipped away. In the last week of August 1939 the Alhambra poster advertised their star attraction, *The Curse of War*, with 'full supporting programme'. A few days later the curse struck.

Over in France, almost overnight, two great armies turned towards each other, poised for battle. But the word to set those armies rolling remained unspoken. The great 'Phoney War' of the American press had started.

As far as Edinburgh was concerned, the 'phoney' part of it went out in a vast rumble of guns on Monday afternoon, 16th October, when two waves of German bombers passed high over the city and made for Rosyth where the Fleet was anchored. If the tiny dots in the sky were noticed at all, they gave no cause for alarm, and moved upon their target, unhindered.

Even as the bombs crashed down, striking ships and killing men, the Spitfires of 603 City of Edinburgh (Fighter) Squadron of the Royal Auxiliary Air Force, rocketed up from Turnhouse to give battle. 'Amateur' fighters, every one of them—a solicitor, a sheep farmer, a mining engineer, a timber merchant. The battle raged over the city, sometimes at roof-top height, and at the end of the day four Heinkels had been destroyed—the first enemy planes to be brought down in Britain. Others came, others fell. For Edinburgh—all unknown—it was the beginning of the new era.

VIII

CEREMONY

A SKIRL of pipes, a roll of drums, a glimpse of swaying tartan—pageantry. Something to stir the heart of young and old. A memory from the past for the present, a flourish of an ancient deed that remains young. Scotland is rich in pageantry. Community pride keeps it alive. The symbols of that pride are all around—the mounted reiver in the High Street of Hawick, gazing towards that once turbulent Border; his comrade in Galashiels, sword at hip, lance on shoulder, guarding the Border town behind him, as his forefathers stood watch and ward on the same spot. Braw lads or lasses, Callants or Cornets at Hawick, Galashiels, Selkirk, Lauder, Musselburgh and more, mount their steeds, and proudly lead their cavalcades around the marches. Peebles crowns her queen and holds Beltane Festival; Kirkcaldy has her pageant week; Lanark her Lanimer Day, while drums and music rouse the folk of historic Linlithgow at the dawn of her own day that brings a memory of an age that has gone.

The Celts hold their Gaelic Mod, the Norsemen of Lerwick shout Up Helly Aa, Stonehaven whirls the fireballs. There are Uppies and Doonies, Gowks and Burrymen, Whuppity Scoorie, Guisers and Guid Nychburris. They are all part of the history and tradition of Scotland.

Edinburgh carries on her own traditions in the old costumes and manner as she always did. Pageantry nowadays, yet somehow not pageantry. It all fits into the scene. The pipes at the Tron on Hogmanay, a trumpeters' fanfare at the High Court, the soft lilt of Gaelic voices at a city *ceilidh,* a convivial evening among the concealing robes of the learned 'Monks of St Giles',' a tourist's stare at the Honours of Scotland, a May Day service in the dawn dew on the summit of Arthur's Seat.

Some are small ceremonies, known only to a handful of citizens, others make news throughout the country. Like the great gathering of ministers in May as Edinburgh is invaded by the dog-collars of the Church of Scotland for the General Assembly, when the kirk is truly in session. The Church of Scotland is Presbyterian, democratic in base, where all men are equal, and no one man may rule. The congregations themselves select the minister of their choice, and 'call' him to take over their church. Elders assist in the running of the kirk, and guidance is given by the district Presbytery, a group of elders and ministers. The head of the Presbytery is called the Moderator. He has title but no power, acting as chairman at Presbytery meetings.

Each year, in May, the General Assembly of the Church of Scotland meets in Edinburgh, under the Moderator of the Church of Scotland; the highest title in the kirk, yet again with no real power. Here all church matters are settled after due debate in which all take part. The Assembly sat originally as a kind of parliament, representing all interests in all parts of the country. It was one of the 'Three Estates' of the national parliament, so had great importance. It could, and did speak with authority.

The "General Assemblie of this haill Realme" met for the first time in 1560. As the king presided over meetings of his national parliament, it was accepted that he would also preside at 'Assemblie' meetings. Mary, Queen of Scots, being Roman Catholic, broke the tradition, rousing the wrath of John Knox.

Those early days were troubled ones, with many a clash between kirk and state. But the kirk grew stronger, attracting some of the highest in the land to the Protestant ranks. King James attended Assembly meetings whenever possible, sending his Commissioner to represent him when he could not attend. He did not always agree with the proceedings, and being a Royal Stuart never left his ministers in any doubt about his views.

The clashes between the churches ripped out the heart of the country through the violent years, but the Church of Scotland became the established Kirk of the nation, and still fills a major role in the public affairs of the North.

Today, the clash is still on, but in a more subtle way. The cry for unity is heard on all sides, and bishops, priests and ministers meet to discuss which does which and who does what. As far as the kirk is concerned, the results of the discussions must be tumbled out in front of the General Assembly each year, to be praised or damned according to individual views of the ministers. Dour provincial ministers and kirk members are already voicing their fears that they are being 'sold' to the bishops and priests. It is an auld sang, an echo from the past, but the kirk was always good for a controversy.

May comes round each year, and the ministers pour towards Edinburgh from the four corners of the land. In the old days many walked or rode great distances, but travel is easier and more comfortable now. As of old, the golden Royal Standard floats above Holyrood Palace to show that the Queen is in residence, and old Edinburgh is royal again. So an ancient order springs into new life—pageantry to the visitor, familiar and matter-of-fact to the people of Edinburgh.

Again as of old, the Queen sends her Lord High Commissioner to take her place when she is absent. He resides in Holyrood, and holds court as his Queen would hold it. Then St Giles' looks down on scenes not so far removed from the days when she was younger. Scenes worth seeing, and something beyond the scenes, for if the old kirk is the heart of Scotland, the gathering of Scotland's ministers is its visible beat.

Soldiers in colourful uniforms predominate as the guard of honour for the Lord High Commissioner marches to St Giles' and forms up, drums beating and pipes lilting. Then come the great and the not so great, in uniforms brilliant and sombre, to pass into the great Mother Church, and worship under the faded regimental colours drooping above the aisles. There are those who have criticized the emphasis on the military arm in a purely religious occasion, as others have frowned upon the array of statues in the city, placed to mark some glorious regimental deed. Those who carp cannot have read the history of Scotland, and must have failed to grasp the significance of the fighting man within the Presbyterian faith. The right to follow God in their own fashion was won by men with the will to fight, something worth remembering.

Not so long ago, the kirk staged a reminder of this very fact. In May 1965 a moving service was held within the ruined walls of Holyrood Abbey. The Lord High Commissioner and the Moderator attended. Before the service began, an officer of the First Battalion The Cameronians (Scottish Rifles) reported to the minister of the Canongate Kirk that his armed picket was in position, and the service could begin. While the hymns rose feelingly from the roofless ruins, men of the Cameronians stood guard outside, as Richard Cameron's men had watched on the lonely moorlands in the old days, while the Covenanters worshipped God in their own way, without the help of bishops. Still on the moors stand the silent cairns that mark where blood was shed in defence against that human right. The faith was there—and the will.

Wills and faiths tend to become worn with the years. The hardy Cameronians, with battle honours stretching across the world, were themselves doomed by London decree, which even the might of Hitler could not achieve, and the Faith is not so ready to make a stand. Here, in Edinburgh, in May, is the place and time to make that stand, bringing unity back to the kirk ranks, before seeking it beyond the kirk. The martial parades and the booming cannon from the castle should inspire a look back and a look around. Alas, John Knox is but a statue now, and the thunderous declamations have shrunk to a yearly pitter patter on the importance of stipends, ecumenical unity, and the rights of female elders and ministers to assume office within the kirk.

There are broadsides, of course, at the wrongs of the world, but the roars are muted. Yet the pageantry remains, and Edinburgh is a city worth living in when the ministers gather, the soldiers march, and the ghosts of the old days stir down the length of the Royal Mile.

So, too, in Edinburgh, the bows and arrows of olden times still have a place in the life of the city. The Royal Company of

Archers, the Queen's Bodyguard for Scotland, have marched with their monarch since 1676, and march to this day. No one can mistake the archers as they pass through the streets—the dark green uniforms and feathered bonnets come from the past, yet they hardly appear anomalous in the Edinburgh of the present.

The Royal Company was created in 1676 in an attempt to keep alive the dying art of archery. Here again was that inherent democracy of the Scot, for the then Lord Lyon, the Honourable Charles Erskine, Bailie George Drummond and John Lindsay, men poles apart in social significance, served together on the first council. Their badge was Cupid and Mars, with the motto 'In Peace and War'. Each year, as a ceremonial occasion, the archers held a competition on Leith Links. Complete with 'shuting graith', and the badge of the company on their 'hatts or bonnetts', they marched with drums beating and colours flying "handsomely dressed in their proper garb, saluted by military guards". The Treasury donated £20 in 1677 to provide an annual 'King's Prize'. Parades were called for the first day of each summer month, absentees being fined half-a-crown.

In 1704, Queen Anne granted a charter giving royal status to the Company. The Provost and magistrates presented a trophy from the town, the Silver Arrow, to be competed for annually. Each year the archers still shoot for that same arrow. It is on record that the Earl of Wemyss won the coveted honour in June 1714, when the contest was shot off before a huge crowd, after the usual impressive march through Edinburgh. The Royal Company paraded at the Shore of Leith when George IV stepped from the deck of the Royal George at the start of his State visit in 1822. They fell in on each side of his carriage, and escorted the royal visitor up Leith Walk. From that incident came their other title, the King's (or Queen's) Bodyguard for Scotland. In due course, the archers provided an escort for Queen Victoria and Prince Albert on their visit to Edinburgh.

It was natural that Sir Walter Scott, with all his love of the old traditions, should become a member of the Royal Company. Robert Burns, the poet, also became a member, while Allan

Part of the impressive quadrangle of Edinburgh University

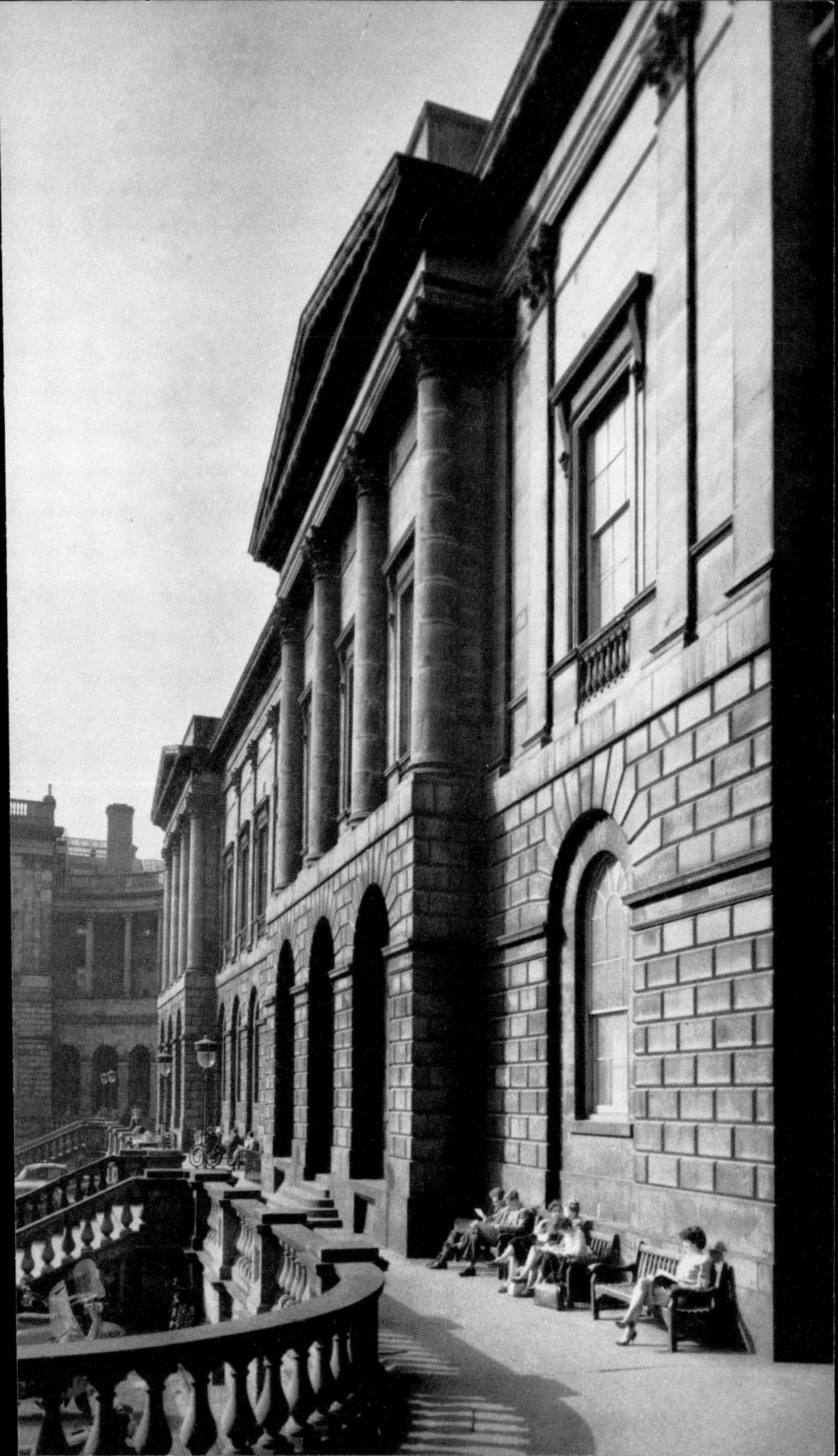

Ramsay, in his time, was acknowledged the company bard. Like calls to like, and the company have had a close link with the Woodmen of the Ancient Forest of Arden in Warwickshire since 1786. Members of both groups still join in friendly contests within the city limits. The bows twang, and Edinburgh's own little army from the past still marches through modern times, somehow in keeping with the Capital scene.

Behind all the pageantry, an integral part at times, sits the Lord Lyon King of Arms. An ancient office indeed, extending beyond records, but traced back to the days of the Druids. Since the beginning, kings and queens have followed his directions, and still do. In Scotland, a name is much more than a name, the clan clashes through the ages emphasize the point. In those early days, arms and symbols distinguished families, and the Scottish social structure grew up under this system. A seal on a deed, a right granted, a right received, determined the ownership of land, of rivers, of mountains, valuable records then, invaluable today.

The necessity of preserving those records was recognized in those old days, and the office of Lord Lyon King of Arms was created. One of those Lyons, Sir David Lindsay of the Mount, wrote *The Book of Blazons* in 1542, the earliest record of arms existing in Scotland. There were other records—lost to that arch plunderer, Oliver Cromwell. Sir David has other claims to fame. He wrote *Ane Satire of the Thrie Estaits*, a bitter look at his times, and the pillars of his times. Not so long ago, the late Robert Kemp, Scottish author and playwright, recreated the *Thrie Estaits* for the Edinburgh Festival stage, and rang the same bell that Sir David rang in the long ago.

The present Lyon, Sir Thomas Innes of Learney, fills the post to perfection. No need to enquire this man's identity when he appears. On ceremonial occasions, standing at the Mercat Cross, flanked by his heralds in uniforms of scarlet and gold, the pride of Scotland stirs again and the ancient pomp and colour of Royal Scotland is not so far distant.

Sir Thomas is absolute authority on all matters relating to Scottish heraldry. At various times he has clashed with London decree—and won. His office is in Register House, looking up North Bridge, where he holds court twice a year, as it has been held since Druid times, at the beginning of May—Beltane—and at Hallowe'en, the end of summer.

Set in St Giles' is a little sanctuary that breathes of Scotland and the chivalry of Scotland—the chapel of the Knights of the Order of the Thistle, one of Scotland's oldest orders. Where the first Chapel Royal was created is uncertain, some say in Scone, in Perthshire. In the reign of William the Lion it was in Stirling, but moved with the Stuarts to Holyrood. Mary, Queen of Scots worshipped in the Holyrood Chapel, rousing the ire of Knox. The sanctuary was destroyed by an Edinburgh mob at a later date. Trials and troubles beset the Order, but it was too deeply rooted to be killed, and rose supreme after each attack.

New Knights are still installed with full ceremony, a spectacle to draw not only Edinburgh folk, but those from all over the world who find satisfaction in being part of something that grew out of the mists of time, and remains still to play a role. On a clear October day in 1962 the old Capital became royal once more, flags streamed from every building, kilted figures strode the streets, pipes lilted, crowds packed every vantage point, and the whole city seemed jammed in Princes Street and round St Giles', where King Olaf V of Norway, and the Earl of Home (who later became Prime Minister) were installed Knights of the Thistle.

The 'royal' epics of Hollywood stand branded as empty sham against the reality. It looked regal—it was regal. Came the Queen, in the robes of the Order of the Thistle, every inch a monarch, Lord Erskine as Page of Honour, the Duke of Edinburgh at her right hand. The Duke and Duchess of Gloucester, the Princess Royal, King Olaf, Dukes and Earls, the Lord Lyon, the Queen's Bodyguard, the Councillors, the dignified Judges of Scotland.

At the great door of the kirk stood the Rev Dr Harry Whitley, minister of St Giles', to greet his royal congregation, while the fanfares rang out from the trumpets of the Heralds. When Edinburgh is royal, she is royal indeed.

A flash of the ceremony associated with Scots law is still seen in the city—but only a flash. In the old days the opening of the High Court sessions was meant to impress. The majesty of the law was a fact, and had to be seen as a fact. The carriages of the judges rolled towards the court, the hooves of the cavalry escort clattering out a warning to all evil-doers on the cobblestones. An impressive gathering waited at the courtroom door, the trumpeters sounded a fanfare, and the solemn macer strode ahead, the judges pacing behind. All stood, the mace was placed behind the Bench—and the court was in session. The atmosphere of any courtroom in a trial involving human life tends to be tense—in those old days it was awesome.

Scottish law was created by Scots for Scots, and differs from English law on many points. Had Scots law accompanied parliament to the south at the Treaty of Union, Scotland would not be as it is today. Parliament Hall, over against the High Court, is the heart of the legal system. Built between 1632 and 1639 as the Scottish House of Parliament, it is an impressive building, history in its every angle and rafter. Sir Walter Scott worked here, as did Robert Louis Stevenson. Here pace the advocates, gowned and wigged, waiting for the stroke of the bell under the great window, to tell them that their case is on in the courtroom, and their presence required.

On the west side is the Advocate's Library, where hangs the standard the Earl Marischal of Scotland carried at Flodden. The library is now the National Library of Scotland. Much of the public ceremony has gone, but the judges, in wigs and colourful robes, still march in procession across Parliament Square to St Giles' for the Kirkin' o' the Court before the Sessions open.

The High Constables of the City of Edinburgh also parade impressively on various occasions, but the years have swept away the more colourful costumes of long ago. The modern uniform is morning dress, with top hat, each member wielding his silver baton of office. Many of the duties of the High Constables have also vanished, but the Society is still healthy and active, taking its place in public ceremonies and civic processions by right.

They were needed in those early days. High Street and Canongate had a black reputation for violence in the sixteenth century.

Brawling was a daily occurrence, the sword flashing into the argument far too often. Men of title set the example; those lower in the social order followed the example in their own way. The law was there, but few to enforce it. Merchants and tradesmen, by that same law, were compelled to keep weapons in their shops to defend their goods—and their lives.

The bailies ruled the town as far as they could, aided by the burgesses. Together they patrolled the streets, but more than patrols were needed. In 1611 the Privy Council ordered the provost and magistrates to enlist suitable persons to guard the streets and take direct action against the violent law breakers, titled or untitled. The Constables of Edinburgh came into existence.

They had a difficult job, but they were tough men. They drilled as an organized force on the Burgh Muir and Leith Links, and showed their intention by marching through the streets under arms, headed by members of the Town Council, pipes and drums in front.

The great city bell was rung forty times at 10 o'clock each night, a signal for all law-abiding citizens to get off the streets, when the constables took over and sent out patrols. They had the power, and used it. Anyone sporting a pistolet, or 'siclike firework engine' was disarmed on the spot and marched to dire punishment, sometimes having the right hand struck off.

Their guardroom was in the Nether Tolbooth, and the 'constable's pairts', or watches, ran from 9.0 at night till 5.0 in the morning. In 1625 the burgesses were pulled in for duty, those named reporting at the Tolbooth in 'their ain gear', steel bonnet, buckler and sword. The leader of the High Constables held the rank or title of Moderator, and it is used to this day.

Discipline was applied in a rough and ready manner that created friction. A constable considered negligent around 1658 was fined five merks Scots, and dumped into jail until he paid up. It was natural that a constable, facing this penalty, should turn upon the citizen whose conduct had brought about the offence, and squeeze the fine from that source. The system spread, and the High Constables became a sort of unofficial official organization for tax collection. It was unorthodox, but the money came in, and the council needed money.

There were other fines and, no doubt, other 'taxes' raked in to meet them. Absentees had to pay 4s. Scots; swearing on duty incurred a penalty of twenty merks; and neglect to attend a colleague's funeral meant a fine of 6s. 8d. Those who refused to pay up had goods to the value of three times the amount seized and sold. All fines collected were distributed by common vote, to various charitable causes. At a later date came the Town Guard, composed mainly of old Highland soldiers with battle experience, solid backing indeed for the harassed High Constables.

The Society of High Constables possess records dating from 1708, and interesting reading they make. Until recently they gathered at Hogmanay, and after supper patrolled the streets until dawn, keeping down disturbances created by late-night revellers. Today the society is still very much alive and ready to serve the city. Behind the morning dress, silk hats and silver rods is a fine record of work over the centuries and an important part in the shaping of modern Edinburgh.

With the Edinburgh Festival comes ceremony of another kind. Stand on Calton Hill or walk down Princes Street in the evening and see the enchantment of the age-old city. High in the darkened sky, the floodlit castle and Royal Mile seem to float upon the darkness, each historic building bathed in soft light above the New Town. So near, so remote. So real, so unreal. The flowers in the gardens bordering Princes Street glow multi-coloured under their own lights, orange, crimson, yellow. . . . There are those who continue to urge that the city should dress up for Festival time, as London dresses, or Paris, Berlin, New York. The sham would shame Edinburgh. The great rock, the castle, the long spire of the Tolbooth Kirk, the grey crown of St Giles', the Royal Mile, the Georgian New Town, the roofs and chimneys of another age, beautiful by day, mystically beautiful by night—this is the finest and most dramatic stage in the world, already dressed.

Edinburgh had a Festival long before 1947. Back in 1488, James IV of Scotland encouraged festival, and started his famous jousts. They lured knights from all over Europe to clash in the lists under the approving eye of the Queen, who sat with her court ladies high on the castle walls to view the chivalry below, while ordinary folk crowded in to watch and cheer. At the end the winners rode proudly forward to receive their treasured award from the King's own hands—a golden-tipped lance.

James supported the cause of the theatre. So did his son, James V, who permitted 'playes' to be performed over by the Calton Hill, despite church opposition. His son, James VI, held the same views and did the theatre signal service by openly flaunting the clergy's bidding when they decreed that a boycott be placed on a well-known company of players arrived from England. The group proposed to stage a show in Blackfriars Wynd, and as was the custom of the day trumpeters and drummers marched through the streets to advertise the performance. The clergy forbade their congregations to attend the 'abomination', which roused the anger of James Stuart. He ordered the church leaders to appear before him—and the show went on.

For a Lowland city the capital of Scotland creates the Highlander's pride in the tartan. A few years ago the massed pipes and drums of the regiments taking part in the Festival's Military Tattoo tried to march along Princes Street. The skirl of pipes, the beat of drum called as the Pied Piper called and thousands pressed in solidly from the side streets until not only the band but the whole street was brought to a complete halt. It was a fantastic sight—one great packed mass of humanity, immovable, while an army of police toiled and exhorted to gain elbow room to force movement. There is the same excitement around the Castle Esplanade each Tattoo night as through that grim portal the tartans come swinging across the drawbridge into the full glare of the searchlights, the throbbing, stirring music of the north catching at the heart. Periodically pipers and drummers from vastly different spheres come to the Esplanade, and still vividly illustrate the universal message of the pipes. Big, bearded Sikhs from Amritsar way, hawk-eyed Pathans from India's famous North-west Frontier, men from Malaysia, Gurkhas from Nepal, Punjabis from Pakistan—playing Scotland's tunes on

Scottish pipes with tartan streamers, marching and counter-marching, shoulder to shoulder with the sons and grandsons of the men who taught them the meaning of the pipes.

Edinburgh also holds her Highland Games each year at Murrayfield, another import from the north, for in the beginning the games were warlike exercises carried out by the clansmen to keep fit and efficient. Tossing the cabar, putting the shot, running, wrestling, jumping, dancing.

Then there are the students from the university who hold their own kind of pageantry in their own way. Capping ceremonies are dignified affairs, as they should be, when graduates come forward to claim their reward for years of study. So are the processions when the men of learning appear behind their bedellus or mace-bearer on academic occasions, impressive figures, chancellor, principal, senatus, honorary graduates in gowns, mortar-boards and bonnets. But installation ceremonies, after a rector has been chosen by vote to represent the students at the University Court, are usually a mixture of dignity and slap-stick farce. The distinguished gathering on the platform behind the newly-elected rector cast apprehensive looks at the students attending the rectorial address, for a broadside of decayed eggs, bags of flour and worse is apt to become a bombardment from the packed tiers.

A more profitable ceremony passes into the streets when the students fall upon the citizens during Charities Week. Fancy dress flourishes in every part of the city and neighbouring towns beyond. Bearded bandits, pirates, cut-throats of every description, Ali Babas, Robin Hoods, Rob Roy MacGregors hold every citizen to ransom, aided and abetted by winsome girl students in costumes ranging from skimpy-clad slave girls blue with cold to circus ringmasters with a full compliment of Noah's Ark performing animals, all can-rattling. Charities Week ends in a blaze of splendour when a legion of students gather under the castle walls, flaring torches held high, and a great procession moves down Castlehill, Lawnmarket, High Street, a long wavering snake of fire heading for the Calton Hill.

There is one ceremony whose popularity has increased and

spread with the years—the Burns Supper. Today it is an institution not confined to Edinburgh, the Burns Country, or even Scotland, but across the world, wherever two Scots meet, in stately homes, village halls, or Highland crofts. Robert Burns, Scotland's National Bard, was born in Alloway, Ayrshire, on 25th January, 1759, and the Burns Supper celebrates the event and what Burns stood for—the dignity, humanity and brotherhood of man, faith and love for Scotland. The supper need not necessarily take place exactly on the poet's birthday, but whatever the date, and wherever the celebration, the ritual is the same: Haggis, neeps, song, the Immortal Memory and good fellowship.

Nothing mysterious about the haggis, a mixture of oatmeal and chopped liver boiled up in a sheep's 'pluck' or stomach bag. When the assembly is seated the haggis is carried in with due ceremony, and marched around the room, a piper pacing in front. Piper and cook are usually rewarded with a glass of whisky. The meal is simple, as it was among the poor folk of Robert's day—haggis, mashed tatties and neeps (potatoes and turnips), followed by kebbuck and bannocks (cheese and oatcakes). Almost every move is marked by the words of the Bard. There are a number of ritual toasts—to the Haggis; to the Lasses, which must please Burns's wraith; to absent friends; and most important, the principal toast, to the Immortal Memory of Robert Burns, which is considered a slight if it lasts much short of an hour.

The person chosen to carve the haggis rises and gives his 'address'—"Fair fa' your honest, sonsie face . . ." and at the words "to cut ye up wi' ready sleight", he dirks the haggis with a flourish. Once asked by an Englishman to describe this part of the ceremony, the speaker graphically replied: "Man, it sits there on the plate in front o' ye, sae plump, sae grey, sae bonnie. Then ye draw yer dirk across its face, an' man, it smiles at ye. . . ."

Edinburgh is rich in such activities. Some are comparatively recent innovations to the Capital's calendar, others have their origins in the mirky beginning days. Some are amusing, some haughtily dignified, some wistfully sad. Whether it is the march of the Edinburgh Police Pipe Band along Princes Street, the songs of the Newhaven fishwives, a registry wedding 'pour oot' for eager-faced children, the castle guard inscrutable as the cameras click, the ancient rites of the masons, the boom of the One O' Clock Gun, the greeting from the morning-dressed ushers at St Giles' on Sunday . . . it is all part of the Capital scene, the tradition, the ceremony, Edinburgh.

IX

CULTURE

FOR those with a taste for irony, the Edinburgh Festival must give remarkable satisfaction. Conceived in genius, it was born in controversy, and has endured in paradox. In spite of its sceptics and occasionally itself and sponsors, it has miraculously reached maturity and entrenchment in a city that has had an inferiority complex about the arts since Walter Scott was buried, in a country that has rarely given them more than the lip service of a few kind words. To Edinburgh people, most of whom never go to a performance, the Festival is for the visitors only, an alien three weeks in the city calendar outwith their ken, an accolade certainly, an honour to be shared which suitably pampers the Capital ego, but a bore nonetheless, a falsification, a glorious apathy. When there is acclamation Scotland recognizes it with a kind of ownership acknowledged; when there is criticism she leads the attack. It is left to the Lord Provost to sing praises, and that hard core of true Edinburgh art lovers who are among the most knowledgeable and discerning in Europe, while the rest of the world, free from that Scottish genius for tearing itself and each other apart, sit back and enjoy themselves, with jealousy. The truth is that the Festival is one of the best things that ever happened to Edinburgh, and neither Edinburgh nor Scotland really deserves it.

Which in no way means that Edinburgh has not done more for the arts than the rest of Scotland put together. Glasgow might like to argue the point, but not if she is honest with herself. Any city that could keep the Burrell collection of art treasures in cobwebbed storage for twenty years savours too much of bingo, football and the engrossment of money-making to spare time for seriously wooing the arts. It is a pity. The competition could be nothing but beneficial to Scotland as a whole. But Edinburgh has the Festival, and even if she offers little of her own or native culture, or lends it patronage, Edinburgh will keep it and foster it, or it will be to her undying shame.

Culture is history, geography, peace, disaster, development. Culture in Edinburgh reflects the fierceness of the Picts who came from the mountainous north and before that no one quite knows from where; the distant calling of Votadini warriors after the Romans had gone; the shrewdness of the Anglo-Saxons and their industry; the dreams of the Celts and their music. It is the flash of sword, the clash of power, the whisper of intrigue, the pomp of pageantry, the purple of royalty. It is nature in the raw, the black rock of Arthur's seat a symbol; it is the magnificence of the wind-swept firth and its islands, the green of the Pentlands, the growl of city winter. It is travel, trade, battle and adventure in Europe, and in the rest of the world beyond. Most of all in the story of Scotland and its Capital it is the girn of poverty, the curse of war, the steel of a Calvinist Kirk.

Edinburgh has always had European longings. Since earliest times there has been a rapport between Scotland and the Continent that England has never established. The Auld Alliance is the best-known link, but not the most significant, although Scotland and France still have binding ties. Trade and commerce throughout Europe won the materialistic riches, but the free-flow exchange of ideas and thoughts reaped their own rewards. The influence is there on speech, manners, customs, painting, architecture, literature, music, medicine, outlook. The Port of Leith in the old days was the open door, and more than businessmen travelled. Artists and writers, philosophers and poets, doctors and engineers came and went, saw and learned. What they brought back is easily discernible. The influence of France on our painting, the impact of the Dutch and Flemish seventeenth-century masters; the skill of the surgeons of Leyden passed to Edinburgh's Medical School and the Royal Infirmary; the beauty of ancient Greece has been transferred in part to stately columns and porches in the New Town. Since the days of David Hume and Adam Smith, Scottish men of letters have been held in high regard on the Continent, and they still are; which has its own importance at a time when Britain is losing its insularity and leaning heavily towards the rest of Europe. Edinburgh has its own ties, especially with France, but the university's Chair of European Institutions emphasizes the interest that Edinburgh itself holds for the Continent as a whole.

The written word was the greatest influence that Edinburgh herself wielded. Literary power is an awesome thing and Edinburgh's writers, poets and philosophers found fame throughout the world and the years, from the beginning days of old Drummond of Hawthornden back in the sixteenth century down to that irascible genius Hugh MacDiarmid himself. Edinburgh's golden age of letters was only one facet of the amazing intellectual activity which awakened Scotland in the eighteenth and early nineteenth centuries, when the Capital suddenly became one of the most exciting cities in Europe, native talent bubbling and spilling into many fields. Those were the days when James Thomson wrote *The Seasons,* when Lady Nairne was singing her sweetest; when the young Robert Fergusson was winning acclaim as a poet, before his career was abruptly cut short in the agonies of bedlam where he died; when David Hume, philosopher of world stature, held open court to the great intellects of Europe; when historian William Robertson wrote his story of Scotland, and Adam Smith his *Wealth of Nations.* Those were the days when Robert Burns rode up from Mossgiel in search of fame and fortune and took the city by storm, becoming the companion of some of the famous names of the day: Henry Mackenzie, the writer and critic; Dr Blacklock; Dugald Stewart; Lord Monboddo; Lord Glencairn; until his libations and tavern cronies made him appear more ploughman than poet. Then came the rise of Sir Walter Scott, the great romantic, who remembered as a boy seeing Burns and his large dark shining eyes, a vision that remained with him until the day he died.

Those were the days, as the century turned, of that highly respected sabre-toothed literary journal, the *Edinburgh Review,* which won grudging praise even from John Gibson Lockhart, who wrote for its stalwart rival, *Blackwoods Magazine,* given life to offset the *Review's* liberal outlook and the caustic comment of Francis Jeffrey. What an extraordinary gathering of literary talent ranged Edinburgh then. Some had already made their names, some found fame later outside Edinburgh and Scottish environs.

The literary stimulus of the Capital set Europe ringing. There was Lord Cockburn, whose *Memorials of his Own Time* remains one of the most observant accounts of contemporary life ever written; Thomas Carlyle; Thomas de Quincey; Dr John Brown; Susan Ferrier; Anne Grant; James Hogg, who found recognition as the Ettrick Shepherd; Dean Ramsay, the wit and moralist; John Wilson, who wrote under the pseudonym of Christopher North; and a legion of others.

With the death of Walter Scott the last of the great creators of the period had gone. Apart from the painters, Edinburgh's literary force was spent after the century-long orgy. Perhaps it was a natural decline, perhaps the rending claws of the critics had cut too deeply on tender would-be literaries who became inhibited and reluctant to expose their work and themselves to the snake pit of criticism. Never have there been such critics. Grand and lordly men, they relentlessly pursued their quest for the negative with the dedication of fanatics, positive themselves only to fault. In the end they consumed even themselves for there was nothing left to criticize.

Edinburgh was left an inglorious paradox. A city with a genuine taste and love for the arts, but lacking the courage to express itself, an inner fear of attracting scorn by laying bare her true feelings. Edinburgh camouflaged its inhibition under a cloak of gentility that remains to this day. That was the curse of the Victorian period. It was left to the tragically short-lived Robert Louis Stevenson to force a minor revival with his exciting tales of high adventure in a style of compelling simplicity, the emotion, sensitivity, and personality of the man in every line. His followers were lesser men, although of a fine literary turn, inspired by Stevenson's leadership into the new freedom. Arthur Quiller-Couch was one of them, Conan Doyle another. His famous Sherlock Holmes, the scientific detective, was born in a test tube at Edinburgh University, where the author was a medical student.

Today there is a prodigious list of writers and poets demanding attention, but hardly in the same category as the old masters. Perhaps we live too close to see the perspective. The quite remarkable revolution in the fields of communications, radio, television, and the unprecedented number of books, magazines and newspapers present unrivalled opportunities for the writer. Most of it may be journalism in one form or another, but journalism is likely to glean respect again after falling into disrepute since the war with the advent of the high-pressured popular dailies.

Hugh MacDiarmid (Christopher Murray Grieve), now living in sprightly old age in his olde-world cottage at Biggar, remains our only major literary figure of acknowledged genius, and his clan of 'Scottish Renaissance' poets have made their own impact on Scotland. What they have done and continue to do is give Scottish poetry a pride again, a place and an aim, which is no miniature achievement, for before MacDiarmid and his tail, Scottish verse had languished for years in the literary desert. His two most notable followers are Albert Mackie, a rhymer of such amazing facility that at one time, as MacNib of the *Evening Dispatch,* he reported run-of-play football matches in verse, sending 'takes' back to his Sports Editor every fifteen minutes in vivid telling quatrains; the other is Sydney Goodsir Smith, who besides several books of verse in Lallans and a use of Scots all of his own, wrote *The Wallace* for the Assembly Hall's open stage in the 1960 Edinburgh Festival, where it was applauded generally, particularly by the Scottish Nationalists. Robert Garioch Sutherland; Sorley Maclean, with his outstanding work for the Gaelic language; Norman MacCaig, who scorned the Lallans and with his two compatriots, G. S. Fraser and J. F. Henry, founded a new movement—The New Apocalypse; and Orcadian George Mackay Brown who studied at Newbattle and the university. They present some of Edinburgh's poetic luminaries of today, who have taken over from the late greats like Will Ogilvie, Alexander Gray, Andrew Young, Lewis Spence and Edwin Muir, the poets of an earlier yesterday.

Edinburgh prose writers of recent years proliferate by the battalion, playing their parts in the whole spectrum of writing activity, from light novels to works of major importance. Over the years the university has provided many a dexterous exponent in the latter field in the tradition of Blair, Aytoun, Masson and Saintsbury: Sir Herbert Grierson with his anatomical study of genius, particularly with regard to Sir Walter Scott, bridged the gap into the present; Dover Wilson the Shakespearian authority; W. L. Renwick the knowledgeable on Spencer; Stuart Piggott a definitive voice on archaeology; Alastair Smart an expert on Allan Ramsay; and many others in their specialized interests have contributed much of worth and note to serious critical study.

In a city with a self-generated sense of history, it is hardly surprising that Edinburgh has produced a host of writers with a fascination for the past. The historic novel has a special role in Edinburgh literature, although many city writers have also expressed the same interests in books of scholarly research. Dr William Beattie, a chief librarian of the National Library of Scotland, has contributed much to Edinburgh's own story, like George Scott Moncrief and Moray McLaren, now a character as much as writer, surrounded in the aura of Georgian splendour with a wistfulness for the more gracious days that have gone or are going, yet still nimbly continuing to keep pace with the present. The past pulls strongly for Marion Lochhead and Dorothy Dunnett, who has contributed some of the best historical novels in recent years.

Women writers have created a place of their own in the Edinburgh context. Between doing the household chores, Mary Stewart, wife of a university lecturer, continues to produce unrivalled thriller best-sellers; and Hannah Aitken, Jean Matheson, Mary Kelly, Elizabeth Holland, and Joan Lingard have already their own established admirers.

So the list of Capital writers continues, without attempt to embrace them all, for there are so many that their names come fast and without order of merit. But numerical strength does not total a greatness and the truth is that since Edinburgh's 'golden age' there has been a steady and distinct decline, an increase in provincialism, a reluctance to experiment or to adventure even in tradition. In an age of science and materialism, Edinburgh remains a bastion of traditional thinking at a time when the rest of the world has thrown tradition out of the window, when convention and conservatism have become the ridiculed symbol words of fusty Establishment. Perhaps in a world that to a large extent has lost much of its sense of values, Edinburgh's unswerving dedication to the old order is a quality. We hope it is so. The university retains an emphasis on the traditional classics, yet this is to be applauded, for others disregard them wantonly, and a true appreciation of tradition is a sound base for development and pioneering.

The Edinburgh Festival has brought a gale of new thinking gusting through many areas—some even outside the arts—and in a city which sponsors the arts to such an extent, we wait with breathless anticipation for some new native talent of stature to stand on the European or world stage. Literature provided in the past, and now we look for the emergence of some young writer to outpace the times and bring a little excitement to the Capital scene again, someone capable of creating and leading a revival, as has already been done in Edinburgh's writing past.

Edinburgh has never been one of the great centres of art, music or the theatre. The whole character and history of the Capital and the country gave the arts little opportunity to blossom. The cold baleful eye of John Knox, with his chill and cheerless Calvinist creed, wrought its own inhibition. The kirk frowned on the slightest deviation from the grim and perilous track across the bubbling oceans of hellfire that it had marked out for the people to follow, and the vivid fear of Satan and his sulphurous abode ensured that few transgressed, at least in public. It would be wrong, however, to over-emphasize the kirk's stifling role, for there are many other factors, and at least Knox preached honesty and truth, which, in a sense, is what the arts have always sought.

In many ways the kirk has tried to make amends for the constrictions of the past, and the old Gateway Theatre begun by the Church of Scotland's Home Board in 1946 in the face of considerable opposition, made a unique contribution to Edinburgh's theatre history. The echoing voice of Knox rumbled over the centuries when some of the Kirk's 'Auld Lichts' damned it as an encouragement to laxity and even immorality, and while most recognized the bravery of the attempt, few gave the Gateway much chance of success, and some were frankly puzzled and suspicious at the church's sudden interest in the arts. In fact, the Gateway Theatre, under the direction of the Rev George Candlish and managed by Miss Sadie Aitken, was a resounding success, taking its place in time in the Festival's official fringe, encouraging Scottish writers and producing many plays of Scottish character, especially comedy. A host of familiar names are associated with the Gateway, but perhaps Robert Kemp did more than any to establish its reputation. Not only a prolific writer, Kemp was chairman of the Gateway Company for seven years, although it is as a dramatist that he will be remembered. His output seemed inexhaustible: *The Heart is Highland, Let Wives Tak' Tent, The Man Among the Roses, The Laird o' Grippy, Conspirators* flash back over the years, and there was Lennox Milne, Tom Fleming, James Gibson among a rare gathering of talent to present them.

The earliest Edinburgh theatre was probably the Tennis Court in the Watergate, down by Holyrood Palace. The occasional touring London company played there, and Mary of Guise once visited it in 1557. For a performance of Macbeth in 1714, a "grande assembly of Scottish Nobility and Gentry" turned out to make it a gala occasion. The Taylor's Hall in the Cowgate was a theatre for a time after 1727, but following a difference among the company, the Canongate Theatre was built in 1747, resulting in a much higher standard of performance. Indeed, the stage of this old playhouse had its moments of real drama, for it was not infrequently the scene of riots and flashing swords, with the audience playing some of the principal parts. Allan Ramsay's theatre in Carrubber's Close was given short shrift by the city magistrates, who in turn suffered the indignity of ego-pricking in one of Ramsay's poems published in the *Gentleman's Magazine*.

The first Scottish theatre recognized by law was the old Theatre Royal. Opened in December, 1769, it soon became a 'resort for polite society', all the big stars of the south coming to play before the critical Edinburgh audience. Even the celebrated Mrs Siddons visited the Theatre Royal in 1781, and such was the acclaim that on her return the following year the troops were out with fixed bayonets to control the booking-office crowds. Sir Walter Scott's *Rob Roy* came to the rescue when times were hard.

Then there was The Temple on top of the Mound, the Royal Princess Theatre, in Nicolson Street, the Edinburgh Theatre in Castle Terrace, the Pavilion in Grove Street, the Tivoli in Stockbridge, and more.

The music halls were another ready attraction. The Southminster's fare was decidedly risque, and eventually gave way to Newsome's Circus. The Gaiety in Chambers Street was turned into the Theatre of Varieties, managed by that doyen of the music hall, Sir H. E. Moss, who in the early days before fame descended upon him was ready to pull the curtains or take part in a 'turn' himself. His ambition to elevate music-hall standards drove him to travel the world and build his vast 2,300-seater Empire Palace in Nicolson Street, the first of a series of similar theatres throughout Britain as the Empire-builder spread his wings. Nowadays, apart from an occasional coming to life again in some semblance of the old manner at Festival time, the Empire has at last fallen to the all-conquering Emperor Bingo, like so many other establishments once considered inviolable.

The much-loved Theatre Royal, burnt down in 1946, perpetuated many of the old music-hall traditions in variety and pantomime, and names like Florrie Ford, Tommy Lorne and the evergreen Dave Willis were old favourites. The Palladium, on a less professional level, carried on a similar role with its own dedicated following, who turned out each week to laugh at the antics of pencil-moustached Johnny Victory, the unsmiling Lex MacLean, Johnnie Beattie and the adored Grace Clark and Colin Murray. Built on the site of the once-popular Cooke's Circus, the Palladium was always a nursery for new acts and would-be stars. They seldom lent the performance polish, but the endeavour and good-natured rapport from the patrons gave the shows a certain club atmosphere that won loyal support.

Just as the Palladium experimented with people, the tiny Traverse on the High Street experimented with writers, plays and presentation. The Traverse Theatre Club opened in 1962, and, like most other new ventures backed by original thinking in a city of tradition, it has become from time to time an exercise in polemics about productions and even its aims. That the Traverse and others like it have a role to play in modern theatre can hardly be disputed, just as it is true that experiments and their results can only be appreciated and understood by the minority of those who help to conduct them, and that even today it is unwise to push tradition too far and too fast. In fact, the Traverse has produced some outstanding work, just as it has on occasion plumbed the depths, which is exactly what is expected from trial-and-error pioneering.

It is only sensible that there should be experiment, for, as in so many other fields, the years have wrought the changes on Edinburgh stages and the theatre-going public. The days when an evening at the theatre was an occasion for bow tie and silver-topped canes have gone, and many of the theatres with them.

The cinema, radio, television and the Festival have had marked effects on the Capital scene, and now the call is for a national theatre and an opera house to keep faith and face with the Festival and its visitors, to replace the inadequacies of the King's Theatre and the poor old Royal Lyceum, which has had a storm of controversy swirling around its ornamented gallery ever since it became clear that it stood in the way of city development, and that it would sooner or later have to disappear to be recreated as something better. But what? And when? The situation continues confused, although the town council showed considerable courage in turning it into a civic theatre, first under old Gateway stalwart Tom Fleming, who later resigned rather than have his policies disciplined when the crowds failed to muster, then under the direction of Clive Perry, who was largely responsible for making a success of the Nottingham venture.

One of the interesting features about the theatre in Edinburgh is apparent during the Festival, when a remarkable profusion and variety of theatres suddenly appear from obscurity to throw open their doors and stages to groups from all over the country. The sad aspect is that as soon as the orgy is over they shut up tight again for another year, and even the quite excellent performances from a number of local amateur groups are not enough to keep them in use. There is still considerable pioneering to be done to find the formula to suit the age and to educate the public into accepting it.

So too in the world of art there is no lack of space when the occasion is right. The Festival brings out in force the galleries of improvisation down dingy cellars, in shop windows, restaurants, on walls, park palings and even *The Scotsman*'s back stairs. They are the displaying grounds of the pen and paint fraternity, the flaunting hopefuls whose enthusiasm rubs off on the city scene, whether the passers-by scratch their heads in wonder at some once-familiar form wrapped in confusion, or brush strokes wielded with the dexterity of the agriculturalist, or the sudden excitement of rare skill shining out from the rest—and all this in a city that for years had only one private gallery to its name. Some restaurants and coffee houses nowadays even continue the exhibitions throughout the year after the Festival has gone, which is indeed a major breakthrough for Edinburgh. For with a wealth of talent in the art college, the image of Playfair's classic National Gallery and the Royal Institute behind to lend the correct look and atmosphere to blend with nature's endowment of Arthur's Seat and the gleam of the Firth below, Edinburgh is still not a centre famous for its contribution to art, or anything like it. Perhaps a measure of the general public's interest in art is that even the street artists have vanished from the city, doubtless to take up more remunerative employment where the coppers are more readily given.

Calvin, Knox and the Reformation worked too efficiently to strangle artistic aspirations and discourage those who may have been attracted. Attitudes change slowly, especially when sown with fear, and the years have not entirely eradicated Knox's influence on Edinburgh. Yet at last there are the stirrings of an awakening, an interest by the public, and the artists' road to London is not quite the same open highway that it once was.

Perhaps it is a result of the efforts in school, of greater education, of the changing social pattern, or because artists are enjoying themselves in a new uninhibited freedom, which has become obvious and catching. If so it is an irony, for traditionally, like the boxer, the artist was at his best when hungry. There are no pale and penurious artists in icicled garrets these days, or at least in comparison to thirty years ago. Perhaps they now suffer inwardly instead, but few are faced with success or starvation when realities are buffered by the Welfare State. From the artists' standpoint it may or may not be a good thing, and we must wait to be objective. The whole concept of art was based on reality and truth, even if not always discernible, and although it does not follow that art should necessarily suffer or change if in the future it is less so, there is the arguable suggestion that foundations are better laid on solid realism.

There are more than 300 artists living and working in Edinburgh today. Those who have reached public recognition or border it socialize in their own tightly-knit circles, for although there is no artists' community in Edinburgh (the villages of Dean or Duddingston would be so picturesquely correct), artists like the company of other artists or those who appreciate art, to mirror themselves and their thinking. Of the few who have found distinction, there is the surprise of the unexpected in their work. Artists in Edinburgh might have reflected the gracious but uncompromising Georgian architecture, the bleakness of the northern climate, the dourness of the Scots or the canniness of Capital folk in particular. In fact, their work is free and sure, and full of warmth and colour and individuality and pleasure. In recent years people like William MacTaggart, Anne Redpath, Joan Eardley, Robin Philipson, Denis Peploe and others have won considerable acclaim for Edinburgh and Scotland as a whole, and presented art in Scotland with a new respect.

The trouble with Edinburgh and the arts is that the Capital *looks* as if it could be one of the great centres, although perhaps the day of "artistic centres" has passed. The skyline of the Old Town, the stately magnificence of the New Town, the superb natural setting, and conjured atmosphere conspire to give the

Capital the appearance of a poet's city or a philosopher's city, or the inspiration of some famous school of art. It is not and there are many good reasons for the disappointment.

It is also not one of the great music centres. The general public in Edinburgh are simply not appreciative of music, and there is no reason on earth why they ought to be, except that somehow unfairly it is expected. Music is supported by a small minority group, just as it is in most other cities. At least Edinburgh's music lovers are not over-frustrated, for beside the Festival there is an astonishing year-long musical interest, reaching a crescendo during the winter-dark months, sometimes with as many as five concerts a week to attend. Unfortunately, if so much activity is one of the city's boasts, it is also a major weakness. Loyal adherents there may be, but their ranks are too thin to support so many competing attractions. Some of those attractions have already fallen by the wayside, and others would feel a chill draught without the considerations of the Scottish Committee of the Arts Council.

Yet there is much enthusiasm with resulting high standards. The university and its Reid School of Music play a leading role, providing madrigal groups, a wind ensemble, a student orchestra, the Edinburgh Quartet, and the far-travelled University Singers, who have won a special following furth of Scotland with their Festival performances. There is also a wealth of wide-ranging local musicians. The professional-like Edinburgh String Ensemble; the Edinburgh Chamber Orchestra; the Youth Orchestra and the Corporation School Orchestra; the excellent chamber music recitals in the Scottish National Gallery; the traditional Hogmanay *Messiah* in the Usher Hall by the Edinburgh Royal Choral Union; outstanding organ recitals in St Giles', St Mary's Episcopal Cathedral, St Cuthbert's and St Mary's Roman Catholic Cathedral. There are many, many more, too many to record as Edinburgh makes music in school, with the Gaels at a city *ceilidh,* in churches, factories, and still, as was so popular in the old days, in the drawing-rooms of some of those stately Georgian residences of the New Town. Of course, because Edinburgh partly owns the Scottish National Orchestra to the extent of some £16,000 in grants, there are regular concerts in the Usher Hall by the orchestra that gains in stature and reputation almost yearly.

Yet like the Edinburgh Festival itself, perhaps its true stature is recognized mostly by those outside Scotland. The Scottish National Orchestra is acclaimed on its tours of Europe's concert halls, some of the finest in cities a quarter the size of Glasgow; here in Scotland it is also hailed, yet with a suggestion of unctuous paternalism that has seen it virtually homeless since Glasgow's St Andrew's Halls burned down and it took up 'temporary' residence in an unsatisfactory but necessary converted picture house—at the time a compliment to Glasgow for acting so swiftly, now a condemnation that the orchestra is still not adequately housed, with no firm date for a flitting. Like the Edinburgh Festival, that is regarded with deference around the world yet with inertia and apathy at home, a civic authority that sings like a canary in praise, then depresses and dulls and undermines confidence with its hyper-awareness of Edinburgh rectitude, an unyielding determination not to adventure except along well-tried, safe paths, with a policy of when in doubt do nothing especially if money is involved. Mercifully, the Festival is bigger than those who girn at it. It survives, although without realization of its potential. Attitudes change, as they have changed since that first Edinburgh Festival back in 1947, and will surely change for the better again. Perhaps we should at least give thanks to the city fathers for maintaining it at all and for having had the vision to give birth to such an unlikely enterprise conceived from the sterility of war, when the dust of the upheaval in Europe had still not settled.

Remember those uncertain days. Food still rationed, a time of coupons, dockets and utility living. War criminals on trial in Nuremberg. The relief of victory over Hitler suddenly stifled in mid shout by the brandishing threat of Russian strength. Europe in tatters. Italy, France, Germany—the fount of so much that was once the arts—all devastated. Britain triumphant but exhausted with the reaction of five years' over-strain producing its own lethargy of thought and action. This was the dark backcloth to the Edinburgh International Festival of Music and Drama.

The whole idea at such a time, of course, was so phlegmatically British as to be almost a music-hall representation of British life and character. While most other countries were in a tizzy of concern about the state of the world, atom bombs, politics, the sinister growling from the Russian bear, here was a small handful of enlightened hopefuls with only a dream to sell. A dream indeed that was not even on the priority list. Their talk was of the things that once gave pleasure: music, painting, drama, opera. Memory stirred. To most people it was a pleasant dream, but only a dream, madness to contemplate at such a time. Thankfully, it was such madness that gave Britain once a greatness.

It began simply enough. John Christie, who had founded the famous Glyndebourne Opera, then closed, and his wife, singer Audrey Mildmay, introduced the idea of a festival of music and the arts in an attempt to brighten the drab life of war-aftermath and rekindle an interest in the arts as soon as possible. They talked over their plan with Rudolf Bing, an impresario of considerable genius, who had been the Glyndebourne's general manager. They even made tentative suggestions of suitable sites for the centre. Chester, Cambridge, Canterbury, Edinburgh. Miss Mildmay's preference was for Edinburgh.

In 1944 Rudolf Bing met H. Harvey Wood, the Director of the British Council in Scotland at the time, and Mr Wood persuaded him to think seriously about Scotland's capital. It had all the qualifications, he stressed, and he felt sure that the city would welcome the idea. Bing travelled north to discuss the plan in Edinburgh with a number of influentials, including the Countess of Rosebery, James Murray Watson, the Editor of *The Scotsman* and, particularly important, the far-sighted Sir John Falconer, Lord Provost. The prospect excited them all. Apart from the prestige of housing the first major post-war gathering of the arts, Sir John, who soon became one of the Festival's greatest converts, also saw it playing a leading role in fostering understanding and friendship between nations. At a time when the horror of war was still vivid, it aimed the Festival's sights at the highest possible ideals.

A sign reminding of Roman times at Cramond
(overleaf) One of the most dramatic sights in Scotland, the Forth's famous twin bridges

CRAMOND
INN

Even the sun shone on that first Festival, so that pre-warned visitors who feared the worst of Scottish weather were agog at Edinburgh's long Indian summer evenings, and such was the spirit of excitement and adventure that no native would whisper otherwise. It was gay and exhilarating and satisfying and full of new pride. It exalted Edinburgh into a real capital city for the first time in centuries, and the city has never been quite the same since.

One of the unexpected developments as the Festival began to grow in years was the rise to some importance of the Fringe, that odd collection of little companies who come to risk their grub-stakes for a reputation in one of the multitude of small halls sprinkled across the city. If the Festival is the sun of Edinburgh's artistic year, the Fringe is the corona, and the amateur drama groups—many from universities—and wandering minstrels and artists who come up from the south, lend the city a portion of their own enthusiasm and excitement. It is good for the Festival. It is adventurous, experimental, occasionally it reveals work of real merit, and it brings a useful gust of fresh thinking to pressure the Festival itself out of any staid entrenchment that might have grown with the advent of those years.

Yet somehow the Festival is a more solemn occasion than it used to be. A festival should have gaiety at the same time as seriousness for the arts. Perhaps as the Festival approaches its quarter century, it is changing in character; more likely that at last the moaners and cynics are impinging. There is a lack of confidence, and dither about the Festival and where it is going. Edinburgh Corporation and too many citizens have given the impression that the Festival is such a financial burden that it can hardly be borne. They understress the money that it attracts. Certainly the parsimony shown the Festival in the past has been almost insulting. The humiliating details of grants, lack of facilities, and the long-awaited opera house is a tiresome tale. It is not less money that the Festival wants, but more; not girning but enthusiasm. Above all, civic imagination and leadership is essential.

It is true that the Festival has never enjoyed the confidence of the Edinburgh public. They have never really believed in it, and

Portobello sands at sunset

few of the cities which stage festivals can make that claim. It is also true that the Edinburgh Festival has failed to encourage local or native talent, and this in a city whose symbol for the Festival could well be the Scott monument. In its search for international stature, Festival policy has followed the course of non-Scottish. If this is parochialism—and it need not be—it is also one of the reasons why Edinburgh citizenry show it so little interest and fail even to understand it.

Yet where would Edinburgh be without the Festival? What of the prestige throughout the world that it has brought, and the pleasure and the memories? The thought is appalling. Time and experience have brought into perspective the remarkable courage and confidence that gave the Festival birth. It is unlikely that today's pusillanimous breed would have the resolution and spirit to emulate the 'happening' of 1947. Yet the Edinburgh Festival has no problem that courage and confidence and a little faith and pride will not solve.

X

TOMORROW

LIKE a not-so-young spinster who suddenly sees time as a fear, Edinburgh peers into the future with some trepidation. She has worn her years well. The ancient past gave the city her faerie skyline, all the way from castle down to Holyrood. The golden Georgian era of 200 years ago created the architectural magnificence of the New Town. But all that sterile modern times have wrought is the jungle of Craigmillar housing estate, the amorphousness of St Andrew's House, a traffic problem that threatens asphyxia of the streets, and a city leadership of rare and feckless timidity. Rising above all other problems is the black imponderable of the future.

Today the centuries bear heavily on Edinburgh, a city of charm and beauty still, but at last showing a wrinkle or two of age. Apathy and indecision are her most leech-like enemies. They have clung to the City Chambers for two vital lost decades. The kind of procrastination and decision-shirking that saw twenty-one years of talk and promise of an opera house still unrealized when the Edinburgh Festival came of age. The obsession for short term profitability with minimum outlay that has curtailed many a worthy project and precipitated as many wails of anguish.

Torpor and ineffectuality were close companions on the road that led by way of the Lyceum Theatre controversy, the cultural centre mirage, the dither of the Empire Games stadium, Festival grants parsimony, the ring-road fiasco, the saga of the Castle Terrace car park, the livid bruises of George Square, and even across the curvy feminine Forth Road Bridge, which is not the longest in the world, but must hold a record for length of debate before action, although perhaps all that can hardly be laid at the corporation's door.

The next twenty years are critical. Either Edinburgh discovers some magic elixir to recall her lost youth, her full faith and pride in herself, or the city must inevitably go into decline, with the abdication of her position as the capital of Scotland, and the loss to Glasgow of some of the seats of power and influence that have been taken for granted for so long: the legal system, the church, banks, business and regional government offices.

Of course, we know that will not happen. We have too much faith in Edinburgh ourselves, and at last there are signs that Edinburgh is taking herself in hand. Perhaps blame should not be levelled in a book, for time and people change while criticism sticks. Perhaps it is too easy to criticize from the gallery and spend public money like water when there is no onus of responsibility. Yet for those who truly love Edinburgh these thoughts are rife. They are there to be said and they are better said. Perhaps it is entirely unfair to maligned but well-meaning town councillors who deserve more than brickbats and insults. Many can little afford time from their own businesses to toil for the city on the trouser-seat punishment of committee work. After all, they are not paid for their efforts, and if we are dissatisfied with them we should do something about it ourselves. But from the marriage between civic authority and the trained professional government officers who run the city there is begotten too much of verbosity, procrastination, faint-heartedness and infuriating pettifoggery to be in any way helpful to the city. The indictment of those who have the reins of Edinburgh in their hands is their ready willingness to live on the achievement of the past and their inability to realize Edinburgh's potentiality. Edinburgh, poor, glorious Edinburgh, is a captive city of her own small thinking.

Aberdeen is the silver city of thrust and gaiety, northern inhibition flung to the east wind; Dundee and Stirling burgeon with new and self-found importance; Glasgow is a warm-hearted spend-it-fast millionaire with a worried bank manager; Edinburgh is a displaying peacock of a city. But now Glasgow's industrious starling and the Dundonian cock sparrow are beginning to steal some of the glamour. Dundee has conjured from the rubble of the old Kirkgate the fine feathers of a new image, and the new road bridge stabbing whitely across the Tay is its open door to the new age. Glasgow is razing its tired old tenements, clearing them away, sowing their foundations with salt and building anew, even if she goes bankrupt in the process. For her it was a bagatelle. Apart from the Victorian legacy there was never much of worth in the first place, only the scars of the industrial revolution.

With Edinburgh it is different. Here is a museum city, but in residential and commercial daily use. The priceless relics of a past age are at every turn. Her beauty is beyond the dreams of other towns. It is irreplaceable. Even to think of change is a wickedness, to tinker with her charms a vandalism, to change her face a crime of vilest rape.

That is Edinburgh's dilemma. The pressures of age, the monstrous thundering herd of the motor car and all the attendant problems of modern times demand change. Decision is overdue. The course of action controversially conceived. The future of Edinburgh concerns not merely the present citizens, but the shadowy untotalled millions still to come. Those vague men and women of next century will be the judges of the future we plan today. They will either praise the present city fathers or shake their heads in sad reproof, or curse them until the end of time.

There is, of course, a plan. The dust clouds of contention swirl around it. They obscure much of the good work and thought that went into its compilation, especially as it included such a hot potato as the inner ring road, a running noose around the city centre, a retaining girdle or a hangman's rope to preserve or throttle. Even the experts are divided on its merits or its threat. On paper, the plan—that is the plan review—is rich in promise for the fine Edinburgh of the future. Unfortunately, the city has lost confidence in so many of the town council's statements of intention. They may be honest and forthright, ambitious of the highest ideals and commended by all, but somehow as the years pass there are alterations, a bit here, a bit there, bending to outside influences, perhaps political, perhaps commercial, perhaps the inevitability that springs from weakness, the inability to stick to course. It has happened time and again. Vehement protestations on every possible public occasion to reassert their unswerving resolve to do such and such a thing, yet in the end the result has so often been the opposite. So it was with their zeal and passionate intent to preserve the character and amenity of the New Town, and they meant it, yet had it not been for the vigilance of the city's multiplicity of preservation societies, much of it would already have been obliterated. Too much of it is already being obliterated.

Planning for the future is essentially a continuing process, creating the provision for review and reassessment at various stages, and alterations if necessary to meet the exigences of time and new thinking. In Edinburgh's case it is quinquennial. But unless there is a solid theme to the plan, a clearly stated aim and coherent policy, free from ambiguity and misunderstanding, then it will founder on those infamous Edinburgh graveyard rocks of dither, delay and indecision.

Let there be no belittling the magnitude and the responsibility of planning the future of a city, especially one with the unique problems of Edinburgh. There are many factors to be taken into account. It cannot be planned in isolation. The Government's own policies must essentially play an integral part, reflecting their view of the development of central Scotland as a whole, striking a balance with the sprawl of Glasgow and its population difficulties, spreading the load of the industrial west. Other towns in the vicinity must be considered, growth points like the Falkirk-Grangemouth conurbation, the rising new town of Livingston, even the influence of the Forth Road Bridge in relation to Fife and the development of the kingdom. Likewise the Government's regional plan is affected by the urgency of Edinburgh's requirements.

The priority is for Edinburgh to have its own problems clearly identified. They must be focused in detail against the backdrop of the city's other needs and trends—population movement, housing, corporation and private building programmes, land availability and its use, the anatomy of the city's industry, its realism and the ideal, traffic studies and road surveys, the determination and ruthlessness by the town council to discipline the motor car, and live agreeably with it.

When all these complexities have been digested, the full panoramic view of the city's problems emerges and is placed in perspective against the Government's master plan. Then, and only then, can the future city structure be decided, bearing in mind the effect of its growth on the character and landscape, and finally the implementation of the policy to make it all possible.

The Edinburgh development plan has already endorsed these views. It sets out concisely the main areas of activity for the future. On paper, apart from the expensive merry-go-round of the inner ring road (it would have cost £250 million to build it underground), the plan is a safe platitudinous document. That is to say there is in it nothing of spectacular drama or planning genius, which suits Edinburgh very well. In the meantime, until the planning department is so improved in quality and numbers that it can produce an acceptable plan that has the confidence of the city to back it and a policy to carry it through, nothing could be more disastrous for Edinburgh than the rush-through of half-baked plans that are rent and torn by the claws of controversy as they go into operation. The Capital is for the most part a conservative town with old-fashioned ideas about how the city should look, and though assuredly the egg-box multiples of the south will arrive in increasing numbers, the plan confirms that Edinburgh will appear to the casual observer still very much like Edinburgh for a very long time to come. Where the danger lurks is in the gap between paper and performance.

How exactly do the planners view the future of Edinburgh? By 1985, they say the population of the city will be approaching a figure of 491,600, which is an increase of some 20,000 more than today. The number of people who live in Edinburgh is, of course, dependent on the number of houses in which they can stay, which in turn bears a direct relation to the amount of land available. Land in Edinburgh is as scarce as water in the desert. Already the sites for private building are almost exhausted. Private builders are forced to scour the city for plots and odd corners at highly inflated prices to build a handful of properties or, if feasible, a skyscraper or two. Land becomes available from time to time as slum property and old buildings are cleared away. With the Corporation's entirely commendable determination to maintain green belt principles, and provide improvements for existing developments, new schools and playing fields, recreational facilities, hospitals, industry, and car parking, most of it is quickly used up. By 1985 there will probably be around 11,500 more houses in Edinburgh, but many more of its citizens will have to stay furth of the city boundaries.

Even now, Edinburgh commuters are on the increase. The Fife coast, Penicuik, Currie, Balerno, the former picturesque villages of another era, are today's newly-discovered country havens and tomorrow's satellites. Soon the city and the Secretary of State's Development Department will have to get together to decide where and how this Edinburgh overspill—between 15,000 and 38,000 of them—will be accommodated.

In the long-term there will be greater decentralization of offices and business houses, although the trend will hardly be apparent during the next few years as developments reach skywards around Tollcross, the West End of Princes Street and what was once the elegant St James' Square. Commercial and shopping interests will follow the same pattern, those situated in the centre of the city, particularly in Princes Street, will be so controlled that at least architecturally they will have harmony. The present successful Sighthill Industrial Estate will advance northwards into South Gyle to provide an attractive climate for new clients, and land reclamation along the Forth will provide further opportunities for industrialists. The siting of new shopping centres will see dispersal to the suburbs and outlying areas of the city, and dependent on the take-over bid by the motor car, some of them may even be vehicle-segregated.

The motor car! Who knows what its sweeping tide will do to Edinburgh—or Britain for that matter. Even before Professor Buchanan presented his frightening time-fuse, one old Sutherland farmer holiday-bound to the Capital had discovered Edinburgh's problem—and answer. He parked his car in Stirling and went the rest of the journey by bus. Yesterday's marvel is today's monster. Already we have seen the nightmare death-throes of American cities like Chicago and Los Angeles, contorting aerial motorways, thruways, multi-lane highways, fly-over and fly-under concrete snakes that gradually crush and strangle their victims to hideous death.

Apart from the morning and evening rush hours when Edinburgh citizenry slowly workward or homeward trundles its weary way, total annihilation by car is still several years distant. Unfortunately, so is any feasible plan to deal with it. The road traffic studies that have been carried out so far have produced a multitude of fascinating facts, but no answers. They have revealed that less than 5 per cent of all traffic entering Edinburgh is completely by-passable. That 74 per cent in the central area has legitimate business there. That the remaining 26 per cent is passing from one part of the city to another. That 80 per cent of traffic in the centre of Edinburgh comes from within the city itself. The research also discovered a hard, realistic fact that would not have been hard to ascertain—there will be a whole lot more cars around as the years go by, and the volume increase is likely to continue until the turn of the century, if not the next.

What will be done is anyone's guess. The mere improvement of the existing principal road network is hardly sufficient. Building entirely new roads and creating more parking spaces centrally would appear to be only a temporary relief. There is also a limitation of money for such schemes. It would be merciful if all that was required was the banning of the motor car from the city centre (except for those belonging to the people who live there) and the improvement of the public bus service at least to efficient standards, with an acceleration of the processes of decentralization of industry and offices. But perhaps that is only the daydream of a layman, and the ensuing chaos on the city boundaries and the screams of bankrupt shopkeepers and businessmen would immediately veto such a preposterous notion.

At the worst, it is to be hoped that Edinburgh will not panic plan to the extent of cultivating that creeping concrete ivy of road complexes so insidious in America, or develop some deviate form of car-pedestrian neurosis that will see us all shinning up ladders, ramps and escalators to airy eyrie-like perches and safe elevated walkways and sequestered winding aerial country paths —anywhere, in fact, in the headlong rush to get off the streets and away from the noise and fumes of clogging locust traffic.

The motor car may alter Edinburgh's face by throwing high the barriers of self-defence, but time inexorably rings its own changes. Time has been kind to Edinburgh. Now as decayed old properties tumble under the weight of years, the lessons wrought by time should be heeded. Today and tomorrow Edinburgh is a city in transition. Perhaps it always has been, but now the processes are spurting. The new buildings are flowering up where the old once stood, and there will be more and more of them until the transformation is complete. Then it will start all over again. Most of what is distinctively Edinburgh remains for the time being—and we hope for always—in the central area. But other parts of the city where the new developments sprout have become indistinguishable from little Londons, Manchesters and Liverpools, New Yorks, and Tel Avivs. No matter how well these new blocks and tiny townships are planned, how artistic and futuristic they look and how pleasant to live in (which is debatable), Edinburgh's change of face is an essay in sameness, conformity and in the final analysis, a monotony conceived in the dehydrated precise minds of southern bureaucracy or, worse still, in America. It is the emasculation of local character or regional character in the environs.

A considerable amount of housing renewal is already complete in the city, and a number of large-scale comprehensive developments are well under way, and some in use. Soon there will be more. At Portobello, Juniper Green, South London Road, Newhaven vast new housing blocks will heave up to create a new skyline and an irony, for although they may be planning perfections (which is also extremely debatable), realistically they are not-very-beautiful sops to convention, an orderly disposal of people, who come second.

As the old familiar places and faces vanish, so does what was once called community spirit. The replacement for the most part is affected sham. As people lose contact with their friends their lives become increasingly insulated. Good neighbourliness is under pressure, hospitality and small kindnesses, for these were traditional, and traditions to the new age are proscribed. Even the 'wee shoppie', where housewives foregather for a blether while they buy cheese and hairpins as they wait for the bacon to be sliced is doomed, like so many of the other local shops time-served to the tastes of the environment where friendship and helpfulness are a long-established individuality. Many of them are still found in the poorer areas, although felicity in shopping is hardly the prerogative of the working class. There are so many instances. The local chip shop that also has a fine line in gold-frizzled hamburgers with heaped crisp white onions, the Tally's that serves ice cream double-sweetened on Sunday, the paint-worn bookshop that is partly a philosophers' forum, the pet shop where the man will give a boy a white mouse if he runs a message, the coffee shop where the beams are oak age-polished to blackness, and where home-baked girdle scones are rushed hot with dripping butter. Each is a little rebellion against conformity, each an eccentricity not tolerated by the moguls of supermarket cut-price living. Each is losing its battle. They will be missed, for there is no place for them tomorrow in the tidy sterilized world of deep-frozen conventionality.

There are indeed problems in the creation of a new community and new environment. The scarred closes of Niddrie and Craigmillar bear witness. It is so easy to create conditions that in many respects are worse than the original. Even the city's expensive new private housing estates have their quirks. Most of them attract young couples, many not long married, anxious to fit into the new social pattern with new neighbours in the bliss of a new semi-detached home. Because most of them are young, the stork is a frequent visitor. The bliss is short-lived. It does not take many moons before these overbalanced communities of under forty-year-olds burst into a soapy bubble Nappy Land, where all the female inhabitants are either wearing smocks or pushing tall, elegant prams, and sometimes doing both. Hell knows no fury like a long street of new pink babies or lisping toddlers whose mothers are determined that no matter what the neighbour's child can do their child will do better. Behind the bland coffee-morning smiles the eyes steel in defensive challenge. Which child will have its teeth first? Which one will crawl first? Walk first? Talk first? Which one, ye gods, will grow his hair last? The sensitive mothers go to the wall. Even the menfolk are not immune. If Mr A forks over his virgin garden for ten minutes of a pleasant summer evening, lo, the first ring of metal on stone sends the curtains twitching along the street. Then casually, after pause sufficient to preserve dignity, out come B, C, D, E and F taking spade to soil for at least twenty minutes. It is a picture exaggerated, of course, and time and nature eventually sorts it all out. But the giant blocks of concentrated filing cabinet humanity which will form Edinburgh's skyline of the future will have particular problems and pressures, not the least living with other families through both walls as well as above heads and below feet, just like the despised tenements of old.

Perhaps the real concern focuses on what is to be done in the central area. Who dares meddle with such magnificence! How easy was the task of Cumbernauld's planners! To create a city from nothing, to place houses and roads and shops and open spaces at will must have been an exciting jigsaw puzzle of a problem. But an ancient city like Edinburgh with its picturesque and irreplaceable setpieces of castle and hills, its historic old and new towns is at the mercy of possible planning errors. The preservation and integration of old and new is a problem of immense complication, the planner's supreme challenge. One wrong move or weak decision and a city famous throughout the world for its beauty could be irrevocably sacrificed.

Edinburgh, of course, is quite likely to erupt when changes to the city's face are threatened. The controversies surrounding Randolph Crescent, George Square and the inner ring road brought the Capital quickly to the boil. Yet the towering new development in the modern idiom slap in the centre of town as a replacement for the run-down St James' Square–Leith Street area passed with hardly a murmur. At this stage the architectural merit is difficult to judge from the public's view, but the general design appears to be acceptable, and, after all, Edinburgh is the most critical city in the world. St James' Square, deteriorating and neglected for years, had become a kind of elegant slum and was better swept away, although in its heyday there were few more pleasing parts of the city. Now a modern counterpart to the grace of the Georgian New Town will soar into seven-storey government buildings, a large pedestrian shopping precinct with a car park below, office accommodation, a hotel, corporation housing for some 200–300 people, and a new Roman Catholic Cathedral—all in the contemporary style. The scheme will provide parking for almost 2,000 cars, employment for 4,000 workers, the government offices will cover 300,000 square feet in giant blocks linked to a central eleven-storey tower, which will include a conference suite and a restaurant opening to a balcony over Leith Walk. The hotel will look to Calton Hill, while the shops and supermarkets will be on one continuous pedestrian pavement above Leith Street. The cathedral, a thing of startling unconventionality in keeping with the new trends in church architecture, will stand on the axis of Leith Walk facing east, with the main entrance on the west side from a new cathedral close. As a symbol of the new order its spire will be a huge sharp needle pointing the way to heaven.

The territory to the south of the castle and the Royal Mile presents the chance to create another New Edinburgh of considerable distinction. In fact, it is the most stimulating building ambition since Craig launched into his New Town or the feat of spanning the Forth estuary was accomplished twice. It is the opportunity to make a major contribution in city development of national importance at least comparable in size and achievement to the Old Town on castle ridge and the New Town below it. In twenty years' time we will know the result. The aim is for an adventure of such exciting twentieth-century civic design that it will become yet another Edinburgh planning and architectural wonder, the inspiration to other towns. It could mean the restoration of Edinburgh's place among the great European capitals. The contrast with the old city would be almost incredible, a magnet for visitors from all over the world. It is the kind of acclaim that Edinburgh so badly needs to restore her confidence.

The New Edinburgh will rise up between Holyrood Park and Tollcross. It will be an academic, cultural and conference centre as well as a hub of commerce, the composite integration of a wide variety of quite dissimilar interests. Apart from shopping and housing facilities, up will go a vast new university complex and art college, the new George Heriot's School, an up-to-date Royal Infirmary and teaching hospital, one of the finest health centres in the world, and a centrepiece for the Edinburgh Festival, including all the trappings that have been lacking for years, in particular the long-awaited opera house, which may be one of the first completions.

There are other developments on the way. Perhaps not on such a mammoth scale, but individually in some respects even more important. Although co-ordinated in the overall plan, what happens to the extremities of Princes Street—Waverley Station in the east, the old Princes Street Station in the west, and their environs—will have direct bearing on enhancing or ruining Edinburgh's greatest asset—the dramatic panorama of the magnificent thoroughfare above the gardens and the castle atop its rock. There must be no shoddy work here, no detraction, no chances taken, no cut-price expediencies. As an eminent planning authority once indicated, a mistake in scaling, an error in elevations, a wrong frontage or an indifferent design and the spectacle could be turned into a "coffin in the valley".

Princes Street itself will, of course, be eroded even further. It is quite feasible that by the turn of the century most of the existing buildings will have gone or be marked for demolition. In their places will stand a long line of stone-faced buildings in the modern style, abutting starkly on top floors. They will be girded by a ribbon walkway at the first floor, providing shopping on two levels. This deck of shops will protrude to cover most of the existing pavement and give umbrella weather protection to road-level shoppers. There will be outlets at the end of each block from the first-storey ledge. The premises of Littlewoods and British Home Stores sets a rough guide of the shape of things to come.

With the long-term in mind, the town council have taken steps to preserve as much of Princes Street's dignity as possible. It is now so architecturally jumbled and disturbed—a romantic miscellany notwithstanding—that preservation would be almost pointless. But the corporation's measures will enforce a uniformity of heights and frontages, still allowing for individuality of design, that may well end in attractive eye-pleasing mediocrity in comparison with what presently exists in the New Town, although by then there may be an entirely new set of values. It is likely that the same pattern will follow in George Street, but more slowly, for it still contains considerable architectural merit and beauty, and the commercial disciplining policy of controlled developments will preserve it for a little longer. Queen Street is another matter, and the measures are hardly sufficiently effective to keep intact what is a clear case for preservation.

Change also breathes down the Royal Mile, but bringing new life with it. Only a few years ago the street was virtually dead on its feet. Eulogy and hope were not enough to embalm history. The very fabric of some of the buildings had become so decrepit that large-scale demolition loomed darkly. Today there is a vigour about the High Street again, a certain bolstered timelessness that could lull into inactivity but does not. The quality shops, the outstanding restoration work, the new spirit of determination to preserve at almost any cost and trouble has worked a wonder. But the critical years have still to come.

Part of the charm of the High Street is in its picturesque haphazardness, its extraordinary contrasts, the surprise of the unexpected, the sudden dramatic vistas of the city seen through a dark close mouth framed by billowing washing hanging from upstairs high Land tenement windows. Whether it is possible to continue the effect with entirely new building is doubtful. It is one thing to restore what already exists, and quite another to create something new beside it that will blend with the centuries, preserving character and style and that indefinable aura of concentrated history that seems to have seeped into the very stonework and atmosphere. It is a rare and delicate problem. It will be increasingly presented in the Royal Mile's tomorrows.

The corporation deserve the highest praise for their preservation achievements to date. Both Chessel's Court and White Horse Close are examples of the best restoration work in the country. But only time will tell if it is possible to design and build successfully in sympathy with the antiques of a past age, and whether there is an architect alive with the background, ambition, ability, knowledge and dedication, given the time, scope, money, and encouragement to do it.

During the next few years Edinburgh will also continue with its face-cleaning movement. The image-conscious bank and insurance offices were first to consider removing the city's grime of ages to reveal the fair bright stone below. Some of the results have been almost startling. The stately castle-like Bank of Scotland atop the Mound, encouraged by the pristine freshness of the R.S.A. and National Gallery and the advent of the less smoky diesel trains in the valley below, achieved a result by blasting Gullane sand at the stonework that is almost spectacular. When its pale green floodlights flash on of an evening, illuminating the ornate frontage and producing a dramatic shadow effect, the Bank of Scotland is immediately transformed into one of the city's most attractive sights. There will be a much gayer Edinburgh in the future, although we hope that the cleaning will be done with restraint. Some buildings, limply dejected under thick unglamorous layers of greasy soot, will burnish into a successful glow. Some will not. Who, for example, would want to see staid old St Giles' with its face washed or the dark brooding mass of Holyrood scrubbed into an advertisement for soap powder.

We dare not look too far into the future. Change is spaceship-fast in the twentieth century, a juggernaut cleaving its way through age-long traditions, conventions and ideals. To speculate randomly is a presumption. Thinking on distant tomorrows is shackled by the limiting values of today. The astronaut in his moon rocket was a gross extravagance of imagination to the 1906 Grand Prix winner as he hurtled the track in his open Renault at a breathtaking 63 m.p.h. James Craig's plan for the New Town of Edinburgh appeared dramatic and revolutionary to the High-streeters in their cramped old high-Lands of 1767. The acceptance of change is education, and, although the shape and style of the Edinburgh of the far future might offend and disturb us today, it may be entirely acceptable to our great-great-grandchildren, who may see in its grotesque contortions the symbols of an Edinburgh architectural renaissance, or even another Scottish golden or concrete age. But perhaps by that time there will be so much money in the pockets of Edinburgh citizens and gold in the coffers of the town council and time on everybody's hands that quality, dignity, craftsmanship and work well done will be virtuous again, and Edinburgh will once more build in the grand manner of 200 years ago, only better. By then there might not even be a ring road problem. Ring roads will loop the city in concentric dozens —but out of sight, underground and out of people's minds.

So the changes will come. Some will be praised, some verbally scuttled. Some will be for the good of the city, others to the detriment. All men cannot see things the same way. We know, of course, what we would like to see. Day-dreaming is an exercise in improbabilities, but there is a certain piquancy for ever so often day-dreams come true. With that hope, we would like to see worthy players once more on Edinburgh's great stage. Events can make the man, and Edinburgh needs a leader sorely. That man when he is found must have support, and we would also like to see an elevation in the qualities of the majority of town councillors to stand by him, and an urgency of interest among Edinburgh citizens in the affairs of their city which could hasten the improvement. Edinburgh is too fine a place, too grand, too beautiful, ever to take second place or languish below her ceiling of potential, if indeed she has a ceiling. Today Edinburgh's limitations are self-generated. We would like to see them removed.

We would also like to see the Edinburgh Festival spill out of its three-week confinement into the remainder of the calendar, so that the city becomes year-long the home of artists, writers, philosophers, poets, musicians, all of international stature who work hard and think big, sharing their thoughts in public, who stay in Edinburgh because it is an acknowledged hub of the arts. We would like to see the arts further cultivated in Edinburgh, tended and cared, until they burst into a crop of flowering native genius, the emergence of latter-day Scotts and Stevensons, Ramsays and Raeburns, Humes and Napiers, to take their place on that great stage.

We would like to see another Edinburgh golden age of planning and architecture, the revelation of some young Adam or Playfair presently guiltless of his city's need. We would like to see the stamp of his ability on the new Edinburgh already envisaged. Perhaps history will make the man. We would like to see the new Edinburgh in the new style with as much grace and dignity and beauty and elegance as old Edinburgh.

We would like to see Edinburgh again one of the great capitals of Europe, which means the undisputed capital of Scotland, the leader, the adventurer, the patriot, the fighter for her country's causes. We would like to see Parliament Hall in use again for the purpose for which it is famous—the housing of the Scottish Parliament. We believe that with respect and pride returned, political or otherwise, the city will flourish with the rest of Scotland. Edinburgh and Scotland are inextricably linked, their destinies one. Theirs for too long is greatness under padlock. We would like to see it set free.

INDEX

A

Abbeyhill, 34, 132
Acheson House, 83
Adam, John, 104
  Robert, 102, 107, 108, 115, 117, 119, 131, 140, 202
Adam Square, 107
Advocate's Library, 163
Ainslie Place, 119
Alva Street, 119
Anderson, Sir Rowand, 109
Ann Street, 120
Architects, 102–24
Argyll Square, 108
Arniston Place, 121
Atholl Crescent, 119
Arthur's Seat, 43, 51, 52, 55, 64, 85
Artists, 180, 181

B

Bakehouse Close, 70, 83
Balerno, 125, 192
Barnton, 106, 125
Beaton, Cardinal, 80
Bell's Wynd, 79
Bellevue Crescent, 118
Bible Land, 82
Blackhall, 132
Blackford Hill, 131
Blackfriars Street, 80
Blackfriars Wynd, 62
Blackie, Professor, 67
Blackie House, 67
Black Turnpike, 79, 107
Blenheim Place, 122
Botanic Gardens, 121
Bothwell, Earl of, 87, 90, 91
Brighton Place, 120
Broughton, 34
Bruce, Robert, 56, 57, 59
Brunswick Street, 122
Bruntsfield, 148
Bruschi, Peter, 63
Bryce, David, 109
Burdiehouse, 129
Burgh Court, 76
Burke and Hare, 144
Burn, Robert, 119
  William, 108, 124
Burns, Robert, 67, 77, 78, 82, 83, 84, 102, 122, 160, 168, 172
Burns Monument, 109
Burns Supper, 168

C

Calton Jail, 128
Camera Obscura, 66
Candlemakers' Row, 65, 66, 70
Cannonball House, 61
Canongate, 43, 65, 81, 83, 85, 95, 98 125, 132, 159, 163
Canonmills, 34, 127
Canmore, Malcolm, 57, 130
Carberry Hill, 79, 90
Cargilfield, 134
Carrubbers Close, 60, 80, 177
Castle, 29, 30, 52, 57, 59, 81, 85, 88, 93, 97, 100, 124, 125, 151, 165, 166, 169, 196, 197, 198
Castle Wynd, 46
Characters, 20–29
Charles I, 59, 60, 64, 87, 92
Charles II, 65, 72
Charlotte Square, 106, 115, 124
Chambers, Sir William, 117
Chambers Street, 108, 149, 178
Chessel's Court, 200
Children's Rhymes, 31–3
Church of Scotland, 41, 66, 79, 93, 95, 123, 124, 157, 158, 159

City Chambers (Royal Exchange), 76, 104, 187
City of Edinburgh Fighter (603) Squadron, 154
Clermiston, 125
Clyde, Lord, 45
Cockburn, Lord, 22
Cockburn Association, 79
Cockburn Street, 76, 79
Colinton, 52, 131
Comiston, 100
Comiston Springs, 62
Cope, General, 74
Corstorphine, 55, 94, 129
Covenanters, 65, 66, 159
Cowgate, 28, 66, 69, 70, 81, 125, 177
Craig, James, 102, 105, 106, 107, 110, 111, 115, 116, 119, 121, 123, 132, 197, 201
Craigentinny, 129, 130
Craigleith, 106
Craiglockhart, 52
Craigmillar, 131, 187, 195
Cramond, 94, 97
Cranley, 134
Crochallan Fencibles, 52, 77, 78
Cromwell, Oliver, 59, 64, 65, 82, 87, 161
Culloden, 75
Currie, 125, 192

D

Daniel Stewart's College, 134, 147
Darling, Sir Will Y., 41
Darnley, Lord, 57, 79, 88, 89, 90, 139
David I, 137
Deacon Brodie, 68
Dean Village, 181
Dott, Professor Norman, 47
Douglas, Dawney, 52, 60, 77
Lady Jane, 61
Donaldson's Hospital, 108
Dowie, Johnnie, 77
Doyle, Conan, 173
Drummond, George, 41, 103, 104, 105, 132, 143
Drummond Place, 39, 118
Drumsheugh, 55, 81, 86
Duddingston, 25, 131, 181
Dumbiedykes, 129
Duncan Street, 121
Dundas, Sir Lawrence, 117
Dunnett, Alastair, 46

E

East Brighton Crescent, 120
Edinburgh Academy, 109, 134
Edinburgh Festival, 60, 161, 165, 166, 170, 171, 176, 178, 179, 180, 183, 184, 185, 186, 187, 198, 201
Edinburgh Medical School, 171
Education, 133–47
Edward VIII, 152
Elizabeth I, 58, 87

F

Falconer, Sir John, 41, 184
Fergusson, Robert, 83, 121, 172
Fettes Row, 118
Fettes School, 134
Fleming, Tom, 47
Fleshmarket Close, 79
Fleshers' Close, 70
Flodden, 70, 71, 86, 88, 163
Flodden Wall, 71, 81
Forth, River, 50, 70, 73, 92, 97, 98, 116, 125, 127, 148, 197
Forth Road Bridge, 187, 190
Forth Street, 119
Footballers, 46
Fountainbridge, 34
Fountain Close, 80
Frizell, J. B., 139

G

Gardner's Crescent, 119
Gardyloo, 54
Gateway Theatre, 176, 177
Geddes, Jenny, 28
General Assembly of the Church of Scotland, 43, 157, 158, 159
George II, 101
George IV, 160
George IV Bridge, 68, 69
George V, 151
George Heriot's School, 64, 79, 134, 147, 198

George Square, 17, 108, 141, 196
George Street, 50, 116, 117, 199
George Watson's College, 134
George Watson's Ladies' College, 134
Gillespie, James, 77
Gillies, W. G., 47
Gilmerton, 125
Gladstones Land, 66
Gloucester Place, 118
Golfers Land, 84, 85
Gorgie, 34, 48, 125, 129
Graham, Gillespie, 109, 119, 124
  John, 110
Grange, 52, 131
Granton, 52
Grassmarket, 18, 27, 61, 64, 65, 66, 70, 73, 96, 126, 154
Great King Street, 118
Great Michael, 70
Greyfriars, 64, 65, 68, 87, 123
Greyfriars Bobby, 65, 66
Guise, Mary of, 66, 88

H

Hailes Quarry, 106
Haldane, Viscount, 139
Hamilton, Thomas, 109, 121
Hanover Street, 112
Haymarket, 112, 125
Heart of Midlothian F.C., 46
Henry VII, 70, 86
Henry VIII, 70, 86
Heriot Row, 51, 109, 118, 119
Heriot Watt University, 139
Hertford, Earl of, 86
Hibernian F.C., 146
High Constables, 163, 164, 165
High Court, 156, 163
Highland Games, 167
Highland Church of Tolbooth St John's, 95, 124
Hogmanay, 156, 165
Holy Corner, 129
Holyrood, 55, 59, 70, 74, 81, 82, 85, 86, 87, 88, 90, 91, 92, 127, 137, 152, 158, 162, 177, 187, 198, 200
Home, John, 110, 111
Honours of Scotland, 59, 157
Hope Street, 112
Hospitals, 53, 68, 101, 103, 109, 142, 143, 144, 145, 146, 171, 198
Howard Place, 40, 128
Hume, David, 68, 102, 117, 171, 172
Hunter, John and William, 102
Huntly House, 65, 83
Hyndford's Close, 80

I

Inverleith Row, 121

J

Jackson, Pilkington, 46
James II, 86, 92
James III, 86
James IV, 70, 86, 165
James V, 76, 85, 86, 88, 166
James VI, 58, 91, 92, 166
James VII, 83, 84, 92
James's Court, 101
James Gillespie's School for Girls, 34
Jeffrey, Francis, 173
Jeffrey Street, 81
Johnston Terrace, 66
Joppa, 129
Juniper Green, 125, 194

K

Ker, James Ingles, 151
King's Park, 85
King's Theatre, 128, 179
Kirk o' Field, 90, 139
Knights of the Thistle, 162
Knox, John, 58, 72, 80, 101, 157, 159, 162, 175, 180

L

Lady Stair's Close, 28, 67
Laing, Alexander, 107
Lamb's House, 17
Lansdowne House, 134
Law Courts, 75, 76
Lawnmarket, 26, 66, 67, 68, 69, 70, 72, 75, 167
Leith, 27, 51, 62, 100, 104, 121, 127, 137, 152, 160, 164

Leopold Place, 122
Liberton, 100, 125, 130
Liberton's Wynd, 62, 77
Lister, Joseph, 144
Loretto School, 134
Luckenbooths, 69
Lyon, Lord, 45, 46, 160, 161

M

MacDiarmid, Hugh, 172, 174
Mackenzie, Sir Compton, 39, 40
Macmorran, Bailie, 68
Magdalen Chapel, 69
Mackie, Albert, 42, 174
McCaig, Norman, 47
MacLaren, Moray, 47
MacTaggart, William, 45
Maitland Street, 119
Margaret's Chapel, 57
Margaret Tudor, 70, 86, 87, 88
Margaret Tudor House, 17
Mary, Queen of Scots, 57–9, 79, 80, 88, 89, 90, 91, 92, 107, 139, 157, 162
Mary Erskine School for Girls, 134
Mary King's Close, 76, 77
May Day, 43, 157
Melville, Viscount, 117
Melville College, 134
Melville Street, 124, 199
Mercat Cross, 62, 64, 69, 71, 72, 74, 82, 87, 152, 161
Merrilees, William, 44, 45
Merchiston, 131
Merchiston Castle, 134
Middleby Street, 121
Miller, Sir James, 41
Milne, Lennox, 47
Mons Meg, 27, 59, 60
Montrose, Duke of, 82
Moray House, 82, 139
Moray Place, 119
Morningside, 95, 100, 120, 128, 129
Morton, Regent, 80, 89
Morocco Land, 81
Moubray House, 80
Mound, The, 22, 40, 98, 111, 114, 127, 150, 178, 200
Morvo, John, 113
Multrees Hill, 110
Murray, Sir Andrew, 41
Murrayfield, 125, 167
Museum of Childhood, 80
Music, 182, 183
Musselburgh, 69, 125, 156

N

Napier Technical College, 131, 139
National Covenant, 65, 83, 123
National Library, 163
National War Memorial, 56
Nelson Monument, 121, 128
Netherbow Port, 54, 65, 71, 74, 80, 81, 87
New College, 124
New Street, 82
Newhaven, 28, 52, 69, 148, 194
Newington, 79, 121, 125
Nicholson Square, 122
Nicholson Street, 122, 150
Niddrie, 96, 195
Nor' Loch, 69, 74, 76, 103, 105, 111
North Bridge, 79, 105, 106, 111
Nova Scotia Territory, 60

O

Old Assembly Close, 79
Old Clubs, 28, 77
Old Fish Market Close, 79
Old Playhouse Close, 82
Old Stamp Office Close, 78
One o'Clock Gun, 121, 169
Outlook Tower, 66

P

Palladium Theatre, 178, 179
Paisley Close, 80
Parliament Hall, 76, 163
Parliament House, 76, 202
Parliament Square, 101, 163
Penicuik, 192
Pentlands, 50, 55, 128, 171
Pets' Cemetery, 59, 60
Physicians' Hall, 109
Picardy Place, 119
Picts, 56

Pilton, 52, 132
Plague, 76, 77
Playfair, William, 108, 120, 121, 122, 124, 131, 140, 180, 202
Population, 16, 17
Porteous Riots, 73
Portobello, 94, 120, 125, 126, 127, 148, 194
Prestonpans, 103, 104
Princes Street, 15, 22, 29, 49, 50, 52, 66, 78, 104, 110, 111, 112, 113, 114, 116, 124, 150, 162, 165, 166, 168, 192, 198, 199
Princes Street Proprietors, 112, 113
Printing, 70
Proposals, The, 102, 103, 104
Proprietors, The, 112

Q

Queen Anne, 160
Queen Margaret, 86, 130
Queen Street, 105, 116, 117, 118, 144, 199
Queensberry House, 84

R

Raeburn, Sir Henry, 102, 120
Raeburn Place, 120
Railways, 112
Ramsay, Allan, 28, 60, 80, 101, 160, 175, 177
Ramsay Gardens, 28, 60, 61, 63
Randolph Crescent, 196
Ravelston, 106
Reformation, 64, 180
Register House, 45, 79, 106, 107
Reid, Robert, 109, 115, 118
Reith, Dr George, 139
Rhind, David, 109, 118
Richard II, 75
Riddle's Court, 68
Rizzio, 79, 89
Romans, 56, 157
Rose Street, 106
Rosyth, 154
Ross Bandstand, 50
Rothesay Terrace, 119
Royal Crescent, 118
Royal Circus, 118
Royal College of Physicians, 143
Royal College of Surgeons, 70, 108
Royal Company of Archers, 159, 160
Royal Edinburgh Hospital, 146
Royal Exchange, 76, 103, 104
Royal High School, 68, 109, 121, 134, 137
Royal Infirmary, 53, 68, 101, 103, 109, 142, 143, 144, 145, 171, 198
Royal Lyceum Theatre, 179, 187
Royal Mile (High Street), 24, 27, 28, 29, 33, 52, 54, 64, 77, 94, 98, 100, 102, 106, 108, 125, 126, 132, 159, 163, 165, 167, 179, 199
Royal Scottish Academy, 45
Ruthven, Earl of, 89, 90

S

St Andrew Square, 106, 117
St Andrew's and St George's Church, 124
St Anne's Street, 111
St Bernard's Crescent, 120
St Cecilia's Hall, 80
St Cuthberts, 43
St Denis School, 134
St George's School, 134
St Hilary's School, 134
St James Church, 124
St James Square, 110, 192
St John's Chapel, 82
St John's Cross, 82
St John's Episcopal Church, 124
St Katherine's Well, 130
St Margaret's Chapel, 124
St Margaret's School, 134
St Mary's Church, 124
St Mary's Metropolitan Cathedral, 124
St Mary's Street, 81, 124
St Paul's, 124
St Serf's School, 134
St Stephen's, 124
Salisbury Crags, 85
Sandford Gardens, 120
Saxe-Coburg Place, 120
Schools, 133–9

Scotsman, The, 17, 46, 47, 180, 184
Scott, Tom, 47
Sir Walter, 67, 153, 163, 170, 172, 173, 175, 178, 202
Scott Monument, 113, 186
Scottish Hospital Centre, 145
Scottish Mint, 80
Scottish National Gallery, 108, 180, 182, 200
Scotus Academy, 134
Shoemakers' Land, 70, 82
Sibbald, William, 109, 118, 123
Simpson, Dr James Young, 144
Simpson Memorial Maternity Pavilion, 145
Sinclair, George, 62
Slateford, 34
Small, Rev Dr Leonard, 43, 44
Smith, Adam, 102, 171, 172
South Bridge, 79, 107, 122
South Gray's Close, 80
Stair, Lady Eleanor, 28, 67
Stevenson, Robert Louis, 68, 128, 131, 163, 173
Stewart, Dugald, 84, 172
Stockbridge, 120, 125, 132
Stuart, Charles Edward, 61, 73, 74, 75, 82, 92, 101, 131, 163, 173
Surgeons' Hall, 140

T

Tanfield House, 128
Telford, Thomas, 102
Tenements, 33–8, 54, 64, 100, 199, 200
Theatres, 82, 128, 149, 150, 151, 176, 177, 178, 179
Thistle Street, 106
Thrie Estates, 41, 157, 161
Tolbooth, 73, 82, 164
Tollcross, 120, 192, 198
Town Guard, 80, 165
Tron Kirk, 27, 72, 79, 156
Turnhouse, 154

U

Union of Parliaments, 76, 80, 92, 101, 163
University, 68, 102, 108, 136, 139, 140, 141, 142, 145, 167, 174, 182
Upper Bow, 54

V

Victoria, Queen, 66, 87, 127, 128

W

Walker Street, 119
Walker, Tommy, 46
Wallace, William, 56
Water, the search for, 62, 63, 64
Water of Leith, 127
Watt, James, 102
Waverley Station, 53, 105, 111, 151, 154, 198
Weatherstone, Sir Duncan, 41
Wells o' Wearie, 64
West Port, 61
Western General Hospital, 145
White Hart Inn, 61, 66
White Horse Close, 85, 200
Whitefoord House, 84
Whitley, Rev Dr Harry, 42, 43, 162
Witches, 61, 62
Wood, Wendy, 40, 41
Woodruff, Professor M. F. A., 144
World's End Close, 81

Y

Youngston, Professor J. A., 102